THE BOSTON MONEY TREE

THE BOSTON MONEY TREE

Russell B. Adams, Jr.

Thomas Y. Crowell Company
Established 1834
New York

Copyright © 1977 by Russell B. Adams, Jr.

Manufactured in the United States of America

LIBRARY OF CONGRESS CATALOGING IN PUBLICATION DATA

Adams, Russell B
  The Boston money tree.

  Bibliography: p.
  Includes index.
  1. Finance—Boston—History. 2. Boston—Commerce—
History. I. Title.
HG184.B67A32   332'.09744'61   76–27338
ISBN 0–690–01209–8

1 2 3 4 5 6 7 8 9 10

For Nancy,
Kathryn,
and Russell, III

CONTENTS

INTRODUCTION

Boston has always occupied a special place in the life of America. It was a central element of Britain's imperial designs in the New World; later, as critical interests of colonies and mother country pulled further and further apart, Bostonians virtually hatched the American Revolution. For generations, the new republic looked to Boston for intellectual, economic, and political leadership; today, the city is the center of a complex of financial and cultural institutions, universities, and high-technology companies that combine to make it one of the most vital and innovative areas in the nation.

There is a certain mystique about Boston, something about the spirit of the city that makes it—even in the minds of those who have never been there—an exciting and desirable place to live. Part of this appeal can be attributed to historical significance and what can only be called charm. The site of the Boston Massacre, marked by a circle of cobblestones, can still be seen, nestled in the shadows of modern skyscrapers; Paul Revere's seventeenth-century house, almost medieval in appearance, still stands, conjuring up visions of earlier, simpler times. And contemporary Boston is still a manageable city, large enough to offer the advantages of a metropolis yet still sufficiently small that neither resident nor the visitor feels overpowered by its scale. Walking the streets of Boston, one is able to feel in control of his environment. Then too, in addition to all its cultural opportunities, the city lies at the threshold of the seasoned splendor of New England, one of the most varied scenic and recreational regions in the country.

Above all, there is in Boston a quiet air of competence and achievement, both present and past. In no field is this more true than in that great American pastime of making and investing money, an enterprise in which Bostonians have a long and honorable record. Indeed, Boston may be one of the few cities in the United States where continuing financial threads can be traced from the very beginnings of America to our own day.

With one notable lapse, Boston money has consistently been in the vanguard of American economic life. Long before the Revolution, Boston merchants were known throughout the colonies for their daring and their enterprise—and yes, sometimes for their greed. In the late eighteenth and early nineteenth centuries, Boston seafarer-merchants pushed past Cape Horn questing for the treasures of the Orient; in some quarters of the globe the inhabitants would for years afterward believe that all Americans were "Boston men." Later, with fortunes laid up in foreign trade, these same Boston merchants sparked the industrial revolution in America, creating whole new towns to support a textile industry that was for years a wonder of the Western world. Seeking fresher, more venturesome outlets for their capital and their energies, Boston builders and financiers supplied much of the money and much of the drive to help push railroads across prairies and through mountains to the western coast of America. The great Michigan copper industry was begun and financed by Bostonians, who in the process magnified and consolidated some of the great fortunes made in trade and textiles. The American Telephone & Telegraph Company, today one of the largest corporations in the world, got its start with Boston money and Boston management, and so did General Electric. It was a Bostonian's management and financial skills that saved the floundering General Motors Corporation in the early days of this century.

Eventually, slowly, almost imperceptibly, something happened to Boston money, to its drive and daring. Fathers who doubted the mettle of their sons and heirs began tying up their fortunes in tightly drawn legacies, preserving them in the impenetrable amber of trusts. Trusteed money, in the hands of ever-so-prudent conservators whose job it was to provide a sure and steady income for its beneficiaries, virtually withdrew from productive enterprise. By the 1930s, Boston money had gone to sleep, sustained by a steady 4 percent return and dreams of days long past. Once-bustling wharves and warehouses were rotting and falling into the harbor. Offices that had echoed to the springy stride of railroad builders and Canton sea captains now heard only the plodding of fiduciaries.

Following World War II, Boston was a certified economic and financial backwater. Across the Charles River in Cambridge, however, where generations of Bostonians had showered their largesse on Harvard and the Massachusetts Institute of Technology, something was happening, something akin to the city's more adventuresome times. Bright young men from wartime laboratories were casting about for new applications of knowledge gained in technological warfare. Soon they were setting up shop in back-alley buildings, tinkering with mazes of wires and tubes, dreaming up sophisticated instruments and electronic gear unimagined just a few years before.

Slowly, Boston money began to stir. Venture-capital firms sprang up to nourish companies dealing with exotic products, companies with exotic names. Spurred perhaps by the same spirit of adventure that had propelled the old captains across the seas, Route 128, that quintessential golden highway of technology, was flung out around Boston like a transistorized necklace. Boston's tradition-bound money managers, seeing what was happening, began cracking old molds, turning ready ears to young entrepreneurs in need of financial backing.

The city, too, gained new life, new spirit. Decrepit buildings came down and were replaced with new office towers; soon even many of the old-line bankers, lawyers, and trustees of ancient wealth had abandoned their old quarters and were doing business high above the city in sleek new skyscrapers. Some of them, though, have decorated their offices in traditional style, with rough-paneled walls hung with pictures and memorabilia of former times. And as they go about their twentieth-century business, they can, from time to time, peer out their office windows and look down at the outlines of the old city and at the wharves and squat granite warehouses— many of them restored now—where it all began.

The story of Boston money—how it has been made, invested,

and preserved—is the story of men who were sometimes daring, sometimes timid. It is also the story of a great city. In large measure, too, it is the story of a nation and its rise from untried republic to economic and technological giant.

And it all began with the merchants—merchant princes, some of them were—though it was hardly what Boston's founders had in mind for their newborn wilderness town.

Chapter One

THE COLONIAL ENTERPRISE

... this is never to be forgotten, that *New-England is originally a planta-tion of Religion, not a plantation of trade.*
   Let Merchants and such as are increasing *Cent per Cent* remember this, Let others that have come over since at several times understand this, that worldly gain was not the end and designe of the people of *New-England*, but *Religion*.

—John Higginson, 1663

The Reverend William Blaxton, perhaps too familiar with the worldly ways of sinners, had a marked preference for his own more saintly company. Thus it was that this rather eccentric Anglican divine scouted the unsettled shores of Massachusetts Bay in 1625 and built himself a small hillside hermitage near a clear and free-flowing spring. The peninsula where Blaxton settled was called Shawmut by the nearby Indians; white men who had passed by sometimes called it Trimountain, after its three crowning hills. Later, it would be called Boston and be known to the whole world for the commercial enterprise of its sons.

But William Blaxton, tending his orchard, hoeing his vegetable garden, quietly reading his books, had few thoughts of such wordly activity. He had come to Shawmut for solitude and had found it in full measure. But not for long.

In 1627, two years into Blaxton's lone idyll, the ill-starred King Charles I chartered the Massachusetts Bay Company. In the eyes of the crown, the company was to be a commercial

1

enterprise, designed to exploit the resources of New England for the benefit of the mother country. For colonialism, almost by definition, is a business venture, a fact recognized by Europeans long before it was pointed out to them by Karl Marx. The company's Puritan leadership, however, had other ideas. Their primary goal was not to function as an outpost of commercial empire but to establish a godly commonwealth in the New World, uncorrupted by the materialism of the old. They would quickly find, though, that a regimen of strictly orthodox worship was not sufficient for survival in a new and savage land.

The first organized party of settlers touched the Massachusetts coast in 1630 and wound up in what is now Charlestown, across the mouth of the Charles River from Shawmut. Perhaps tiring of his own company, and noting that the fledgling settlement lacked a good supply of fresh water, William Blaxton suggested that the new arrivals pack up and move over to his well-watered peninsula. The newcomers gladly accepted the offer, and by the fall of 1630 they had dubbed their new home Boston, after the Lincolnshire town from which many of them had originally come.

Soon, English-style frame houses began to rise on the barren ground in the shadows of the three hills, and Boston took on the appearance of an almost medieval village. Soon, too, it was apparent that the devout agrarian life envisioned by the Puritan founders could not be sustained for long. Unlike Virginia and the other southern colonies, Massachusetts lacked the endless reaches of lush and fertile land necessary for large-scale agriculture. Indeed, two years before the arrival of the first Bostonians, Christopher Levett had written, in *A Voyage to New England*, that the soil in the region was "good for nothing but to starve so many people as comes in it."

No, Boston and its hinterland were not destined to compete on equal terms with Virginia, Maryland, and the Carolinas to the south. Boston would be a seafaring and trading town. It was to be, in the words of the Englishman William Woods as early as 1634, "fittest for such as can Trade into *England*, for such commodities as the Countrey wants, being the chiefe place for shipping and merchandize."

So it was perhaps inevitable that merchants, men of business, not farmers or country squires, became the dominant figures in the new town. In a wilderness, goods such as cloth, nails, cooking utensils, and other necessities of civilized life are of critical importance, and those who provide them to the populace assume natural positions of leadership. From the first Boston town elections, in 1634, in fact, the great majority of town officials were drawn from the merchant class; in the town meeting elections of 1636, at least seven out of ten selectmen and three representatives to the General Court, or legislature, were merchants, though control of the colonial government was gripped firmly by orthodox Puritan hands.

For merchants of the Puritan persuasion, Boston offered a congenial combination of circumstances. Not only was it a sanctuary for the practice of a religion that was despised in the mother country, but it also held out promises of great personal profit. And while Puritan ethics and merchant values would quite early come into open conflict, it was believed by many that the laying up of reasonable profits was in some way a well-merited bestowal of God's favor. It was a belief that would persist among Boston's merchants and manufacturers, and among much of the general population, into the nineteenth century.

In the town's very earliest days, the sale of goods was conducted in the most haphazard fashion. Word would spread of the arrival of merchandise-laden ships, and customers would troop aboard to bargain for whatever struck their fancies, either for their own use or for possible resale. This soon proved unsatisfactory—not only did it drive prices up in short order, but it also lacked continuity—and in March, 1635, the government authorized a representative from each of Massachusetts' nine towns to buy cargoes and sell them to the public. Significantly, these agents were restricted to a 5 percent profit margin. This didn't work either, and the practice was suspended after a four-month trial.

Now the independent merchants began coming into their own, often with an assist from merchant relatives in England who would consign goods to Boston on credit. John Cogan, for example, reputed to have been Boston's first shopkeeper, had a brother who was a merchant in Exeter; Henry Grey and Valentine Hill each had merchant brothers in London; Joshua Hewes got shipments from his uncle, Joshua Foote, a member of London's Ironmongers' Company. And while no London merchants of the first water migrated to Boston, some of the town's early merchants had plied the same trade, on a small scale, in the mother country—men like William Alford, John Cogswell, and Edward Tyng—and men like Robert Keayne, who would not only become one of Boston's first major merchant-benefactors but would also be among the first to feel the sting of Puritan disapproval of overgenerous profits.

In 1639 Keayne was hauled into court by the Massachusetts government and charged with overcharging customers for such sundries as nails, buttons, and thread. Found guilty, he received a £200 fine, later reduced to £80. But so strong was the feeling against Keayne that he later wrote that "if some could have had their wills they would have had the fyne mounted up to 1000 lb. . . ." Not content with this mere judicial punishment, the church also admonished him "for selling his wares at excessive Rates, to the Dishonor of Gods name . . . and the Publique scandal of the Cuntry."

Like many future American businessmen, Keayne seemed flabbergasted that his commercial practices should have come to disapproving attention of the law. In his will he observed that "the newnes and straingnes of the thing, to be brought forth into an open Court as a public malefactor, was both a shame and an amazement to me."

Embittered as he was by his treatment by church and state, Keayne held no grudge against Boston. On his death in 1656, he left a £300 bequest for construction of the first Town House, stipulating that the building be provided with space "for Merchants, Mr of Shipps and Strangers as well as the Towne . . . to meet in." For more than half a century after its completion in the following year, it remained the center for both town and commercial affairs in Boston.

Two years after Keayne's misadventure with the authorities it became apparent even to the Puritan leadership that the colony's future rested with the merchants. Civil war in England all but shut off the flow of foreign goods, and prices of domestic commodities took a nosedive. Assaying the situation, Puritan Governor John Winthrop wrote that "These straits set our people on work to provide fish, clapboards, plank, etc., . . . and to look out to the West Indies for a trade. . . ."

With this simple statement, says Samuel Eliot Morison, "Winthrop explains how maritime Massachusetts came to be."

By 1643, the first Boston-built ship, the *Trial*, had returned to home port from its maiden voyage. In its travels, the small vessel set patterns of trade that were to stamp the activities of Boston seafarers and merchants for the next two centuries. At Fayal, in the Azores, Captain Thomas Coytemore traded his cargo of barrel staves and fish for wine and sugar, then headed for the West Indies, where he exchanged his burden of wine for cotton, tobacco, and iron salvaged from wrecked ships. Sailing again, under Captain Thomas Graves, the *Trial* sailed for Bilbao, in northern Spain, and returned with wine, fruit, oil, iron, and wool.

Soon other Boston ships were plowing the same furrows, and by 1676 Edward Randolph would write of the town that "It is the great care of the merchants to keep their ships in constant employ, which makes them *trye all ports to force a trade*, whereby they abound with all sorts of commodities, and *Boston may be esteemed the mart town of the West Indies.*"

TWO. "A BOSTONIAN WOULD SEEK HIS FORTUNE IN THE BOTTOM OF HELL"

The emphasis on trade in Boston very early began to shape the social development of the town. The Puritan founders, to maintain their godly commonwealth, required insulation from the sinful ways of the Old World as well as complete obedience to their authoritarian rule. But such strictures were not conducive to trade, which required free movement of both goods and people. For the merchants, it would not do to have newcomers put to a litmus test of Puritan orthodoxy.

As trade prospered in the mid-seventeenth century, men untouched by Puritanism began moving to Boston to seek their fortunes. They came despite the railings of Puritan stalwarts such as Edward Johnson, who in 1650 warned his brethren against merchants "being so taken up with the income of a large profit that they would willingly have had the Commonwealth tolerate divers kinds of sinful opinions to intice men to come and sit down with us, that their purses might be filled with coyne, the civil government with contention, and the Churches of our Lord Christ with errors. . . ."

The final blow against the Puritan oligarchy came in 1660, with the restoration of the British monarchy. Soon the Boston merchant class was peppered with royalists who patterned their lives after the fashion of Restoration England rather than on the austere ways of the native Puritans. More in tune with the mother country than their predecessors had been, these men soon emerged as a virtually separate class, a class cemented tightly by intermarriage. Thus, the influential Tyng family became related by marriage to the equally influential Bradstreets, Brattles, Dudleys, and Whartons, setting a pattern that would be followed in later generations when Cabots and Lowells, Lees and Higginsons, Appletons and Lawrences would become tied together by family bonds that would tax the ingenuity of a whole brigade of genealogists to trace and unravel.

Unlike the stern Puritans of an earlier day, these new merchants enjoyed life, often in ways that offended the sensibilities of Boston traditionalists. In 1687, for example, Samuel Sewall noted disapprovingly in his diary some of the high jinks indulged in by the wealthy merchant Samuel Shrimpton. Shrimpton and a party of friends, wrote Sewall, "come in a Coach from Roxbury about 9. aclock or past, singing as they come, being inflamed with drink. At Justice Morgan's they stop and drink Healths, curse, swear, talk profanely and baudily to the great disturbance of the Town and grief of good people. Such high-handed wickedness has not been heard of before in Boston."

Wicked or not, merchants were leaving their imprint on the physical growth of Boston. As early as 1639, they had built a "Wharfe and Crayne" to unload ship cargoes that had in the beginning been lightered ashore at a natural cove, and by 1645 the town could boast fifteen private wharves. Within a few years the buildings required by a flourishing world trade were vying with church steeples as hallmarks of the Boston spirit, and in 1654 an observer could note that "the chiefe Edifice of this City-like Towne is crowded on the Sea-bankes, and wharfed out with great industry and cost, the buildings beautiful and large.... The wonder of this modern Age, that a few yeares should bring forth such great matters by so mean a handful.... This Town," he added, "is the very Mart of the Land, *French, Portugalls* and *Dutch*, come hither for Traffique."

So important had trade become to the town that the magistracy was even willing to forgive wickedness if it seemed good for business. The widowed tavern keeper Alice Thomas, whipped and banished from Boston in 1672 for giving her patrons "opportunity to commit carnall wickedness," and for being "a common Baud," was readmitted the following year when she subscribed money to help build a protective seawall in the harbor.

The tempo of daily life was set by the needs of merchants, too. No matter what his station or calling, no Bostonian could fail to hear or gauge the hour by the tolling of the 11:00 A.M. bell ordered by the selectmen in 1664 to summon merchants to gather at Robert Keayne's Town House "For the more convenient and exspeditious dispatch of Marchants affayres...." And as they grew in wealth, merchants freed of Puritan restraints began to display their prosperity. The squat and Spartan dwellings of early times gave way to more substantial structures, and by 1675 William Harris could observe that Boston's merchants "seem to be rich men, and their houses are handsomely furnished as most in London."

They certainly deserved their share of worldly comfort. Separated from their home country by a broad and treacherous ocean that made sailings haphazard and communications uncertain, these merchants on the distant shore of a mercantile empire conducted their business amid great risk and danger. Here was no place for the kind of ordered specialization that can make an efficiently managed business enterprise almost run itself. These early Boston merchants were both wholesalers and retailers of a broad variety of goods and commodities, and they were constantly trying to find ways to dispose of new kinds of goods, to find new goods for new markets. During a single year in the 1640s, Valentine Hill trafficked in pork, peas, fish, wheat, cattle, corn, pipe staves, clapboards, fish, indigo, sugar, and tobacco. Others dealt in a bewildering array of iron, crockery, wines and spirits, cloth, and haberdashery, with sometimes less than satisfactory results.

"You send me such a multitude of hatts," wrote John Hull in 1671 to a London supplier (who just happened to be his cousin), "y^t unless I will give y^m away or trust y^m to such as will never pay, I must keep them to my very great trouble Hazard & charge." Some of them, said Hull, couldn't even be unloaded at cost, "especially the french hatts they are so big y^t noe heads heer Are bigg enough for y^m."

Because of the hazards of transatlantic crossings under sail, Boston merchants were forced to pay hefty freight costs for their goods, so it was natural that some of them would begin to buy their own ships, either outright or on shares with fellow traders. Hull, a typical merchant of the time, owned a small vessel of his own in 1663, and between 1665 and 1670 had part ownership in eight ships plying the West Indies, London, Bristol, Spain, and France. Usually his share came to one-quarter, but he held a one-third share of one and half of another. Between 1670 and 1683, he had ownership in at least fourteen ships, his share ranging from one-twelfth to three-quarters.

If the seventeenth-century Boston merchants traded in a wide-ranging variety of goods freighted on ships with multiple owners, they were also forced to contend with a confusing blend of currencies that made bookkeeping a troublesome chore. For domestic commerce, Indian wampum was legal tender until the early 1660s, and while trade with the West Indies introduced silver into the Boston trading scene, such hard currency usually had to be remitted to London creditors in payment for goods. The same was true of the Portuguese, Dutch, and French coin that found its way into the counting room coffers of Boston's wharves. Among themselves and their customers, the Boston merchants frequently had no recourse but barter.

As the seventeenth century neared its end, Boston was the premier shipping and trading port in North America. Its merchants reckoned their volume of trade at four times that of New York, and in 1698 the royal governor, Lord Bellomont, claimed that more sailing vessels belonged to Boston than to Scotland and Ireland combined. Daring Boston mariners, setting out for ports in the West Indies and Europe, trading all the while, had charted a course of enterprise for generations of Boston traders, setting them apart from their fellow colonials in other parts of America. Indeed, early in the eighteenth century, noting the differences in temperament between the northern and southern colonies, Felix de Beaujour would observe that "A Bostonian would seek his fortune in the bottom of hell, but a Virginian would not go four steps for it."

And if a Boston merchant ever did find himself in the pits of hell to drive a bargain, it is likely that Satan would have met his match. Writing of Boston in 1699, Londoner Edward Ward said that "he that Knows how to deal with their Traders, may deal with the Devil and fear no Craft." And according to Ward, those who dealt with them on unequal terms had much craft to fear from Boston traders. He told a story, which may or may not be apocryphal, of a group of Boston merchants who, behind in their remittances to British creditors, secretly moved their goods from their warehouses, torched the buildings, and claimed that they'd lost all they owned—including their record books. "And so at once [they] Ballanc'd their Accounts with England," Ward observed.

Unkindest of all, Ward snickered at the pretensions of Boston's newly rich merchants, some of whom, he claimed, were building themselves stately houses to the tune of £2,000 to £3,000; "which, I think, plainly proves Two old Adages true, viz: That a Fool and his Money is soon parted, and set a Beggar on Horse-back he'll Ride to the Devil; for the Fathers of these Men were Tinkers and Peddlers." And like many of the newly rich, Boston's prospering merchants were single-minded in their pursuit of gain. Another observer, visiting the town in the final year of the seventeenth century, noted of its merchants that "Interest is faith, Money their God, and Large possessions the only Heaven they covet." The town's sternly Puritan founders must have rested uneasily in their graves.

The Boston of the 1700s was far different from the barren peninsula dotted with unpainted wooden houses that had greeted visitors during much of the previous century. Its growth had been slow, almost imperceptible, unmarked by singular bursts of building. Wood gave way to brick and stone as the favored construction material, and three-story brick dwellings had become commonplace, with merchant William Clark's twenty-six-room, richly appointed house on what is now North Square being the most imposing.

By the third decade of the century the town could boast of more than forty wharves; the largest, lined on one side with warehouses, reached nearly two thousand feet into the bay. Soon the shops and warehouses along the bustling waterfront began to expand into adjacent residential areas, and merchants who had lived hard by their countinghouses began inching farther inland. Growth of trade had brought an influx of new inhabitants, and by the 1740s Boston was the largest town in British North America, trailed by Philadelphia and New York.

At the same time, the town's commercial life was coming to be dominated by great merchants who would leave a lasting imprint on the development of both Boston and America.

THREE. "THE TOPINIEST MERCHANT IN ALL THE TOWN"

As Andrew Faneuil's funeral cortege wound its way through the crooked, narrow streets of Boston toward the Granary Burying Ground, windowpanes throughout the town rattled at the roar of cannon salvos from ships anchored in the harbor. Down at the wharves, warehouses and counting rooms stood shuttered and still as their proprietors paid respect to a prince among mercantile princes. Boston's richest merchant was being entombed with the full honors due a man of his achievement and position.

Peter Faneuil, Andrew's favorite nephew and heir, limping ever so slightly from a hip defective since birth, led the train of mourners trailing the black-draped coffin. As the procession passed King's Chapel, Faneuil surely lifted his head and glanced across Tremont Street to the great house on a hill that was now his own. He must have marveled that fate had placed his uncle's vast holdings in his hands. It may have been out of gratitude as much as respect and bereavement that Faneuil distributed a staggering three thousand pairs of mourning gloves to honor his dead uncle, and later gave out two hundred mourning rings to close friends.

And as they gathered at the graveside, as they watched the casket being borne into the fresh tomb, as they moved slowly back to their countinghouses, some of these friends, the grandees of Boston business, must have whispered to one another: "And now, we'll see how Peter fares on his own." Actually, when Andrew Faneuil died in February, 1738, his nephew Peter had been on his own for about two years. Andrew, a French Huguenot refugee who had been a Boston merchant since at least 1691, had long been bedridden with a serious illness, leaving the management of his affairs to his brother's son. But now, at Andrew's death, the portly thirty-seven-year-old Peter Faneuil was to take over his uncle's vast mercantile empire in fact as well as in practice. In his will, after making bequests to a number of relatives and retainers, Andrew concluded that "I give, bequeath, and devise all the rest of my estate, both real and personal, whatsoever and wheresoever 'tis in New England, Great Britain, France, Holland, or any other part of the world to my loving nephew Peter Faneuil eldest son of my late brother Benjamin Faneuil, to hold to him and his heirs forever."

If Peter Faneuil had worked hard for his inheritance, he had also been lucky. When his father died in 1719, Peter and his younger brother, Benjamin, had been sent from New Rochelle, New York, to Boston, where their uncle Andrew had already amassed a considerable fortune from warehousing and real estate speculation. At his wife's death in 1724, the childless Andrew seemed to transfer all his affections to his two nephews, and he determined that one of them would be his heir. But it was the younger Benjamin, not Peter, who was tapped for this benefaction. There was, however, a strict condition governing the ultimate disposal of the Faneuil fortune.

Andrew Faneuil was a quirky man, and one of his quirks was that the nephew who was to succeed him in his business, be the heir to his far-flung holdings, must not be married. Perhaps the old man was jealous of his nephews' affections; perhaps he simply didn't want them to take on a responsibility that would interfere with a merchant's obligations. Whatever his reasons, he would not be budged from his position.

It is not known how or where Benjamin Faneuil met Mary Cutler. Perhaps it was at one of the glittering balls given by an official of the provincial government, or it may have been while walking at sunset through the bucolic Boston Common. Wherever it was, Benjamin was smitten by this gentle, pretty girl, the daughter of a Church of England clergyman. She was educated—rare in a woman of those times—and was an amateur poetess. Benjamin was in love, so in love that he was willing to risk his birthright; he asked Mary to be his wife, and she accepted. Benjamin tried to keep his plans a secret from his uncle, but a town gossip learned of the furtive engagement and told one of the Faneuil servants. The servant passed the word on to Andrew.

The next day at breakfast with Benjamin, Andrew pushed his chair back from the table, hooked his thumbs in his brocade waistcoat, and looked his favorite nephew in the eye. "I hear you plan to get married," Andrew said.

"Yes, Uncle, I do," said Benjamin, knowing full well the penalty of treasure he was about to pay.

"Then you will leave my house," Andrew shot back.

It is said that the two were not together again until 1785, when Benjamin was buried in the family vault—with considerably less pomp than was accorded his uncle. In his will, Andrew bequeathed to his once-favorite nephew "five shillings and no more" and specifically excluded from any other share of his estate both Benjamin "and the heirs of his body forever."

After dispensing with Benjamin, Andrew called Peter to his

countinghouse and told him the news. Peter, he said, was to be the heir to all the Faneuil fortune. But he must stay single. Peter agreed, and for the rest of his life he was known as Boston's Jolly Bachelor.

At one point, though, he came close to suffering the same fate as his brother. In about 1730, Peter attended a reception for Jonathan Belcher, newly arrived royal governor of Massachusetts. There he met Mary Jekyll, a daughter of John Jekyll, collector of the port of Boston. He continued to see her from time to time after this first meeting, and he fell in love. But in 1733, when her father died, Mary and her family moved back to England to settle the estate, entrusting the care of their Boston property to Faneuil. Several years later Mary and her sisters returned to Boston, where they lived for a time in the Faneuil mansion. Mindful of his brother's disinheritance, Peter kept his distance, but still kept his interest in Mary. When it appeared that she might marry one Lord Linnington, Peter arranged for the Jekyll sisters to go to Haverhill, to the north of Boston, for a lengthy stay, and took it upon himself to warn Mary's brother, Richard, in London, about the prospective bridegroom. Linnington's character and reputation hardly merited repeating, wrote Faneuil, saying only that "he is a worthless pretender to a good deal of money and witt, without, according to the best accounts I can learn, any of either...."

Mary Jekyll found Haverhill a welcome change from Boston. Within a short time after her arrival, she met and married Colonel Richard Saltonstall. A little over a year later, she died, leaving no children, and there were those who said that Peter Faneuil never fully recovered from the loss.

Peter worked hard for his uncle, probably harder than he had worked on his own trading and real estate ventures. Shipments of fish, tobacco, tar, and barrel staves were dispatched to major ports in Europe and the West Indies, where they were exchanged for wine, cloth, crockery, rum, sugar, molasses, and other necessities of civilized colonial life. From England, France, and Portugal came cargoes of goods on consignment, which Faneuil warehoused and sold for a 5 percent commission. Smuggling, too, helped swell the Faneuil coffers, and while Faneuil and other colonial merchants did not consider it a sin to cheat His Majesty's government out of import duties, they were fully aware that it was a crime, and were at great pains to avoid getting caught at it. To a southern port in 1737, for example, Faneuil shipped sixty-two dozen fine Barcelona handkerchiefs, worth about £435, and didn't even let his ship's captain know about it. "You cannot be insensible," he wrote to his southern agent, "that they cannot be imported openly, therefore I desire yr. care in gettg. of them on Shore Immediately on yre arrival."

The most visible jewel in Peter Faneuil's inheritance was the spacious white-painted brick mansion which his uncle had built about 1709 on a seven-acre plot opposite King's Chapel. With its lush, terraced gardens and pagodalike summer house with a broad view of the town and harbor, the Faneuil estate was a showplace of Boston. Peter gave frequent parties there for the elite of colonial Massachusetts, and among the delicacies that he was able to serve them were tropical fruits grown in his own hothouses.

Faneuil's guests were also given nothing but the best in wines, and the Jolly Bachelor was careful to make sure that he poured from his own decanters better stuff than he sold to his customers. Just three weeks after his uncle's death, Faneuil wrote to Pope & Company, on the wine island of Madeira, specifying exactly what he had in mind: "Send me by the first opportunity for this place five pipes of your very best Madeira wine, of an amber color, of the same sort which you sent to our good friend De Lancy of New York." And he added, "As the wine is for the use of my house, I hope you will be careful that I have the best...."

On the same day, Faneuil took steps to insure that he would travel the streets of Boston in fine style. "Be so good as to send me a handsome chariot with two sets of harness," he wrote to Lane & Smithhurst in London, "with the arms as enclosed on the same in the handsomest manner that you shall judge proper, but at the same nothing gaudy...." Handsome, but not gaudy. High quality, but not flashy. These were to remain watchwords for well-heeled Bostonians even to the present day. Faneuil also took great care in selecting his clothes, writing frequently to London to order the latest fashions; "all to be of the best, you must mind," he admonished his tailor. Not for nothing did fellow merchant Thomas Hancock call Faneuil "the topiniest merchant in all the town."

For all his love of the good life, Peter Faneuil was a generous, charitable man. Indeed, at his death, the *Boston Weekly Newsletter* called him "the most publick spirited man, in all regards, that ever yet appeared on the Northern continent of America." And his eulogist observed that "It was to him the highest enjoyment of riches, to relieve the wants of the needy.... His acts of charity were so secret and unbounded that none but they who were the objects of it, can compute the sums which he annually distributed among them. His alms flowed like a fruitful river...."

These private acts of Faneuil's philanthropy have long since been forgotten, interred with the bones of their beneficiaries. But his major public gift to the town of Boston still stands, in somewhat altered form, after more than two centuries.

Faneuil, like most other Boston householders, was constantly pestered by door-to-door produce sellers arriving at erratic intervals. On the other hand, it was equally bothersome when some item was not in his larder and servants had to be sent scurrying around town to find what was needed. For Boston had no central market for foodstuffs; country people, fearing that prices would be driven down if they all brought their goods to one place at the same time, had successfully blocked the establishment of a common marketplace. When such a market had been built in 1737, in fact, its opponents, disguised as clergymen, tore it down one night.

To Faneuil, with his well-managed, wide-ranging enterprises, lack of a central place to sell farm produce was simply inefficient and a great hindrance to business. The solution was clear. Faneuil would build a market for the town at his own expense, with the proviso that the town would in turn "constantly support it for the said use." A petition favoring the plan was signed by 314 Bostonians, and after much squabbling the town meeting agreed to let its foremost merchant proceed. In September, 1742, more than two years after the initial approval, the building had been completed to the town meeting's satisfaction, and it was voted to name "this most generous and noble benefaction" after its donor and to place a full-length portrait of Faneuil in the meeting hall above the market area.

At the opening of the annual meeting of the town on March 14, 1743, John Lovell, master of the Boston Latin School, rose in this hall and began to speak. "I stand in this place, my fellow townsmen . . ." he said, "to condole with you for the loss of your late generous benefactor, the founder of this hall. . . ."

For just four days before, Boston's topiniest merchant, felled at the age of forty-two by a "dropsical complication," had been buried in a black-velvet-covered coffin in his uncle's tomb in the Granary Burying Ground. Faneuil left no will, and his business empire died with him. The grand house that had been his pride was sold; his considerable store of silver and jewels was divided among his sisters and his brother, Benjamin, who must have been thankful that Peter had not drawn up a will guided by the dead hand of his uncle Andrew.

Not so thankful for Peter Faneuil's intestacy was John Lovell, speaking for his fellow townsmen. "For I am well-assured, from those who were acquainted with his purposes, that he had many more blessings in store for us, had heaven prolonged his days."

If heaven did not see fit to preserve Peter Faneuil, it has preserved his benefaction to Boston. Gutted to the walls by fire in 1761, the market hall was rebuilt to become the gathering place of colonial dissidents plotting revolution. Enlarged in 1805 to its present size, it still serves its original double function of market and meeting place, its walls echoing with debate over issues undreamed of by its donor.

FOUR. "CHOICE PARCELS OF NEGRO BOYS AND GIRLS"

Ironically, one of the issues that would be debated in Faneuil Hall was slavery. For Peter Faneuil, like most early Bostonians, saw nothing amiss in what was later to be termed the "peculiar institution" of the South. Indeed, just a few weeks before the death of his uncle, Peter had consigned a shipment of fish to the West Indies, instructing that its proceeds be used to "purchase for me, for the use of my house, as likely a strait negro lad as possibly you can, about the age from twelve to fifteen years. . . ." Not wanting his young slave to fall victim to a most common disease of the period, Faneuil recommended that preference be given to a boy who had already survived a bout with smallpox. Among the effects in Peter's estate at his death were five slaves.

But it was primarily as slave traders, not slave owners, that Bostonians were to make their mark in the history of human bondage in America. Having no vast lands to till, and having a ready supply of cheap immigrant labor close at hand, Boston's merchants had little need for great numbers of slaves; those that they did own, primarily for use as house servants, were probably prized as much for their exotic effect as for their labor. And even this novelty value must have paled after a time; as early as 1687, a French visitor to Boston had reported that scarcely any Boston household of consequence didn't have at least one slave.

Trading as they did with the West Indies, Boston's pioneer merchants stumbled upon the traffic in human beings almost by inevitable accident. In those tropic regions, slavery had quite early become all but necessary for the cultivation of sugarcane; Boston's enterprising merchants, always on the lookout for commodities to serve their markets, turned naturally enough to trading slaves for sugarcane, which was brought back to home port for processing into rum and molasses. It took little imagination for these diligent traders to sail off to Guinea with cargoes of rum to be exchanged for Negroes who were then transported to the West Indies where they were exchanged for more sugarcane to be turned into more rum. It was a neat trick, this triangular trade in cane, rum, and men, and it took on a new twist toward the end of the seventeenth century with the introduction of rice and indigo culture in South Carolina and the great expansion in cultivation of Virginia tobacco, all of which required slave labor. So diligent were the Bostonians and merchants from neighboring ports in supplying this demand that the second Colonel Richard Byrd of Virginia was moved to lament in 1736 that "the Saints of New England import so many Negroes hither that I fear the Colony will some time or other be Confirmed by the name of New Guinea."

How many of Boston's leading merchants were included

among Byrd's New England slaver-saints is impossible to determine. To this day, there are Bostonians—some of them still living off the fruits of fortunes that had their genesis at a time when it was possible to traffic in human cargoes—who maintain that the direct participation of their forebears in the slave trade was minimal and that the bulk of this business was engaged in by the more uncouth merchants of Providence and Newport. To some extent, this may be true, though it may also be true that Boston slavers and their descendants were more careful than others in destroying incriminating records of their slave trade days. But early Boston bristled with rum distilleries, and while some of the output may have been for home consumption or trade for more conventional commodities, much of it was no doubt destined for Africa to be bartered for Negroes. In the mid-eighteenth century, a flourishing time for the slave trade, one observer noted that "The quantity of spirits which they distil in Boston from the molasses they bring in from all parts of the West Indies is as surprising as the cheap rate at which they vend it . . . but they are more famous for the quantity and cheapness than for the excellency of their rum." Such a product would seem to be ideally suited for passing off to undiscriminating blacks who must have prized spirituous liquors more for intoxicating effects than for mellowness.

Thomas Amory, one Boston merchant who was big in the slave trade and who succeeded in helping to found one of the city's latter-day first families, calculated in 1724 that "a good likely fellow that speaks English sells from £70 to £80." Unfortunately for Amory, his involvement in the triangular trade led indirectly to his untimely death at the age of thirty-five; inspecting one of his distilleries in 1728, he fell into a cistern and drowned.

Peter Faneuil, too, tried his hand at the slave trade more than once, perhaps most notably in a venture whose abortive end he didn't live to hear about. Not long before his death Faneuil sent a slaving ship, owned half by himself and one-quarter each by a neighbor and the captain, on an expedition to the coast of Guinea. Before it was fully loaded, the ship—appropriately dubbed the *Jolly Bachelor*—was boarded by a party of natives who killed the captain and two sailors, stripped the vessel of its stores and provisions, and liberated the blacks already on board. A short time later, the *Jolly Bachelor* was salvaged and sent to Newport by George Birchall of Sierra Leone, who had managed to buy back some of the ship's stores and twenty of the freed slaves from their rescuers. Ship and slaves were sold at auction, a portion of the proceeds going to the estate of Peter Faneuil. The buyer of the highest-priced slave, a "negro boy" who went for the princely sum of £134, was one Mr. Chaning, who may or may not have been an ancestor of the latter-day abolitionist William Ellery Channing.

Despite efforts to discourage it on moral, economic, and other grounds—a £4 head tax imposed in 1704 on each slave imported into Massachusetts was intended "for the Better preventing of a spurious or mixt issue"—the holding of slaves persisted in Boston, and Bostonians continued to trade in them. Well into the 1700s Boston newspapers advertised the arrival of "choice parcels of negro boys and girls," and as late as 1785 an English resident of the Guinea coast wrote that "They now have here, from Boston and its vicinity, six vessels, five of which, I am told, have positive orders to take slaves only." And just the year before, two British slave traders on the Gold Coast had complained that the Boston slaver *Commerce*, captained by John Dudley Saltonstall, had tried to buy slaves directly from the Africans, thus circumventing the British-claimed monopoly on the trade. What was worse, the irate Englishmen said, was that in his dealings with the native African slave traders the crafty Saltonstall "used every Argument to influence the Minds of the Blacks, and instill in them that spirit of Republican freedom, and Independence, which they, through Rebellion, have established for themselves. . . ." Saltonstall prevailed, they held, "As no Arguments are so powerful with the Natives as a plentiful supply of Rum, of which he has not been sparing."

In 1807 both Britain and the United States passed laws forbidding their citizens from engaging in the slave trade, and in 1819 Congress declared that slavers would be considered pirates. But there are those who say that some Boston merchants continued in the trade until as late as 1850.

FIVE. "THE GOOD LORD PROTECT YOU & OUR INTERESTS"

Though he owned a least one slave during his lifetime, the great merchant Thomas Hancock does not seem to have taken part in the lucrative slave trade. But this archetypal eighteenth-century Boston businessman bought and sold nearly every other commodity available in his day and laid up one of the largest pre-Revolutionary fortunes in America. He did not live long enough, however, to see his nephew and adoptive son, John Hancock, become an architect of the revolt that would destroy British rule over the American colonies.

Hancock, the son of a Lexington clergyman, was indentured in 1717, at the age of fourteen, to Boston bookseller Samuel Gerrish. After his indenture, with capital supplied probably by his father, he went into business for himself, selling and binding books and dealing in stationery supplies. The Boston of his day was small, with a population of just 15,000 or so, and it wasn't long before the industrious young Hancock was rubbing shoulders with the town's leading citizens. It wasn't long, either, before he began branching out of the book business to become a general merchant.

Lacking hard cash—coins still had to be sent back to Britain to cover debts, and colonial paper currency was printed in such quantities that it was all but worthless—Hancock made many of his transactions with money substitutes such as goods or services. The whale oil that he shipped to London was sold for sterling, which was used to buy British goods for the Boston market. These goods were then often exchanged for such things as beef, hemp, cotton, rum, and other commodities, which were in turn bartered for more whale oil.

The whale-oil trade was profitable for Hancock, and he didn't hesitate to make display of his newly acquired wealth. By 1735 he had bought an acre of pastureland on Beacon Hill, adjacent to the present State House, where he laid out elaborate gardens and an orchard. Eventually, he would expand his holdings until he owned the whole of Beacon Hill, and in 1737 he built a large house on his original plot of ground, sending to

England for sumptuous furnishings. The following year he paid £160 for a slave named Cambridge.

Like many businessmen before and since, Hancock found that wars make profitable business. During Britain's war with Spain in 1740, having already trimmed his overseas trade in anticipation of the conflict, Hancock became a major supplier of beef and pork to the British forces in the Caribbean. And like many a merchant of later Revolutionary times, he dabbled in privateering, taking out shares in ships with letters of marque entitling them to seize merchant vessels on the high seas. One of these privateers, the *Young Eagle*, took two Dutch ships off the Spanish colony of Tenerife within a few days. Holland was a neutral nation, but under the rules of war even a neutral ship was fair game for privateers if it was trading with the enemy, and Hancock got a handsome share of the booty.

With the end of the war, Hancock resumed his foreign trade, sending fish-laden ships to the West Indies to pick up cargoes of logwood, lignum vitae, indigo, and molasses and take them to Amsterdam, where they were exchanged for paper and other European goods. Many of these cargoes were brought to home port without benefit of inspection and collection of duties by customs officials, and Hancock commonly instructed his captains to send word ashore when they arrived off Cape Cod or Cape Ann so he could arrange to have the goods carried ashore in secrecy. And he was not above asking the Almighty to watch over his smuggling, closing a letter of instruction to Captain Simon Gross of the ship *Charming Lydia*, in which Gross is advised to evade customs by unloading at nearby Nantasket, with the hope that "The Good Lord protect you & our Interests, from all Dangers & Enemies. . . ."

By the middle of the eighteenth century, smuggling had reached almost epidemic proportions in Boston. There were few merchants who didn't give it a try now and again, some of them on virtually every voyage, and such illicit trade was probably greater than legal trade. For while the key to their prosperity was the British Empire and its all-powerful navy, colonial merchants bristled at the ever tightening restrictions placed upon them as tribute to the mother country.

In the beginning, such restrictions had been of little moment. The original merchant-colonists were, after all, loyal Englishmen, and no doubt agreed with that prime tenet of mercantilism that the home country should be the funnel for the import and export of colonial goods. To these men, Boston was a place to enrich themselves while at the same time enriching the crown. The various navigation acts of the seventeenth century, specifying that colonial goods had to be sent to Britain in British ships, were not viewed as all that restrictive, since this was the pattern of trade followed by most merchants anyway. Besides, the rules weren't very strictly enforced, and there was ample opportunity for an enterprising trader to avoid them.

By the early 1700s, however, there were great numbers of merchants who, if they considered themselves Englishmen, felt that they were a hybrid variety, with roots not in England but in America. And they did not take kindly to the notions that they seemed to toil primarily for the benefit of a nation that some of them had never seen and that England's primary interest in the colonies was to siphon off the wealth of America.

Unfortunately for Britain, it was during this time of disenchantment that His Majesty's government saw fit to begin cracking down on smuggling and imposing even stiffer customs duties on imported goods. Smoldering with resentment, the merchants would continue to resist and evade the restrictions pressed upon them by the crown; eventually, their resentment would catch fire and lead to the drive for independence.

In the meantime, though, there was still opportunity for enterprising merchants like Thomas Hancock to profit from the colonies' ties to England and do a thriving business in government contracts. During King George's War (1744–48), Hancock was heavily into outfitting the forts of Nova Scotia. Here in Newfoundland—"the Land," as it was called—the British were throwing up fortresses for protection against the French, and desperately needed building materials. Hancock obliged, and noted that he "nearly sank 4 vessels with the bricks I put in 'em." Getting these fat government contracts could be a tricky business, and Hancock pulled out all the stops in trying to pick bigger and better plums for himself. If he didn't scruple to smuggle, he didn't balk at bribery, either. Drum up as much business as you can with government officials, he wrote to his London agents, and "if a few Guineas be necessary to Expend on the Affair, let it be done."

Done it was, and Hancock made a considerable fortune out of the war. In celebration, he wrote to London for a four-horse chariot and chaise—"such a one as Sir Harry Frankland bought"—taking care to note that what he wanted should be "not gaudy but neat and fashionable." He also sought a coachman; "not an overgrown fatt fellow, nor an old one."

Supplying provisions to troops during the French and Indian War proved to be another bonanza for Hancock, and it was during this time that his young nephew, John, came to work for him to learn the merchant trade as a clerk. In 1763 John was made a partner and virtually took over the business. All did not run smoothly, however. In 1764 a British officer at the fortress of Annapolis Royal in Nova Scotia filed a report in which he stated, "This is to certify that having carefully surveyed a Barrell of Pork in the Stores sent here by Thomas Hancock Esqr & Co. . . . we found same Stinking, decay'd and intirely unfit for use." Undaunted, the wiley Hancocks unloaded their ripe pork on the French, who apparently were not so squeamish.

By the 1760s Boston's merchants had firmly established themselves as social, political, and economic leaders of the town. Beyond that, they had planted seeds of charity, commerce, and enterprise that would flourish for generations. Robert Keayne's Town House had been followed by the gift of Faneuil Hall. Peter Faneuil, not content to depend on the ups and downs of trade, scanned the *Boston News Letter* for the latest London stock quotations, and invested considerable sums in Bank of England shares and in East India Company stocks and bonds; Thomas Hancock put money in a short-lived copper mining venture, presaging the great Calumet & Hecla lode that would enrich Bostonians in the coming century.

And despite their smuggling and bribery, their slaving and hard bargaining and occasional bad parcels of meat, these colonial Boston merchants were as upright and honorable—and perhaps more so—as the commercial ethics of their era required. If Peter Faneuil was relentless in seeing to it that others "act the Honest and Just part by me," he was also honest and just in his own dealings. And Thomas Amory was speaking for more than himself when he advised an agent in the Azores to take all necessary steps to discharge Amory's financial obligations there, explaining that "I had rather be a loser in any way than have my reputation in question abroad."

In the revolutionary decades to come, many of the established merchant families of Boston would be swept away, replaced by newcomers sprung from different roots. And though the war would bring with it a round of greed and profiteering, the old spirit, the old standards of conduct, would survive.

Chapter Two

COMES THE REVOLUTION

When you come [to Boston] you will scarcely see any other than new faces . . . the change wch in that respect has happened within the few years since the revolution is as remarkable as the revolution itself.

—James Bowdoin, 1783

Walking into the council chamber at the State House on August 1, 1764, Thomas Hancock dropped suddenly to the floor, struck down by a fit of apoplexy. Within two hours he was dead. In his will, he left his house and lands, his carriages and horses, and £10,000 sterling to his widow. To Harvard College, Hancock bequeathed £1,000 for a chair of Oriental languages. Much of the estate, which totaled some £100,000, went to John Hancock, along with control of his late uncle's mercantile house.

For the history of America, it was a propitious time for the sometimes impetuous Hancock to become head of a great mercantile enterprise. Boston's merchants had long been unhappy with the restrictions pressed upon them by Britain, which was now determined to start cracking down on evasion of customs duties. As early as 1750 some of these dissidents had begun to meet informally in the front room of a tavern, the British Coffee House, on King Street near Long Wharf. By 1763 they had organized themselves as the Society for Encouraging Trade and Commerce within the Province of Massachusetts Bay, and determined to meet annually "to consider the state of Trade. . . ."

There was much to be considered. The postwar depression
that followed the French and Indian conflict had cut the
number of ships plying the lucrative West Indies trade routes
by 80 percent. A heavy duty was placed on sugar, not simply to
regulate commerce, but to raise money to meet colonial expenses and expansion. New or higher duties were clapped on a
wide variety of goods, and while the duty on molasses was
halved to three pence a gallon, this did not really amount to a
reduction. The old duty had been evaded with impunity; the
new one was to be carried out. Boston merchants alleged in
1764 that British enforcement of customs laws would cause
them a total annual loss of at least £164,000 and leave ships
worth £100,000 rotting at their moorings.

A final straw was the Stamp Act, concerning which John
Hancock prophetically wrote his London agent in early 1765:
"I hear the Stamp Act is like to take place it is very cruel we
were before much burthened we shall not now be able much
longer to support trade, and in the end Great Britain must feel
the ill effects of it." In the fall of 1765 Boston's merchants
agreed to import no more British manufactured goods until the
act was repealed, and early in the following year Britain gave in.
But things had gone too far. Motivated more by economic
self-interest than by any feelings of patriotism, Boston merchants continued to defy the crown and to urge their colleagues
in the other colonies to do likewise. It all moved Edmund Burke
to tell the British Parliament that "By these acts of oppression
you have made Boston the Lord Mayor of America."

On April 7, 1768, John Hancock's ship *Lydia*, heavily laden
with spring orders from London, slipped into its berth at Hancock's Wharf. The British customs officers, suspecting that the
cargo included paper, tea, and other dutiable items, sent two
men aboard the following day to check over the contents of the
hold. Learning of this intrusion, Hancock rushed to the wharf
with a small group of followers, possibly from the Sons of Liberty, in which he had become active at the urging of John
Adams. When he boarded the ship, he asked the customs operatives to explain what they were up to; told that they had been

sent to examine the cargo, he ordered the captain not to allow them below deck. The following night, one of them, Owen Richards, decided to get to the bottom of things, and sneaked aboard the ship and went down to the hold. Hancock got wind of this, too, and a short time later showed up with a lantern-bearing slave and eight or ten friends. Hancock ordered the surprised Richards off his ship; Richards refused to leave, and Hancock then demanded to see his commission and orders. Claiming that they weren't in order, the fiery Hancock ordered two of the crew to throw the trespasser from his vessel. While one of Hancock's friends bellowed, "Damn him, hand him up! If it was my vessel, I'd knock him down!" the crewmen grabbed the shaken Richards's arms and legs and wrestled him out of the hold and onto the deck.

There, as the *Lydia* bobbed gently in the dark harbor, Hancock asked Richards if he still wanted to search the ship. When he shook his head and said no, Hancock smiled and said, "You may search the vessel, but shall not tarry below." Richards, his mission aborted, scrambled down the gangplank to report to his superiors, who turned the matter over to an attorney general who eventually determined that while the law allowed customs officials to go on board a docked merchant vessel, it did not necessarily give them the right to inspect the hold. As for Hancock's high-handed ejection of Richards, the ruling was that "though Mr. Hancock may not have conducted himself so prudently or courteously as might be wished, yet from what appears it is probable that his intention was to keep within the bounds of the law." It is probable, too, that his intention was to avoid paying duties on contraband goods.

Hancock, a leading merchant of Boston and a member since 1766 of the Great and General Court—the colony's legislative body—had taken a fateful step that night. He had become the first substantial citizen in all the American colonies to offer physical resistance to an officer of the crown.

Even before he was found faultless in the *Lydia* affair, Hancock clashed with the customs authorities once more. When his ship *Liberty* arrived on May 9 freighted with wine from the island of Madeira, customs officials suspected that there might be more wine on board than had been reported to them. It was a fair suspicion, as it had long been the practice for merchants to avoid duties by underreporting their cargoes and unloading the excess under cover of darkness. The inspectors who looked over the *Liberty*, however, reported that no wine had been removed from the Hancock ship. The matter seemed closed until a month later when one of the inspectors, Thomas Kirk, stepped forward and confessed that he had lied. What had really happened, he said, was that on the night of the so-called inspection his partners had got drunk and gone home. While Kirk had been poking about the ship alone, he said, the captain arrived and strongly suggested that it would be a good idea if Kirk turned his back while a quantity of wine was removed from the hold. When he refused, Kirk said, the captain and some crew members stuffed him down a hatch into a small cabin and nailed it shut. The resourceful Kirk proceeded to break down the cabin door into the steerage, and was trying to creep to the deck when he was caught and hustled back into steerage, where he was held for three hours. Huddled there in the creaking darkness, he said, he could hear the unmistakable sound of wine casks being rolled off the ship. At the end of this operation, he told the customs commissioners, the captain had pledged him to secrecy by threatening his life and property if he ever told what had happened. Meanwhile, the captain had died, and Kirk now felt moved to tell the truth.

The commissioners believed Kirk's tale, which was probably true, and seized the ship. But not without incident. It took the help of the crew of the British man of war *Romney*, anchored nearby, to push through a shouting, cursing mob that had gathered on Hancock's Wharf—perhaps encouraged by Hancock himself—and assert the king's dominion over those who would flout his laws and threaten the lives of his minions.

Although Hancock took no actual part in hammering the hatch on the hapless Kirk, he was held responsible for spiriting the wine ashore. It was, after all, his ship, and the captain was surely acting under his orders. Hancock was arrested and charged with assisting in the illicit landing of a full one hundred pipes of wine, valued at £3,000. This leading citizen of Boston was released from custody on £3,000 bail, and the customs commissioners demanded that he pay a penalty of £9,000 for his transgression. John Adams defended his friend in the Dickensian court proceedings which dragged on and on and on, even until the first blood was drawn in the War of Independence. A "painful drudgery I had of his cause... ," wrote Adams later, "this odious cause was suspended at last only by the battle of Lexington, which put an end, forever, to all such prosecutions."

TWO. "ENEMIES TO THE CONSTITUTION OF THEIR COUNTRY"

Merchants in the years immediately preceding the Revolution may have smarted under heavy import duties and restrictions on where and with whom they could trade, but they still prospered and displayed their prosperity. So opulent was the establishment of Nicholas Boylston, in fact, that John Adams was almost breathless when he dined with the wealthy merchant one day in 1766. He recorded that he "Went over the house to view the furniture, which alone cost a thousand pounds sterling.... The Turkey carpets, the painted hangings, the marble tables, the rich beds with crimson damask curtains and counterpanes, the beautiful chimney clock, the spacious garden, are the most magnificent of anything I have ever seen."

Still, all was not well in the town. By the eve of war, Philadelphia, with its more central location and deep expanse of well-settled hinterland to supply with goods, had moved ahead of Boston as a port, and as early as 1760 Boston had dropped to third place in colonial population, trailing Philadelphia and New York. Part of the reason was a series of epidemics that had felled large numbers of townfolk. In addition, the high cost of fuel and the steep taxes on real and personal property—67 percent in 1760—levied to pay for the care of the poor and to support city services, had driven many citizens out of town. One merchant who fled, to set himself up as a country store proprietor in Sudbury, was Joseph Barrell, who noted that conditions

in Boston were so bad that he was "heart sick," and "flying from
this Dying town to an agreeable Retreat."

If the imminent demise of Boston—a refrain that was to echo
even until the present day—agitated some of the town's merchants, most were more concerned about burdensome customs
duties on their goods. The situation came to a head of sorts on
August 1, 1768, when the Society for the Encouragement of
Trade gathered in Faneuil Hall and resolved to retaliate. All
but sixteen of the town's merchants agreed that for a full year
after January 1, 1769, they would import nothing from Great
Britain except essentials such as coal, wool cards, duck,
cordwire, shot, and fishing equipment. Further, they pledged
to refuse all dealings with any merchant who brought in tea,
glass, paper, "or other goods commonly imported from Great
Britain." By the following May, the Boston town meeting expressed its satisfaction that the boycott was working and called
on the citizenry not to patronize merchants who broke the
agreement. In August, meeting once more in Faneuil Hall, the
town's merchants voted that those among them who continued
to defy the import ban "must be considered as Enemies to the
Constitution of their Country."

In the spring of 1770 word reached Boston that Parliament,
loath to lose the American market for British goods, had repealed the onerous duties—except the one on tea. But repeal
had not come before John Hancock himself had run afoul of
the Sons of Liberty when one of his ships was found to contain a
number of goods barred by the nonimportation movement.
This cost him a good deal of popularity among those who put
their politics above business.

The remaining tax on tea, and the 1773 act giving the
British-controlled East India Company a virtual monopoly on
tea sales in America, was the nettle that led to the Boston Tea
Party. For even though merchant William Phillips snorted that
the effort to corner the colonial tea market merely proved
mismanagement on the part of the East India Company—"a
paltry transaction," he said of the move, "unworthy of one of
the greatest associated bodies of Europe"—the granting of this
exclusive franchise meant that the British monopolists would be

able to undersell even those merchants who smuggled tea past the watchful eyes of the customs inspectors. It was a bitter brew for Boston to swallow, though most merchants were aghast when a gang of their fellow townsmen steeped bale after bale of high-quality tea leaves in the briny harbor waters. It wasn't the defiance of the crown that bothered them, though; it was the waste of £12,000 worth of choice merchandise.

One of the few merchants who applauded the tea party was Hancock, even though the British, in retaliation, all but sealed the harbor and invested the town with troops. By this time, though, Hancock's interests had switched from business to Revolutionary politics, and while he continued to dabble in trade his heart wasn't really in it. Then in 1774 he was elected chairman of the Provincial Congress and, as the virtual ruler of Massachusetts, had little time to devote to commercial affairs.

Besides, he was already a wealthy man, one of the wealthiest in all of Boston, and could well afford to live off the income from his capital. In 1771, for example, he had £11,000 lent at interest. And toward the end of the war, he made such a display of his riches that a correspondent of the *Pennsylvania Ledger* noted that "John Hancock of Boston appears in public with all the pageantry and state of an Oriental prince...."

The musketry at Concord on that early April morning in 1775 sounded loudly in the counting rooms of Boston's merchants. Many of them, Tories to the core, had already fled the town; more than two hundred Loyalist merchants joined British troops in the evacuation of Boston the preceding month, and many would later press the British government for reimbursement for the property they left behind. Not all of them would be successful, and the motives of some would be severely questioned. A claim by distiller Thomas Apthorp, for one, was rejected by a royal commission, which declared his suit "a very extraordinary Application from a Servant of the Crown in whose Loyalty there is no Merit and who confesses that he has made as much by the War as he has lost by it...."

The war brought legal trade in British goods to a virtual standstill, and Britain's mastery of the seas severely limited other foreign trade as well. There was still money to be made, however, and not the least opportunity for profits was in outfitting the Continental army with clothing—much of it brought in from France and Spain—and other supplies. But they drove hard bargains, these Boston merchants, even when selling to the army that was battling for their commercial independence. One government purchasing agent on a buying trip to Boston in early 1777 complained bitterly of "the many Dificulties we have mett with in this Business from People whose station in life ought to make them above the Art & Chicanery going forward; the grasping disposition of these people to seize every Opportunity in their Power to increase their private Interest, & the Duplicity daily carried on makes this Business exceedingly disagreeable." Salem merchant Elias Hasket Derby boasted that wartime profits of 100 percent were made on cocoa, sugar, and gunpowder, and margins of 150 percent were "more than common" on linen, cotton, and paper.

Not everyone took this profiteering in stride, and in 1777 John Scollay related with some relish what he described to a friend as a "high Scene in this town." A group of women, it seems, had heard that merchant Thomas Boylston had received a shipment of scarce coffee, and they went to his dockside store to inquire about it. The women explained that they operated some small shops for poor people, and would like to buy some coffee—if the price were right. Boylston growled that his price was more than they could pay and turned them away. But the women soon returned, insisting that the merchant sell at their price. When he refused, they dragged him from his counting room and wheeled him up the wharf in a cart. Perhaps fearing what the women might do next, Boylston tossed them his keys, and they relieved him of a large cask of coffee beans. "Poor Boylston," said Scollay, "was never so Swetted since he was born."

Despite the congressional ban on importing British goods, canny merchants who had made a career out of evading colonial trade regulations found ways to get around the restrictions imposed by their own embattled government. The war year of 1777 found Salem's William Cabot in England "on business" that must surely have involved rounding up a shipment for the home market, and in 1782 Jonathan Amory wrote to his brother that even though there was a law against bringing in English goods, "yet I think they might be so managed that by Invoice and mixed with Holland goods, that there would be but little difficulty" in sneaking them ashore at Boston. "And English goods," Amory added by way of justification, "sell best. . . ."

In the same year, merchant John Welsh, also noting that Americans continued to favor English wares, advised an agent that it might be a good idea if French textiles could be "pack'd & marked the same as tho' manufactur'd in England. . . ."

THREE. "SEVERAL WEST-INDIAMEN, TO THE VALUE OF AT LEAST £100,000 STERLING"

Trade—licit or illicit—was not the only avenue to wealth during the Revolution. For the venturesome and the lucky, there was also privateering, and the foundations of some of Boston's greatest fortunes were to be built with the booty from British merchant ships seized with cannon and cutlass on the high seas. Generations later, commenting on the progenitors of his family's vast wealth, Godfrey Lowell Cabot would observe that "They were pirates, but now we're so refined we call them 'traders.'" And the captain of the British ship *Mary & James*, captured in the fall of 1776 by the eighteen-gun Cabot privateer *Rover*, would complain that his captors behaved "worse than pirates."

John and Andrew Cabot were not the smallest operators in the sleepy fishing village of Beverly, some fifteen miles up the coast from Boston, but they were far from the largest. They owned two of the town's thirty fishing vessels, and had another two ships specializing in foreign trade. Most of their business was with Spain where they exchanged cargoes of fish for cordage, linen, iron, salt, liquors, and silk.

Andrew Cabot, a member of Beverly's Committee of Correspondence in the period leading up to the Revolution, was

quick to see that privateering was a way not only to aid the cause
of independence but to enrich himself in the bargain. Sometimes alone, sometimes with other Cabot family members,
sometimes with friends, the firm of J. & A. Cabot was to have an
interest in at least thirty-nine privateers before the British surrender at Yorktown.

It was a risky business, sending armed ships flying the flag of
an untested nation into hostile seas ruled by an enemy with the
mightiest navy in the world. But if the risks were high, so were
the possible rewards, and men bought and sold shares in
privateers in much the same way that they would later buy
common stock in industrial corporations. It was a gamble, high
speculation, but for men of daring and resolve it was an exciting way to make a living.

It was nothing, however, compared with the deeds of pirates
of earlier days who had swept through the Spanish Main raid-
ing galleons heavy with gold bullion and silver bars. For Revolutionary privateers, the prizes were often more prosaic than
those seized by their spiritual forebears; George Washington
himself once counted it as good news to learn that "Capt.
Adams in the *Warren* has taken a schooner laden with potatoes
and turnips." And the *Oliver Cromwell*, one of the most successful of the privateers in which the Cabots had an interest (it took
eleven prizes on its first voyage), once captured a small sloop
loaded with butter and sheep guts.

But it was volume that counted. If enough potatoes and turnips, butter and sheep guts were sold, an investment in a
privateering vessel would show a profit. By 1777 Andrew Cabot
was able to put £1,000 into a fund to lend the state of Massachusetts money to build and outfit two cruisers to protect the coast
from enemy marauders.

One of the secrets of Cabot's success at privateering was that
he was a good judge of men, a trait that would be highly prized
by latter-day Boston merchants and industrialists. The Cabot
captains were among the best of those who plied the seas in
search of British merchantmen, and the best of the best was
probably the Irish-born Hugh Hill, a cousin of Andrew
Jackson's. This great bear of man, who has been called the very

"beau ideal of privateer captain," was courageous and daring almost to the point of rashness. Once, while drinking at a cabaret in L'Orient, France, Hill roused the ire of a Frenchman who felt that he had been insulted by the dashing American seaman. "I will send my seconds to you in the morning," said the French gentleman, scrupuously abiding by the time-honored *code duello*.

Unruffled, the impetuous Hill reached inside his coat, pulled two loaded pistols from his belt, and offered the butt of one to the startled Frenchman. "What is the matter with here and now?" he asked.

The Frenchman withdrew his challenge.

During the final two years of the war, the British coastal blockade was drawn more tightly, and privateering became an even more risky enterprise. Many investors, lured by the promise of quick riches, wound up losing all they had. Not the Cabots, though. Captained by the likes of Hugh Hill, blessed, perhaps, by pure and simple luck, the Cabot privateers made a fortune for their owners, moving an envious Loyalist to remark to a friend in 1780 that "The Cabots of Beverly, who, you know, had but five years ago a very moderate share of property, are now said to be by far the most wealthy in New England." And the war wasn't over yet; still more rich prizes would fall into the Cabots' hands. Writing after the war of the "extraordinary spirit of enterprise and great success of the Messrs. Cabot," a French traveler noted that "Two of their privateers had the good fortune to capture in the European seas, a few weeks previous to the peace, several West-Indiamen, to the value of at least £100,000 sterling."

It was wealth that would in coming generations find its way into enterprises much more respectable, if not more profitable, than privateering.

Peace dawned in 1783 on a Boston vastly different from the town of pre-Revolutionary times. The exodus of Loyalist merchants had left a social and economic vacuum, a void that had been filled by out-of-towners lured by dreams of riches. One, John Lowell, had come down from Newburyport in 1775, almost on the heels of the retreating British and their train of adherents to the crown. Lowell, an already prosperous provincial lawyer, was soon doing a thriving business advising the commission that was disposing of confiscated Tory estates; his juiciest plums, however, were to come from handling the legal work involved in the sale of prize vessels brought into harbor by privateers. Of the eleven hundred prize cases handled in Boston during the course of hostilities, Lowell was counsel in seven hundred and assistant counsel in nearly half the rest. All told, Lowell surely made more from privateering than most of those directly engaged in it.

Like many of the newcomers to Boston, Lowell was able to take over a fine house abandoned by a departed Loyalist. Others—Higginsons and Cabots, Lees and Jacksons—would do the same, and begin fashioning an economic aristocracy that was to remain dominant even into the twentieth century.

It would be an arduous task. Even under the best of conditions, foreign trade in the eighteenth century was a hazardous and uncertain business, and the coming of peace had left Boston's merchants to operate under conditions that were far from ideal. During the first few months following the war's end, Boston Harbor bristled with the masts of scores of ships bearing cargoes of foreign goods, but these were not Boston ships. They were French and English, mostly, and they arrived in such numbers and with such huge ladings to satisfy the demand built up by wartime shortages that the market was soon glutted. Prices fell so low that some merchants could clear their warehouses only at ruinous auction, and in 1784 the house of J. & J. Amory was offering goods for sale at a scant "2 or 3 per cent. over costs and charges."

Barred from the British commercial system which had been the keystone of colonial trade—England was not yet ready to permit ships from its former colonies to put into British-controlled ports—the Boston merchants saw the once-rich commerce with the West Indies dwindle to next to nothing. In a way, this turned out to be a blessing; to take up the slack, the Bostonians began trying other ports, other avenues of trade. As early as 1780 the venturesome Cabots had led the way to Sweden, and by 1784 both the Cabots and Elias Hasket Derby of Salem were sending ships to Russia, where they were followed two years later by Thomas Russell, who with his brother-in-law John Codman had been active in privateering ventures during the war. By the time trade with the West Indies was restored in the late 1780s, Boston ships were familiar to nearly every major port of Europe. And they were soon to become known in distant ports of Asia and at many an anchorage in between.

Chapter Three

VOYAGES OF ADVENTURE:

THE OLD CHINA TRADE DAYS

"Father," your great-grandfather said to him, "don't worry. A vessel of mine has just come alongside the wharf with a cargo which can buy the whole town of Sudbury."

The old man groaned and turned his face to the wall. "To think," he said, "that I must die and know my son a liar."

—The Late George Apley

Making her way through Boston Harbor on a fine early August day in 1790, the ship *Columbia* fired a federal salute to honor the colors fluttering over the fortifications on Castle Island. Soldiers on the ramparts replied in kind with thirteen guns, one for each state in the infant union. As the ship eased into her moorings, Captain Robert Gray ordered his men to repeat the patriotic gesture, which was echoed with three cheers from the throng of Bostonians gathered at the wharves to greet the safe return of the eighty-four-foot vessel that had set sail from the Nantasket roads nearly three years before. Two days later, the *Columbian Centinel* reported that the ship had arrived back at her home port from "a voyage of adventure...."

A voyage of adventure, indeed. Bankrolled by six merchants—three from Boston, one from Cambridge, one from Salem, and one from New York—the *Columbia* had put to sea with a sister sloop, *Lady Washington*, before dawn on September 30, 1787. A year later, the ships bobbed at anchor in

Nootka Sound on the Northwest Coast of America—2,500 miles from Boston as the crow flies, but some 22,000 round-about miles by sail around Cape Horn through scantly charted waters. There, in territory under the nominal dominion of His Most Catholic Majesty, the king of Spain, the Bostonians bartered a cargo of cheap iron chisels for the sleek black sea otter pelts so coveted by the mandarins of China. In Canton, the ship's cargo of 1,050 otter pelts brought $21,410 from the trading firm of Shaw & Randall. But after deductions for commissions, repairs, and other expenses, only $11,241.51 was left to invest in the return lading of 21,462 pounds of Bohea tea. The tea was damaged in transit to Boston, and the backers wound up losing money on the venture. But the *Columbia*'s globe-girdling voyage had inaugurated the great China trade that was to be a fount of Boston's wealth for nearly half a century to come. It had also helped set in motion the great western migration that would in time push the boundaries of the United States across prairies and mountains to the far shores of the Pacific Ocean.

Boston is more closely linked with the China trade than is any other American city. Its ships, however, were not the first American vessels to put in at the bustling anchorage of Whampoa, some twelve miles down the Pearl River from the trading city of Canton. That honor belongs to the aptly named *Empress of China*, a New York vessel that returned to home port in May, 1785, with a cargo of tea and silk. And before the *Columbia* arrived at Whampoa, some fourteen American ships, from New York, Philadelphia, and Salem, had preceded it.

The owners of these ships had faced the common problem of finding a suitable medium of exchange for trade with the Chinese, who in general would accept only hard cash or Oriental goods with which they were already familiar. For the Celestial Empire to which American ships set forth with such great enterprise was not a savage land where ignorant natives would exchange their treasures for a few trinkets and tools. The Chinese were a highly developed and self-sufficient nation with little need and less desire for what goods the Americans might offer them. The British, with outposts in India and other parts

of Asia, could offer the Chinese the produce of their own continent, and were also in a much better position than the Americans to come up with silver for the purchase of silks and teas. So
short were the American traders when it came to trade goods
that the British at first had little fear of competition from them;
assessing the possibility of American commerce with China
shortly after the Revolution, Lord Sheffield remarked that it
just wouldn't happen, since the newly independent colonies
had "neither money with which to buy Oriental goods, nor
cargoes to supply this deficiency."

For a time, ginseng seemed to be one answer. This harmless,
totally useless root, prized by the Chinese as a restorative drug,
was native to Manchuria and Korea, and also to the Hudson
River valley. But ginseng was limited in both supply and market; some other commodity was needed if the Boston merchants were to capture a share of the China trade.

John Ledyard, a divinity student turned vagabond seaman,
had long been telling tales of having seen furs purchased on the
Northwest Coast of America for six pence sell in Canton for
$100 or more, and similar stories came from other sources.
Fired by these reports of relatively easy riches, the *Columbia*
made its pioneering voyage and charted a course to fortune
that would soon be followed by legions of others.

TWO. "THE FINEST NATURAL OBJECT
IN THE WORLD"

While the *Columbia*'s crew was busily bartering with the coastal
Indians for a supply of sea otter pelts, John Ledyard, the prophet of the Northwest fur trade, lay dying in Cairo, half a world
away; he would not live to see even the first faint buds of this
thriving commerce. But the eighty-four-foot ship's arrival at
Whampoa was marked by another man, Thomas Handasyd
Perkins, who was destined to bring Boston's trade with China to
full flower, in the process planting the taproot of many of the
city's largest family fortunes.

The twenty-four-year-old Perkins, grandson and namesake of
Thomas Handasyd Peck, a prosperous pre-Revolutionary mer-

chant and fur exporter, may have caught sight of the *Columbia*'s sails from the deck of the *Astrea*, which had dropped anchor at Whampoa two months before. Owned by Salem's Elias Hasket Derby, the ship was under the command of the Irish-born James Magee, a former privateer captain who had once poured brandy in his boots to save his feet from freezing after a wintertime shipwreck that left eighty-three of his crew dead from exposure. Magee, who was Perkins's uncle by marriage, had formed a business partnership with his young nephew not long before the *Astrea* set sail for Canton, and had persuaded Derby to hire Perkins as supercargo for the voyage. Later, Perkins was to look back and recall that this year-and-a-half trip had changed the whole course of his life.

As supercargo, Perkins was charged with lining up shippers and then supervising the sale of their goods and the purchase in Canton of a return cargo. Lacking relatively stable investment opportunities—the United States was not yet a nation of manufacturers—holders of capital in post-Revolutionary times were willing to put money in high-risk trading ventures because the only alternative was to let their wealth lay fallow, and Perkins and Magee were able to round up some eighteen shippers for the voyage. By the time they got under way in February, 1789, the hold of the *Astrea* was laden with a cargo that included 32,000 pounds of butter, 100 tons of Russian bar iron, 8,933 spermaceti candles, 6,300 pounds of salt codfish, 1,729 gallons of rum, and a variety of miscellaneous goods. Owner Derby, who at his death in 1799 was said to have the largest fortune in America, sent out a lading of Philadelphia beer, English iron, and 75,000 pounds of ginseng; Governor James Bowdoin entrusted Perkins with four thousand Spanish dollars for the purchase of fine hyson tea. In exchange for their labors, Magee and Perkins were to pull down a 5 percent commission on the sale of the cargo at Canton or other foreign ports, and half that amount on sales of the return freight. In addition, their firm of T. H. Perkins & James Magee shipped out goods of its own.

On the way to Canton, Magee steered as planned to the Dutch colonial city of Batavia, on the northwest coast of Java, where Perkins intended to exchange part of his cargo for goods suitable for the Canton market. Finding that a ban had been clapped on trade with Americans—the shrewd Dutch had little desire to aid and abet competition from the new nation's merchants—Perkins cajoled the governor general into permitting him to sell his goods, and the *Astrea* rounded out its cargo with hides, sugar, coffee, and rice. The ship lifted anchor at Batavia on August 18, and a few weeks later sighted the Portuguese outpost of Macao, at the mouth of the bay that opened Canton to the South China Sea and to the Western world.

The trading conditions that Perkins found in his maiden commerce with China were unchanged since Major Samuel Shaw, supercargo of the *Empress of China*, had sold the first American cargo at Canton five years before. And they were to remain unchanged for a half century to come. The Chinese, while they coveted the profits to be made in trade with Europe and America, made no secret of their scorn for white men. *Fan-Kwae*, the Chinese called them, foreign devils, foreign devils with repulsive ivory skins and barbaric ways, men beyond the very pale of civilization. The Chinese were willing to trade with such savages, but at the same time they believed that they were doing the *Fan-Kwae* a great favor by selling them, among other things, tea and rhubarb to relieve the chronic constipation which the Chinese inscrutably imagined was a chronic affliction in the Western Hemisphere.

Foreign devils could hardly expect to be given a free hand in their dealings with merchants of the ancient Celestial Empire, and the Chinese severely restricted the conduct of trade. When the *Astrea* had passed Macao, a Chinese pilot was taken aboard to guide the ship up the bay to the Tiger's Mouth, the opening into the Pearl River. Passing the Bogue forts guarding the river's mouth, the ship glided through a wasteland that slowly gave way to sweeping spreads of well-tended rice paddies, and before long Perkins could see ahead the anchorage of Whampoa, twelve miles downstream from Canton and its rows of mercantile houses, or *hongs*. By imperial decree, Canton was the only city where foreign trade could be conducted; by imperial decree, too, Whampoa was as near as ships of the *Fan-Kwae* could approach to the walled metropolis.

Whampoa was crowded with foreign ships, a number of them American, and the *Astrea* was soon joined by three more of Derby's vessels which had been rerouted to Canton from the Ile-de-France in the Indian Ocean in hopes of finding a better market for their cargoes. The glut of American goods soon drove their prices down, while the price of tea rose, and the Derby men decided that the only way to dodge a ruinous loss was to sell two of the four ships, cram the remaining two with tea and other China goods, and head for home. This they did, selling their cargoes and buying the return goods through the hong merchants, a group of about a dozen traders who paid their government dearly for the exclusive franchise to do business with foreigners. Before leaving, however, Perkins was put on the scent of profits that would eventually make him a prince among the merchant princes of Boston.

First a British ship, the *Iphigenia*, then Boston's own *Columbia* put into Whampoa with cargoes of sea otter pelts bartered for trinkets on the far Northwest Coast of America. Smuggled into Canton—and smuggling was as common in this Chinese city as it had been in Boston—these coal black furs could fetch as much as $70 per skin, a stunning profit that would be even more magnified by the markups tacked onto the teas and textiles for which they would be traded in Canton. Small wonder that Captain William Sturgis once said that "Next to a beautiful woman and a lovely infant, a prime sea-otter fur is the finest natural object in the world." All that, and staggeringly profitable, too.

Their appetites whetted, Perkins and Magee got together with Joseph Ingraham, first mate on the *Columbia*, and pumped him for details of the epochal voyage. They shortly agreed that on their return to Boston, Perkins and Magee would send out a ship of their own, captained by Ingraham, to follow in the wake of the *Columbia*.

When they got back to Boston in May, 1790, after a 125-day voyage from Canton, Magee and Perkins immediately began laying plans for their next venture. Magee, perhaps as a token of earnest to his captain-to-be, presented Ingraham's wife a gift of tea; then he and Perkins joined the *Columbia*'s owners in an anxious vigil for that vessel's safe return. Little more than a month after its August arrival, Magee, Perkins, and fellow merchant Russell Sturgis registered their newly purchased ship, aptly dubbed the *Hope*, at the Customs House. Even by the standards of the time, it was an almost pitifully small vessel, a two-masted brigantine just a fifth the size of the *Astrea* and considerably less than half as large as the tiny *Mayflower* that had carried the Pilgrim fathers to Plymouth more than a century and a half before.

It was a craft well suited for poking about coastal inlets questing for furs, however, and most of the ships that would follow it around Cape Horn to the fur coast and then on to Whampoa to be freighted with teas and silks and chinaware would continue to be relatively small. It was a hazardous enterprise, and while the old China traders were willing to take great risks, they hesitated to chance the loss of large cargoes.

Working against time now—the *Columbia*'s owners, undaunted by the losses on their first voyage, were fitting out for a return trip, and other adventurers had similar plans—the partners provisioned their tiny vessel and loaded it with trade goods; by September 17 all was ready, and the *Hope* cleared Boston Harbor and put out to sea with a company of fourteen men and a boy.

Rounding Cape Horn, Ingraham made for the Marquesas Islands to trade with the natives for provisions, then moved on to Hawaii and took on wood and water. There, too, he said good-bye to Opie, a Hawaiian native that he had taken on as a servant when the *Columbia* had stopped off at the islands two years before. On June 4, nearly nine months out of Boston, he hoisted sail once more and set out for the Northwest Coast.

In his first stab at trading there Ingraham found the Indians little interested in the tools, cloth, and other items brought along to exchange for furs. Previous trading expeditions had left the natives amply supplied with such goods, and Ingraham despaired of the whole venture until he came up with the makeshift solution of making collars out of twisted iron rods. For some reason, the Indians were quite taken by the collars, which weighed in at as much as seven pounds, and were soon giving three fine sea otter pelts for them. Word of the fashionable ornaments spread along the coast, and while the Indians still preferred the collars to other goods they began accepting some of the more conventional items offered by Ingraham. By August the crew was carefully packing the furs in the hold, and Ingraham was plotting his course to Canton.

Back in Boston, Perkins and Magee had no way of knowing how their captain had fared, but they had ample reason to be optimistic about their venture. Just twelve months after clearing Boston, the *Hope* was set to sail for Canton with a cargo of 1,400 sea otter pelts, more than 300 sable skins, and a variety of miscellaneous pelts. On its first voyage, the *Columbia*—which was even now, along with the ship *Hancock*, ranging the coast questing for more furs—had managed to lay in just eight hundred skins, and had taken more than twice as long as the *Hope*.

Indeed, perhaps the two partners *did* know, by some shrewd merchant instinct, that their paths to fortune were being charted by their tiny brigantine, and that this was no time for doubt. On October 24, 1791, with Ingraham less than two weeks out from a provisioning stop at Hawaii on his way to Canton, another vessel, the *Margaret*, moved out of Boston Harbor on the way around Cape Horn to the Northwest Coast. More than twice the size of the *Hope*, the ship was owned by Perkins, Magee, and several other investors, and was captained by none other than Magee himself.

Unfortunately for Ingraham—not to mention partners Perkins and Magee—the *Hope* arrived at Canton at a time when China, at war with Russia and believing that the fur trade had a Russian tinge to it, was barring fur-bearing ships from Canton. Skins that Ingraham had dreamed might sell for as much as $80 were now going for as little as $15, and buyers were hard to come by. He at last teamed up with another fur ship captain, and together they sold their skins, invested in teas, and chartered a vessel to carry the cargo back to Boston.

When Ingraham got back to the Northwest Coast he learned that the fur situation was little better than it had been in China. The Indians were now demanding more and different goods for their otter pelts, and Ingraham—Perkins would later dub him an incompetent—was doomed to sail back to Canton with only about a third of the pelts it had carried there on the previous voyage. The *Hope* had far from lived up to the high hopes of its owners.

The *Margaret* was a different story. Magee, perhaps luckier or harder-working than Ingraham, managed to stuff the hold of his vessel with as many as 15,000 sea otter pelts, which at the going price at the time of something like $30 to $40 apiece reaped a return of some $500,000. The teas, textiles, and chinaware that no doubt made up the return cargo probably produced a handsome profit for the owners, though no record survives.

For the ambitious Perkins, the message was clear: his road to wealth was through the Orient, that shimmering vision that had beckoned fortune seekers for centuries. Christopher Columbus, after all, had not braved the unknown Atlantic to chart undiscovered worlds; the goal of his epic passage had been the court of the Great Khan of Cathay. John Smith, Henry Hudson, and scores of other adventurers had not risked their frail ships to find new lands, but to seek a seaway to China, the elusive Northwest Passage. Generations of explorers had sought for the fabled wealth of the Indies; now the quest was completed.

THREE. "THEIR VESSELS HAVE FREELY NAVIGATED THOSE SEAS"

Back in Boston, Perkins was not spending his time scanning the horizon to spot the returning sails of tea-laden ships. Born to a goodly mercantile heritage—his father had married the daughter of Thomas Handasyd Peck and had later gone into business on his own; when he died, young Perkins's mother took over the business and ran it with no little success—Perkins had a number of other enterprises to keep him busy. His older brother, James, had gone to work in the 1780s at the thriving house of W. & J. Shattuck, and after apprenticing for a year in one of the Shattuck retail stores Thomas had joined him there, though James had shortly gone to Cape Francis on the island of Santo Domingo (now Haiti) to seek his fortune with a firm of commission agents. Advised by his doctor to spend the winter of 1785–86 in a warmer climate than Boston's, Thomas, too, headed south to Cape Francis. By spring, he and his brother, along with Walter Burling, had set up their own commission business there, with Perkins acting as the Boston agent for trade in such goods as fish, flour, and horses. The firm also dealt in slaves, and in July, 1786, Perkins, who spent most of that year in Cape Francis, was pleased to inform a Boston customer that "agreeable to your desire we have already made some advances in establishing such a place for the disposition of Slaves in this quarter as will be attended with safety and advantage to the proprietor." And taking a leaf from the colonial experience in Boston, Perkins sometimes advised clients how best to smuggle goods in and out of the French colonial port.

By the time Perkins formed his partnership with Magee in 1788, he had considerable mercantile experience, and many interests besides the trade in furs and tea. And even as Magee and Ingraham were cruising the Northwest Coast seeking a cargo of skins, these interests were about to be expanded and solidified into a wide-ranging commercial establishment that would enrich first the Perkinses and later a number of other Boston families as well.

The Perkins interests at Cape Francis had fallen upon bad times, due largely to a vicious slave insurrection that had all but suspended economic activity in the French colony. So it was that in July, 1792, Perkins wrote to his brother proposing that James return to Boston and that the two pool their resources and talents and form a business house together. It would be an ideal arrangement, said Perkins, noting that partnerships of strangers or even friends often break down because of jealousy and lack of confidence. ". . . [O]n the other hand," he added, "a connection between brothers is both natural and beneficial; they have fewer distrusts and are more communicative, which strengthens their confidence and makes their business but amusement." By September Perkins had announced to the Boston public that "Brown Sugars, and loaf sugars, cotton, Madeira wine in pipes, Sherry, and etcetera" were being offered for sale at the store of James and Thos. H. Perkins at number 64 Long Wharf. It was not the first time, nor would it be the last, that a Boston business would be a family affair.

The brothers Perkins threw themselves wholeheartedly into their growing commercial enterprises, trading with China and sending cargoes to the West Indies and to Europe. By the end of 1792 they owned sizable shares in seven vessels, this on top of the already heavy investments in the *Hope* and the *Margaret*. Two years later, Thomas Perkins himself sailed to Paris, where he speculated in ferrying cargoes of European goods to French ports where trade by native vessels had been severely trimmed by the efforts of other European powers to help put down the French Revolution. As the representative of a scrupulously neutral nation, Perkins skillfully played both sides of the fence in that conflict, proving once more that war can be good business for those whose principal loyalty is to profits. But Perkins did not devote himself solely to business; while in Paris, he took time to see the guillotine at work, observing the action through opera glasses and coolly noting that a group of seventeen men was dispatched in a scant fourteen minutes.

Trade with the West Indies and with Europe was profitable enough, but the China trade remained the mainstay of the Perkins enterprises. Indeed, by the third decade of the nineteenth century, Perkins was said to control as much as half of the entire U.S. trade with Canton. And while the sea otter pelts of the Northwest Coast continued to be an important medium of exchange for the teas and silks of the Orient, the Chinese merchants were also partial to specie, or cold, hard cash. As the novelty wore off the trade in furs, specie became the preferred item of trade, and by the trading season of 1804–5 it accounted for nearly $3 million in the U.S. traffic with China, compared with less than $700,000 in furs and other commodities.

As conditions changed, the Perkinses soon saw that it would help their interests in China to have their own man stationed year round in Canton. This would formalize their business there and give them much more continuity than the earlier practice of counting on captain and supercargo to anchor at Whampoa, make the best deal they could with the hong merchants, then sail for home and return to start trading from scratch once more a year or two later. A permanent branch office in China would also enable them to earn commissions from other China merchants.

To head the Canton outpost, the Perkinses chose Ephraim Bumstead, who had apprenticed in their countinghouse and proved himself on a Canton voyage as supercargo on board the ship *Thomas Russell*. As his assistant, they tapped young John Perkins Cushing, son of their sister Nancy. Only sixteen at the time, Cushing had been virtually raised by Thomas Perkins following Nancy's death from smallpox shortly after she had been abandoned by her shiftless husband, Captain Robert Cushing. John P. Cushing, who would live to hear of the shelling of Fort Sumter and the Battle of Bull Run, was to become one of the giants of the China trade, and through his later investments would come to typify the rising Boston investor class.

Bumstead and Cushing arrived in Canton on New Year's Day of 1804 and were soon doing business as Ephraim Bumstead & Co. Firmly entrenched in China now, Perkins decided to concentrate the bulk of his energies in that thriving business, and by year's end had six ships on their various ways to China, bearing specie, furs, and other goods. One, the newly built 358-ton *Mandarin*, put out from Boston on December 10 bearing $300,000 in specie.

For the Perkins interests, it looked like nothing but smooth sailing ahead, but events were to take an unexpected turn. Bumstead, though not yet thirty, became sick and died, leaving the Boston firm's China business in the untried hands of the adolescent Cushing. It was April, 1805, when Perkins first learned of Bumstead's death; and the home office had heard no word from young Cushing since his departure for Canton more than eighteen months before, a singular omission even in a time when letters from that Chinese city took five months or more in transit to Boston. By the following month, however,

Perkins's doubts about Cushing were put to rest when the young man's first letters, composed in a businesslike manner and with great attention to detail, arrived. And so did the ship *Hazard*, freighted with teas bought and loaded under Cushing's supervision. It was, according to Perkins, the best of his China cargoes to arrive in Boston in all his years in the trade. Before long, Cushing, not yet twenty, was a principal in the firm, newly named Perkins & Company.

The importance of the China trade, particularly as it hinged on the fur trade of the Northwèst, was not lost to the government in Washington. In the beginning, this coastal trade with the Indians had been opened and sustained by the British, but by the close of the eighteenth century it was virtually monopolized by Americans, primarily Bostonians; English traders on the coast were called King George men by the Indians, but Americans, no matter what their home port, were known as Boston men. This flourishing trade on the shores of the Pacific led to an increasing awareness that these lands, though separated from the eastern seaboard by thousands of miles of unmapped territory, were or could be a vital part of the American nation and its growing commercial empire. President Thomas Jefferson was well aware of these possibilities when he instructed the explorers Lewis and Clark in 1803 to map the streams and rivers of the West to find "the most practical and direct water communication across the continent for the purpose of commerce." This done, thought Jefferson, the long, hazardous voyages around Cape Horn, and hence home by way of the Cape of Good Hope, would no longer be necessary, and China traders would in the bargain be able to harvest furs from deep in the interior of the continent as well as on the coast. When mapping those waterways that no white man had seen before, he told Lewis and Clark, be sure to bear in mind "the practicability of taking the furs of the Rocky Mountains direct to China, upon the line of the Columbia River and the Pacific Ocean."

Later, as the Russians moved south from their Alaskan settlements and threatened to bar ships from the United States and other nations from the waters of the Northwest Coast, Secretary of State John Quincy Adams, certainly not unmindful of his home state's stake in the China trade, would sternly warn the Russian minister in Washington that "From the period of the existence of the United States as an independent nation, their vessels have freely navigated those seas, and the right to navigate them is a part of that independence." Adams was not about to let the Russian bear cut off American access to the sea otter.

Later still, in 1844, New York railroad builder Asa Whitney, petitioning Congress for a grant of land from Michigan to the Columbia River, would claim that unless this were done Oregon might declare as a separate nation, monopolizing the rich Orient trade at the expense of the United States.

The great Northwest Territory was not the only slice of the North American continent that Boston's China-bound traders were to stake out for eventual union with the United States. California, too, then a bauble of the enduring Spanish Empire in the New World, was first breached by a U.S. vessel as early as 1796 when the Boston ship *Otter*—under the command of Ebenezer Dorr, Jr., who had sailed six years before as supercargo on board the Perkins-owned *Hope*—put in at Monterey for provisions on the way to the Northwest Coast. The Spanish, wishing to keep California trade restricted to their own colonial family, forbade their subjects from trading with outsiders, but to little avail. Yankee traders managed to carry out a thriving contraband commerce in California, easily justifying it with the claim that the people wanted it, and were in any case oppressed by their Spanish rulers and well deserved the bounty of illicit trade.

Boston's old China traders did more in their voyages of adventure than simply line their own pockets. Far beyond that, they helped set the ultimate frontiers of their nation on the farthest Pacific shores of the continent and even beyond to Hawaii, where Boston men put in for provisions and cargoes of aromatic sandalwood for the Canton market. Later, Boston missionaries would stake out their own peculiar claims in the Hawaiian Islands, claims that would eventually be extended to annexation and statehood. With good reason has the great western movement of the United States been credited in large measure to what Sydney Greenbie so felicitously termed "the aureate sheen of the East," a promise of riches that had drawn Boston merchants to the Orient like pilgrims to a holy shrine.

FOUR. "THE PERSEVERING INDUSTRY OF BOSTONIANS"

The Boston that had seen the proud return of the *Columbia*, that had cradled the robust infancy of the China trade, was a Boston little changed from the 1740s of a half century before, and with good reason. From 1743, when the tight little peninsula's population stood at 16,382, the population of the town had grown only to 18,038 by 1790. No need here for much new building, except perhaps to erect more stately mansions for prosperous merchants whose fortunes were made, not from home-based enterprises, but from voyages to the West Indies and beyond. By 1810, however, the number of inhabitants had swelled to nearly 34,000, and considerable physical changes had taken place or were in the planning stages. Boston had ceased to be a mere town—it was on its way to becoming a modern city.

The insular character of the place—only a narrow neck of land connected it with the interior—was broken in 1786 with construction of a forty-two-foot-wide toll bridge across the Charles River to Charlestown, and this was followed by another bridge seven years later, spanning the river to Cambridge. Parts of the town that had lain all but fallow since the days of the first settlement now became thoroughfared gateways to the outside world, opening up fresh areas for residential and commercial development. By 1808, a visitor returning to Boston after a long absence could note that "The great number of new and elegant buildings which have been erected in this Town, within the last ten years, strike the eye with astonishment, and prove the rapid manner in which the people have been acquiring wealth." The wealth of China and the Indies, brought home in wooden ships, was beginning to blossom in stone and brick.

Happily for Boston, the spate of building activity in the waning years of the eighteenth century and the first decades of the nineteenth century coincided with the early career of one of the most talented architects America has ever known, and the work of Charles Bulfinch was to leave a lasting stamp on the appearance of the city. Bulfinch, who had studied his craft in France and England, returned to Boston in 1787, just in time to make a small investment in the voyage of the *Columbia*, and just in time to apply his architectural genius to reshaping the face of his native city.

Bulfinch's first major project, finished in 1795, was the Tontine Crescent, a gracefully curving block of sixteen brick houses located on what is now Franklin Street in downtown Boston. Though difficulties in lining up buyers in time led to Bulfinch's bankruptcy—forcing him to shed the guise of gentleman designer and take on the role of hard-driving architect hungry for commissions—the Tontine project was a magnet that opened up a little-used section of the town to further residential development.

Another Bulfinch building, the new State House capping Beacon Hill above the Common on pastureland bought from the heirs of John Hancock, shifted residential patterns still further. With the seat of state government now removed from the Old State House at the head of State Street—site of Robert Keayne's wooden Town House—Beacon Hill lands that had previously been regarded as the outskirts of the city soon became desirable for dwelling places.

Foreseeing the changes that were in the wind, a group of merchants organized as the Mount Vernon Proprietors purchased in 1795—three years before completion of Bulfinch's gold-domed State House—a large plot of adjacent Beacon Hill land as a real estate speculation. In the bargain, they touched off a bitter feud with the previous property owner, portrait painter John Singleton Copley, who had left Boston in 1774 to live in England. Copley accused the Mount Vernon Proprietors of grossly underpaying him for his Beacon Hill acreage, charging that they knew in advance that the State House would be built nearby and that land values would soar. He further

claimed that his trusted agent, Samuel Cabot—of the privateering Cabots—had connived with the real estate speculators to sell
them the property at a price far below its true worth. Bostonians generally chalked the charges up to the painter's "discon-
tented spirit," and when Cabot was sent to London a short time
later as an aide for the United States commission that was pressing war-damage claims against the British, a group of prominent Boston merchants fired off to the chief commissioner a
testimonial letter to counter the "foul aspersions" that Copley
was publicly hurling at Cabot.

Unfortunately for Copley—the land was soon worth more
than he would ever make from a lifetime of painting—Cabot's
deal proved binding, and by 1799 the Mount Vernon Proprietors were laying out streets that exist to this day, in the process
shearing some sixty feet of earth from atop Mount Vernon, one
of the three hills that had given the peninsula its early name of
Trimountain. Presaging future projects that would greatly expand the land area of Boston, the dirt from Mount Vernon was
dumped into coves and inlets at the bottom of the hill to create
new land for development. Bulfinch-designed mansions were
soon sprouting on Beacon Hill and on other streets near the
State House, and it was not long before this area became the
favored residential area for prosperous Boston merchants.

In addition to the State House, Bulfinch designed the town's
first theater worthy of the name—one of the investors was
Thomas Handasyd Perkins—and built a new courthouse and a
number of churches, some of which still stand. And while
ministering to the domestic, civic, religious, and entertainment
needs of his townsmen, he did not neglect the needs of commerce which had given life to the city. In 1805, he directed the
enlargement of Faneuil Hall; five years later, he completed two
new market buildings in other quarters of the town. And at
about the same time he began overseeing a nearly total reshaping of the waterfront, a reshaping that turned a hodgepodge of
wooden wharves and warehouses into an impressive rank of
solid structures that would stand for generations as testimony
to the seaborne wealth of Boston's merchant princes. His India
Wharf, built in 1805, was a marvel of the age, the most ambi-

tious waterfront development in the United States at the time. Here, in a lengthy five-story tier of stores, warehouses, and counting rooms, with ships heavy with cargoes from distant ports, Boston merchants went about laying up fortunes beyond all dreams of avarice. In 1817, Shubael Bell, senior warden at Christ Church, would write to a long-absent friend that the even larger Central Wharf, completed just the year before, "is a proof of the enterprize, the wealth, and persevering Industry of Bostonians."

Proof, too, of that industry and enterprise was the continued leveling of Beacon Hill, which had by 1824 been reduced to its present height, the earth being used to help fill in the adjacent Mill Pond and add some fifty acres of land to the city. But the crowning proof, destined to change the face of Boston more than any project before or since, was the completion in 1821 of a causeway running from the foot of Beacon Street at the Common and across the Back Bay to Brookline. Proposed originally to replace the source of water power that was lost when the Mill Pond was filled in, this causeway—which was topped with a toll road—walled in some six hundred acres of the tidewater Back Bay. Later in the century, it would form the outer limit of a land-fill project that would vastly increase the land area of Boston and create one of the city's most exclusive residential areas, rivaling Beacon Hill as the home of Boston merchants and their well-heeled heirs.

While Charles Bulfinch was busily changing the face of the town where Boston merchants lived and labored, events in Europe were conspiring to change the complexion of their commerce. The on-again, off-again war between Britain and France, which would not be ended until Wellington bested Napoleon's host on the field of Waterloo, had greatly upset the sea-lanes plied by Boston merchants. Flying the flag of a neutral nation, their ships were prey to the depredations of both sides in the European conflict, each of which suspected the Americans of favoring the other. Indeed, Boston merchants, with their close ties to London bankers on whom they relied for credit, frequently took the part of their former colonial masters, and when France in early 1798 declared open season on American ships that had touched at British ports or carried British goods, a group of merchants that included the Perkins brothers, Stephen Higginson, John Codman, and Thomas Amory pledged $136,500 to build and outfit a protective ship of war for loan to the government.

For a time, Boston's merchants and their counterparts in other American port cities managed to outwit the belligerents in the European wars and carry on a steady commerce with the West Indies, Portugal, Denmark, Russia, and a variety of South American and Mediterranean ports, as well as to keep up the thriving China trade. But it was all too good to last.

In June, 1807, refused the delivery of four British deserters alleged to be on board the American warship *Chesapeake*, His Majesty's Ship *Leopard* opened fire on the American vessel, killing three and wounding another eighteen. Removing the four men, the British ship then left the battered *Chesapeake* to limp back to home port. War fever swept the country as a result of this outrage, but President Thomas Jefferson chose another course. Warned by the British that the Royal Navy had no intention of easing its policy of impressing suspected deserters and that British ships would seize any vessels trading at ports barred to the Union Jack, and learning that the emperor Napoleon had ordered his navy to confiscate any ship that gave in to the British threat, Jefferson opted for discretion over valor. Henceforth, he ordered, American vessels would stay out of harm's way by the simple expedient of staying home. Effective December 22, 1807, no American ship would be allowed to leave an American port for a foreign destination.

For Boston's merchants, the Embargo Act was a heavy blow. Now not only were they barred from belligerent ports, they were also forbidden even to set out for China—and by their own government. The merchants felt sure that Jefferson, for political reasons, was trying to destroy their commercial power, and for a time there was even talk of seceding from the Union.

Some trading continued—there was nothing in the act, after all, to prevent ships at sea or already in foreign ports to go about their business in anticipation of the embargo's end—but in the main, the once-busy Boston merchants were reduced to unwonted thumb-twiddling. Ships designed to bear the wealth of the world to Boston lay idle at quiet wharves that stood now as tombs of the town's commerce.

Resurrection was not to come for more than fourteen months, when Jefferson, on the last day of his administration, permitted a congressional bill lifting the embargo to become law. Soon, Boston ships were plowing the oceans once more. But the great orgy of trade and speculation that followed the end of the embargo was doomed to be short-lived. With U.S. ships again roving the high seas, Britain resumed the impressment of seamen serving aboard American vessels, leading in 1812 to a declaration of war, a war that was neither wanted nor supported by most Boston merchants. For a time, some trade continued under special dispensation of the British squadrons that effectively blocked the Atlantic ports of America. By the end of 1813, however, times had changed. The British blockade was tightly knotted; during the entire year, only a paltry five Boston vessels cleared the port for foreign shores. In December, chary of losing ships and cargoes to the enemy, Congress passed—and rigorously enforced—yet another embargo, this one banning not only foreign traffic but domestic coastal voyages as well.

Some two hundred and fifty ships stood stripped and rotting at the Boston wharves, their naked masts and spars outlined against the harbor like so many winter trees. Capital, too, lay idle, capital that in former times had gone into more ships, more cargoes for distant ports. But it would not lay idle for long. Soon, in the hands of new men schooled in trade but ever-willing to study new fields, Boston money would be channeled into new enterprises, close to home, that would shore up the shipping fortunes and prove once more the abiding industry and enterprise of Bostonians.

Chapter Four

MILLS ON THE MERRIMACK:

THE TEXTILE KINGS

In 1813, Mr. F. C. Lowell having returned from Europe, he and Mr.
P. T. Jackson came to me one day on the Exchange, and stated that
they had determined to establish a cotton manufactory. . . .
—Nathan Appleton

John Lowell, the "Old Judge" who had come to Boston from
Newburyport in 1775 to make a fortune handling the legal
affairs of privateers and disposing of the estates of departed
Loyalists, died suddenly in 1802, at the age of fifty-nine.
Though he had made numerous investments in currency
speculation and various canal and bridge projects in and
around Boston in the closing decades of the century, his estate
was not spectacularly large. And it was complicated somewhat
by the fact that Lowell, who had so painstakingly drawn up last
testaments for his clients, never got around to writing a will of
his own. In this oversight he was in good Boston company.
More than half a century before, the great merchant Peter
Faneuil had died intestate; on John Hancock's death, nearly a
decade before Lowell's, it had been found that this merchant-
politician, whose bold signature would one day be used as a
symbol of financial probity and responsibility by the insurance
company that bears his name, had never quite got around to
affixing his John Hancock on a will. With at least three such

dismal failures at estate planning in mind, it is perhaps no accident that wealthy Bostonians of future years would become famous for the care with which they composed their wills.

Happily, a considerable portion of the Old Judge's total estate of some $80,000 was in the able hands of his merchant son Francis Cabot Lowell, who had ventured it on cargoes aboard eight ships—the *Hannah, Horace, Indies, John, Ocean, Perseverance, Regular,* and *Thomas Russell.* Francis Cabot Lowell's older half brother, John, would later credit this merchant Lowell with "the restoration of my father's dilapidated fortunes." And in the process, Lowell would go on to inaugurate the industrial revolution in America and establish one of Boston's greatest fortunes and family dynasties.

Born in 1775 to his father's second wife, Susanna Cabot, Francis Cabot Lowell was considered something of a mathematical wizard at Harvard, where he was a member of the class of 1793. It was a facility that would stand him in good stead, both as a merchant and as an industrialist. After graduation from college, he shipped out as supercargo on one of Thomas Russell's ships bound for France, where he witnessed a curious event which demonstrated both the cheapness of life in Republican France and an extreme dedication to business affairs. "A duel yesterday was fought at 'change time between two Gentlemen by the Riverside," he wrote his father from Bordeaux on August 28, 1795. "After trying with the sword for some time they took their pistols. One of them shot and killed his adversary. Left him and went immediately on Exchange again." It must have been a shocking spectacle to a young man from Boston, where devotion to commercial matters was seldom coupled with such hotheadedness.

Following a few more voyages as supercargo on other men's ships, Lowell struck out on a mercantile career of his own, with a store and counting room on Long Wharf. Here, in addition to buying and selling a wide variety of goods—cotton was a big item in the Lowell establishment—he got into real estate speculation; in the first decade of the century he bought nearly two dozen properties on India Wharf, Long Wharf, and in nearby areas. With characteristic Boston verve, Lowell threw

himself so energetically into his business affairs that he was
soon driven close to a nervous breakdown, and decided in 1810
to spend a few recuperative years abroad with his wife and
children. It was a common enough resort for those suffering
from what was called a "nervous disorder"; seven years before,
Lowell's older brother, John, had gone the same route after a
trying court case which had sent his client to the gallows.

For Francis Cabot Lowell, however, the foreign journey was
to be more than a mere pleasure jaunt. As a dealer in both raw
cotton and cotton cloth from the recently established spinning
and weaving mills of England, Lowell was painfully aware of
the effects of the U.S. embargo on British goods. With virtually
no manufacturing industries of its own, the new nation was all
but totally dependent on the output of British mills for its
supplies of textiles. While in Britain, Lowell intended to learn
as much as he could about the power looms that had revo-
lutionized the process of cloth-making there, with the aim of
transplanting that revolution to America.

It would not be an easy task, this midwifery of industrial revolution in America. The British jealously guarded the secrets
that had changed spinning and weaving from cottage industries, carried out by women in their spare time, into a large and
lucrative enterprise. The sprawling mills of Lancashire had
given England a commanding lead in the world textile market,
and the British government was not about to lose this advantage; the export of textile-making machinery, or plans for such
machinery, was strictly forbidden, punishable by heavy fines.

There was opposition at home, too. America was an essentially agrarian society, endowed with a strong and persistent
strain of anti-industrialism. Yeoman farmers were cherished as
the backbone of a fragile democracy that could ill-afford the
presence of a proletarian class laboring in dark satanic mills.
"Cultivators of the earth are the most valuable citizens," said
Thomas Jefferson in 1785, adding that "I consider the class of
artificers as the panders of vice and the instruments by which
the liberties of a country are generally overturned." Besides,
there were plenty of purely practical arguments against an industrial America. Here was no great mass of surplus labor;

there was not even a huge domestic market to satisfy; nor were there ready supplies of liquid capital available to pump into manufacturing enterprises. Ships and cargoes were sufficient to soak up mercantile profits, and in any case large-scale domestic manufacture would eat into the business of the established foreign traders.

The commercial disruptions culminating in the War of 1812 had changed this picture considerably, however, and by that fateful year even the gentleman farmer Thomas Jefferson had changed his tune. "To be independent for the comforts of life," he said now, "we must fabricate them ourselves.... He, therefore, who is now against domestic manufactures must be for reducing us, either to a dependence on that nation [England], or to be clothed in skins.... Experience has taught me that manufactures are now as necessary to our independence as to our comfort."

While Jefferson was articulating the philosophical and political necessity for a native textile manufacturing industry, Francis Cabot Lowell was touring the British cotton mills, watching the water-driven spindles and looms as they magically twirled cotton into thread and wove thread into cloth. For if it was illegal to export machinery or plans, there was no law to bar a substantial American merchant, a potentially major customer, from seeing first hand how the product was made. What was the harm? This amiable, dignified Bostonian took no notes and made no drawings of what he saw. To be sure, he asked a lot of questions, but Americans were well known for their curiosity. What was the harm in satisfying it?

Lowell was not the only curious Bostonian in Britain at the time. Nathan Appleton—no mean merchant in his own right, and a distant relative of Lowell's—had arrived with his ailing wife a few months before Lowell, and while he spent much of his time buying goods for shipment home, he also looked in on a few cotton mills. But he lacked Lowell's mechanical gifts and was more interested in such things as prices and prospective profits than in the nuts and bolts of the machinery. In 1811 the two merchants crossed paths in Edinburgh, and after talking over what they had seen, decided that it would be a good idea if

Lowell continued with his observations. Not that Lowell's mind wasn't already made up: "We had a good deal of conversation upon the subject of the cotton manufacture," Appleton recalled later, "and he told me that he had determined to make himself fully acquainted with the subject with a view of the introduction of it at home." For his part, Appleton agreed that if anything should come of the scheme, he would come up with some of the required capital investment. For the future of American industry, it was a fateful encounter, this chance meeting of two traveling Boston merchants.

Lowell, who had already spent some time checking out the mills in Lancashire, went on to Birmingham and Manchester, roaming for weeks among banks of looms and spindles, always probing, questioning. How does this work? Why is it done this way instead of that way? How does it work? How does it work? The British operatives obligingly answered, never dreaming that this Boston merchant was all the while storing the inventive genius of the industrial revolution in his brain.

TWO. "THIS NEW AND WONDERFUL MACHINE"

When he arrived home shortly after the outbreak of hostilities, Lowell stepped ashore in a country that was ready to see this genius put to work. Population growth, especially in the West, was opening up new markets that could no longer be satisfied with severely curtailed shipments from abroad. Deprived of its customary outlets, shipping capital was languishing, and enterprising men accustomed to risking substantial sums for the promise of profits were eagerly seeking new fields for their energies.

Lowell wasted little time in providing an outlet for this capital and energy. With his kinsman and business associate Patrick Tracy Jackson—Lowell had married Jackson's sister, Hannah, and had left his Boston business affairs in his brother-in-law's hands during his sojourn in England—he incorporated as the Boston Manufacturing Company in early 1813. Like Lowell, Jackson had entered the ranks of Boston merchantdom by the supercargo route, eventually rising to captain before setting up his own mercantile business. But he was more than ready to try his hand at something new.

Shares in the new company—though its charter called for capitalization of $400,000, just $100,000 was raised initially, to give the venture a trial—were sold in multiples of $1,000, and the bulk of the subscriptions were taken up by Lowell, Jackson, and Jackson's brothers. Appleton, whose zeal had cooled somewhat from the time of his enthusiastic talks with Lowell in Edinburgh, was asked to chip in $10,000 for ten shares, but quibbled his investment down to five shares. Theoretical prospects for the venture seemed favorable, he explained, but he had nagging doubts about its practicality.

Appleton was not alone in his misgivings. Many of Lowell's friends and relatives tried to convince him that his plan to launch a cotton manufacturing industry was a "dangerous and visionary scheme" that wise heads would do well to avoid. There were certainly sufficient examples of previous failures—or at best, indifferent successes—to support these caveats. Spinning mills had been tried before in America, with less than spectacular results. One, operated by horsepower, had been built in nearby Beverly in the late 1780s, and was considered notable enough to be visited in 1789 by President George Washington. Despite its novelty—or perhaps because of it—the Beverly operation lost considerable money for its investors, who included several of the brothers Cabot. It is hardly surprising that Lowell's Cabot relatives argued against his interest in cotton mills, and that no Cabot money was invested in the Massachusetts textile industry until 1828, long after the new mills had proven themselves successful beyond all reasonable doubts.

At about the same time that the Beverly operation was getting off to its shaky start, the firm of Almy & Brown, in Providence, Rhode Island, set up a bank of machine spinners, and invited the Englishman Samuel Slater to manage it. By 1791 this mill was turning out quantities of satisfactory yarn, and before two decades had passed there were some thirty small-sized spinning mills operating in Rhode Island, Massachusetts, and Connecticut. All of these mills, however, had faced a common problem: there was simply not a large enough market among housewives and hand weavers to support large-scale operations. Even the best-run plants were only marginally profitable. The Almy & Brown mill, overseen by a man who knew more about machinery than anyone in the country at the time, squeaked by with a profit of only $18,000 during the ten best years between 1793 and 1803.

Speaking from past experience—which is not always a sure guide to the future—those who tried to talk Lowell out of his plan were probably right. But they did not reckon with Lowell's determination and vision. For Lowell was no mere mechanic, enthralled by the workings of wheels and gears, spindles and looms. He looked far beyond machinery and equipment and saw a whole new system of industrial organization. What he had in mind was nothing less than the prototype of the large modern corporation, the precursor of American big business. And he was operating in a time and place where the stars seemed uniquely conjoined to bless his undertaking.

Geographically, Boston was in an ideal spot for the birth of modern industry in America. Its already-developed port made it a simple matter to import raw materials and ship finished goods to distant markets. Perhaps even more important, sources of water power—vital in the days before steam and electricity—were within easy distance of the city. To be sure, Boston was not alone in access to these advantages. Philadelphia, too, was a major port city, a city with the added bonus of being centrally located on the eastern seaboard, closer to the growing markets needed to sustain large-scale manufacturing operations; Philadelphia also had abundant water power. Unlike Boston, however, Philadelphia had a strong tradition of hand craftsmanship, and balked at mass production. What is more, with its all-important shipping industry virtually paralyzed and with no deep hinterland to fall back on as a market for available goods, Boston had a restless economic drive unmatched by any other American city. Boston's capitalists were ready and able to chance a part of their fortunes on visionary and even dangerous schemes, particularly when the chief schemers were men like Francis Cabot Lowell.

Brushing aside the warnings hurled in his path by well-meaning if unimaginative associates, Lowell proceeded apace. Buying the property of a failing paper mill alongside the Charles River at Waltham, a few miles upstream from Boston, he began the ticklish task of designing and building his machinery, using as a guide the memory of what he had so carefully observed in his tours of the British mills. For months, with the help of an ingenious master mechanic named Paul Moody—the first employee of the new company—he labored at a rented store on Boston's Broad Street, re-creating and making refinements on British spinning and weaving machinery. There, as a hired hand turned a crank to set the mechanisms in motion, Lowell and Moody tinkered into the nights, adjusting a gear here, whittling a spindle there, building models of some of the most sophisticated machinery of the time.

Not content with merely tapping his own recollections of distant machines, Lowell also inspected equipment built by other American mechanics, with sometimes unexpected results. Learning that a Mr. Shepherd of Taunton, Massachusetts, had patented a winding machine that was considered the best then available, Lowell and Moody called on the proud inventor to see his device in action. It was truly a marvelous machine that wound a "cop" of thread onto a spool, from which the thread was then fed to the bobbin of a power loom. Lowell dickered with Shepherd for a reduced price for rights to the machine, arguing that he deserved a discount because he would be using it on such a large scale. Shepherd, sensing that he had the Bostonians over a barrel—after all, they wanted an efficient operation, and his was the most efficient winding machine going—held out for his price.

"You must have them," he said, as Moody and Lowell peered at the whirring spindles and spools. "You cannot do without them, as you know, Mr. Moody."

But Moody, who had been apprenticed to a mechanic at the age of twelve and had later worked as a handweaver, was now several steps ahead of the stubborn Shepherd. "I am just thinking," he said slowly, "that I can spin the cops direct on the bobbin."

Now Shepherd, seeing that his golden goose was about to drop a leaden egg, retreated sharply. "You be hanged," he said to Moody, and turned to Lowell. "Well, I accept your offer."

But Lowell, too, had calculated that it would be possible to bypass the winding machine, and coolly replied, "No, it is too late."

After more than a year of such work, the new building at Waltham was completed, and the first loom was installed and ready to go on steam. It was only then, in the fall of 1814, that Lowell invited his friend and close associate Nathan Appleton to make the trip to Waltham to inspect what the Boston Manufacturing Company had wrought. Years later, by then made rich beyond his wildest dreams by investments in numerous mills, Appleton would recall "the state of admiration and satisfaction with which we sat by the hour, watching the beautiful movement of this new and wonderful machine, destined as it evidently was, to change the character of all textile industry."

It would do that and more. The British, while they had invented power loom weaving, did their spinning, their thread-making, in separate facilities. At Waltham, Francis Cabot Lowell had put the entire textile-making process under one roof, bringing in cotton at one end and shipping out bolts of cloth at the other. It was a pattern that would later be followed in other industries as well—Henry Ford was to carry it to its zenith—and it was the first demonstration of the great genius and promise of American industry. Though he couldn't know it at the time, as he sat there in the Waltham mill with Lowell, enchanted with the steadily clicking loom, Appleton had seen the first tentative stirrings of a giant, the greatest industrial nation that the world has ever known.

THREE. "THE WHOLE POWER OF THE MERRIMACK POURED DOWN"

Like so many new enterprises, the mill at Waltham got off to a stumbling first start. Accustomed to cotton goods imported from England and India, the public balked at buying untried

American-made sheeting, even though the manufacturers had added an extra bonus inch to the standard thirty-six-inch width. This hesitation was soon overcome, however, when Appleton had a few bolts of the material sent to B. C. Ward and Company, a newly formed dry goods firm in which he was himself a partner. The cloth was sold at Lowell's suggested price of twenty-five cents a yard to an auctioneer, who turned around and auctioned off the goods at a shade over thirty cents a yard. With that, the Ward firm was made permanent sales agent for the output of the mill, at a standard commission of 1 percent. It was a minuscule percentage, but as the industry prospered and grew, that steady 1 percent to the selling houses, skimmed off millions of dollars of annual volume, made for a profitable business indeed.

In 1815, its first year of operation, the Boston Manufacturing Company managed to unload only a scant $412 worth of goods; by 1820, it was selling $260,000 worth, and this despite the postwar slump and the dumping of British goods on the market. There could be no doubt that Boston's road to wealth, built on the foundation of overseas trade, was now to be paved by the textile industry. Between 1817 and 1821, investors in the Waltham mill were paid dividends that averaged 19¼ percent a year; in 1822, the ante hit 27½ percent. In less than ten years, stockholders scooped up dividends totaling better than 100 percent of their investment. Now, many of Lowell's reluctant friends and relatives, those nay-sayers who had warned him of his folly, were scrambling to pick up shares in the company at a premium of 40 to 50 percent above the original subscription price. Better late than never, they reasoned, and in this case, late was soon enough.

Even as the mill at Waltham was churning out a stunning thirty miles of cloth per day, it was becoming apparent that this was not enough to meet the swelling demand of a growing population. New and larger mills were needed; needed, too, would be whole new communities, organically mated to the looms and spindles that brought them into being and gave them life. And Francis Cabot Lowell, whose brain had borne the machinery of industrial revolution across the Atlantic, had augured this social revolution as well, perhaps even as he paced to and fro among the looms of Lancashire and Birmingham.

It is doubtful, but not known, whether he also visited Robert Owen's utopian community on the banks of the river Clyde, or whether he had even heard about it. Like other Americans of his time, however, Lowell was concerned about the effects that large-scale industry might have on the character and morals of the workers. For this was an age when modern relativism was unknown; "character" and "morals," particularly in New England, were palpable qualities whose slippage a well-run society could permit only at its peril.

Based on the British model, there was ample reason to fear that the introduction of mass-production industries in America would cause a dangerous erosion of traditional—if not always observed—values such as thrift, temperance, churchgoing, hard work, education, and sexual circumspection. And America's pioneer capitalists, even for the sake of profits, did not want to be responsible for setting the scene for Hogarthian degradation in the United States. "The introduction of the cotton manufacture in this country, on a large scale, was a new idea," Nathan Appleton recalled years after the event. "What would be its effect on the character of our population was a matter of deep interest.... The operatives in the manufacturing cities of Europe were notoriously of the lowest character, for intelligence and morals. The question therefore arose, and was deeply considered, whether this degradation was the result of the peculiar occupation, or of other and distinct causes."

The considered answer to this burning question was that European workers were in all likelihood degraded to start with—and they probably were. Operatives in the early English mills, in fact, had been levied from the poorhouses; later recruits—whole families, more often than not—were driven to the mills by the abject poverty of squalid urban slums, having no alternative but starvation. To be sure, conditions in America were quite different; there was no lumpen proletariat willing to toil for a marginal living because there was no other choice. No, workers in the new mills would have to be pulled in from rural areas, not by necessity, but by the desire for gain. And yeoman farmers, Jefferson's backbone of democracy, would not give up their daughters—their sons were needed to till the land, and besides, weaving was a woman's work—to the cotton factories unless assured that they would return to the family hearth in the same pristine condition in which they left.

With this in mind, the prescient Francis Cabot Lowell had envisioned not only a new system of industrial organization but a new type of community as well. The central element, the place where the operatives would spend a good twelve hours of their day, would of course be the mill itself. Surrounding it would be banks of boardinghouses where young girls fresh from the farms of Massachusetts and surrounding states would live under strict supervision while serving their time at the looms and spindles—Lowell did not anticipate that the millworkers would become a permanent working class; the girls were expected to spend only a few years in the mills, earning enough money for a respectable dowry, or perhaps to help put a brother through college. With such an arrangement, Lowell hoped to overcome the native American prejudice against the factory system, to build an industrial utopia.

The need for substantial expansion put the Boston cotton manufacturers on the threshold of a new industrial and social order that would for decades be a wonder of the Western world. In time, that observer of the human condition Charles Dickens, visiting the crowning jewel of Lowell's achievement, would say that what he found there would bear comparison to the British factory system only as between "the Good and Evil." But Francis Cabot Lowell—"the informing soul," in Nathan Appleton's words, "which gave direction and form to the whole proceeding"—did not live to see it. In 1817, at the age of forty-two, he died, never having fully recovered from the debilitating ailments that had led him to sail for England in 1810. Eventually, he would be followed in the industry by two of his sons and a nephew; for the moment, leadership fell to his brother-in-law, Patrick T. Jackson, and to Nathan Appleton.

In Appleton, Lowell had a worthy associate who had long since been purged of misgivings about the future of cotton manufacturing. Indeed, Boston newspapers would soon dub him the Great Manufacturer, and his children would some- times teasingly address him by this grandiloquent title. Born in New Ipswich, New Hampshire, in 1779, Appleton arrived in Boston in late 1794, his spare clothes knotted in a handker- chief, to join his older brother, Samuel, who had just set himself up in a tiny retail store in the town's bustling Cornhill district. Along with minding the store while his brother was on a buying trip to Europe, Nathan studied double-entry bookkeeping and learned to speak fluent French while boarding with a French family. In 1800, following a European business trip of his own, he was taken into his brother's by-now flourishing firm as a partner, and in the following year went once more to France and England. In England, he visited some of the textile towns, where he was shocked and revolted by the living and working conditions of the operatives.

Back in Boston by 1804—it was Samuel's turn now to be the firm's man in Europe—Nathan busied himself with shipping out potash and pearl ash for making lye to finish fine British woolens. Late in the year, he found time for a trip to Savannah and Charleston, where he bought rice and cotton. To get a look at the countryside, he returned from Charleston by stagecoach, stopping along the way at Richmond, Washington, Baltimore, Philadelphia, and New York. He found Philadelphia to be "un- questionably the finest city in the United States."

The Appletons were hard hit by the embargo, but Nathan still managed by 1808 to buy a handsome town house at 54 Beacon Street, fronting on the Common, as a home for himself and his new wife. The young man from New Hampshire, not yet thirty, had done quite well for himself in the merchant's trade.

Samuel Appleton, the elder brother who had made it all pos- sible, returned to Boston from Europe in 1810 after spending most of the past decade abroad, and decided to retire. Nathan, meanwhile, continued in trade, going into partnership with his younger brother, Eben, and Daniel P. Parker. Eben Appleton, who had previously been in business with Parker, was already in England, and took over as the new firm's British agent, based in Liverpool. Nathan visited with him there on his way to his encounter in Edinburgh with Francis Cabot Lowell, and early in 1815, shortly after the end of the War of 1812, Nathan would write to Eben to inform him that "Our manufacturing establishment in Waltham is just getting under way," and to ask that on his next visit to Manchester he "buy and send out to us a few lbs. of cotton twist of different numbers, from 15 to 60, with a few pieces of grey calico of the different qualities and the same bleached, in the rough. They will be very useful to us to calculate how we can compete with them."

As early as 1821 the Waltham establishment was competing so well that demand had far outrun capacity, and Nathan Appleton and Patrick T. Jackson began casting about for a place to grow. The Waltham mill had already been crammed so full of machinery that the waters of the relatively sluggish Charles River were hard pressed to power the equipment that was already there, so the only solution was to seek out a fresh site, a new source of water power. A new face was needed, too, someone to take charge of the new operation that the Boston Manufacturing Company had determined to launch. Appleton was still conducting a thriving import business, and his primary interest in manufacturing was as an investor—he had neither the time nor the inclination to take on the building and running of another industrial complex. And Jackson was busy with his responsibilities as treasurer and agent—which in the management parlance of the time meant that he was both chief financial officer and manager of production—at the Waltham mill. They found their man in Kirk Boott, a somewhat eccentric Anglophile who affected a riding crop, which he sometimes used to whack impudent boys about the head and shoulders. Born in 1791, Boott had been educated in England, where he became an officer in the British army. His love for Britain was not so deep that he would fight his own countrymen, however, and with the outbreak of the War of 1812 he returned to Boston and went to work in his father's importing firm on State Street. By coincidence, it was at the Boott store that John Amory Lowell, nephew of Francis Cabot Lowell, was to get his first taste of business before moving on to become one of the leading figures in the textile industry.

After a disappointing inspection of a site in southern New

Hampshire, Appleton and Jackson learned that Paul Moody, the mechanic who had collaborated with Lowell in the building of the Waltham mill's machinery, had found a likely location at the fork of the Merrimack and Concord rivers, some twenty-five miles north of Boston. There, at a thirty-foot fall, "the whole power of the Merrimack poured down," producing a theoretical drive equal to 27,000 horsepower. If this wasn't attractive enough, the spot was also served by two canals. One, the Pawtucket, bypassed the rapids, and had been dug late in the eighteenth century by Newburyport merchants who hoped that it would help funnel the commodities of the New England back country down the Merrimack to their wharves. It had been a good idea, but Newburyport had lost out a few years later when a second waterway, the Middlesex Canal, was built to connect the site directly to the more desirable Boston Harbor. Moody can hardly be blamed for his excitement when he told Appleton and Jackson of his find.

Light snow powdered the ground on the November day in 1821 when Appleton and Jackson viewed Pawtucket Falls and the surrounding village of East Chelmsford for the first time. With them were Paul Moody, Warren Dutton, Kirk Boott, and his brother Wright, all of whom were to be directors of the projected company. There were fewer than a dozen buildings in the neighborhood of the falls, and as the men paced back and forth on the river shore, envisioning the new mill and town that would soon be rising on the site, somebody mused that there might be one among them that day who would live to see the place inhabited by twenty thousand people.

FOUR. "CAN THE GOVERNOR OF MASSACHUSETTS PRINT?"

Moving with a dispatch that would have done credit to Francis Cabot Lowell himself, Appleton, Jackson, and Boott went about acquiring the needed property. The Pawtucket Canal was purchased for some $30,000, and adjacent farmland totaling about four hundred acres was picked up for $40,000 or so. Much later, Kirk Boott, whose riding crop and ill-disguised Anglophilia—one Fourth of July he ran up a British flag atop the United States colors and, refusing a demand by angry citizens to reverse the order of the flags, he watched with amusement while they did it themselves—hardly endeared him to the populace, would be accused of fleecing unsuspecting landowners out of their property by assuring them that he intended to use the land only to plant orchards and raise a few sheep. Actually, though the buyers did not exactly trumpet the fact that their aim was to build a new industrial city, they probably paid a fair price for the undeveloped tracts. And in any case, Boott had little to do with the initial purchases; they were handled by an agent whose willingness to include untillable swampland in his acquisitions made some residents believe that he must be insane.

As the new city began to expand after its initial success, both millmen and property owners were sometimes outsmarted by speculators. Thomas Hurd, for example, overhearing in Boston a conversation about the need to buy land for additional mills, took options on considerable surrounding acreage, which he held and sold at inflated prices. A latter-day chronicler would describe Hurd as "one of those sagacious and scheming men who seek, and whose keen sense discovers and appreciates an advantage, while other men rub their eyes and listlessly wonder what he is doing." Hurd was not all that clever, however; he invested his profits in a brick business that went bankrupt.

With water rights and land secure, Appleton, Jackson, and Boott incorporated the Merrimack Manufacturing Company in February, 1822. Shares were sold at $200 each; Jackson and Appleton, with 180 shares apiece, took the largest individual blocks. Kirk and Wright Boott got into the company with ninety shares each, and Paul Moody bought sixty shares. The Boston Manufacturing Company, the parent firm of the Merrimack mill in more ways than one, subscribed to 150 shares of the first offering, which called for an authorized capitalization of $600,000. As planned, Boott was given complete control of the operation, serving as both treasurer and agent. His first task, though, was to build a mill, and a city.

It did not take him long. Using the factories at Waltham as a guide—two additional mill structures had been raised on the banks of the Charles by 1820—Boott set to work constructing a mill complex of five buildings grouped functionally along the Merrimack. By September 4, 1823, not yet two years after he and his associates had first viewed the barren, snow-sprinkled ground, Boott was able to record in his diary that "After breakfast, went to factory and found the wheel moving round his course, majestically and with comparative stillness."

Ranged around the mills, within an easy walk of the factory floors where they would put in at least twelve of their waking hours, were the boardinghouses for the millworkers who would soon be streaming to the new city to tend its spindles and looms. More than mere dormitories, these dwellings—supervised by strait-laced housemothers—were equipped not only with sleeping rooms and kitchens but with common parlors as well, many of them featuring pianos as tokens of the cultured, respectable life envisioned for the mill girls. For himself, Boott built in the center of town a porticoed mansion appropriate for the autocrat who was sometimes called His Imperial High Mightiness. When it came time to give the new city a name, there was little question what it would be. It was called Lowell.

The Merrimack mills prospered beyond the wildest dreams of their backers and paid their first dividend—of $100 a share—in 1825. Not a bad return on stock that had sold for $200 just three years before. And management was willing to pay dearly for the talent needed to keep those dividends rolling in. To find a competent head for the new calico printing operation, Boott went in 1825 to Manchester, England, where he tried to convince the masterful John Dynely Prince that he should come to Lowell. Prince was interested in the challenge, but held out for the then-staggering salary of $5,000 per year. "Why, man," said the incredulous Boott, who himself pulled down only $3,000 a year as treasurer and agent, "that is more than we pay the governor of Massachusetts." Said Prince: "Well, can the governor of Massachusetts print?" He got the job.

As profits and dividends kept up their steady pace, stockholders in the Waltham and Merrimack mills saw the need for still more expansion, and were soon joined by merchants who in the beginning had been reluctant to invest outside their own narrow spheres of knowledge, or to sully themselves in manufacturing. A great explosion of growth followed as pioneer and newcomer alike poured capital into new mills at Lowell. The Hamilton Manufacturing Company was organized in 1825; the Lowell and Appleton companies in 1828—the Appleton concern with capital resources of one million dollars. In 1830, three new companies, Suffolk, Tremont, and Lawrence, were formed and by the time Kirk Boott fell dead on the main street in the spring of 1837—his stately home was converted into a hospital for millworkers—the city of Lowell was just a shade away from the twenty thousand population that had been so optimistically envisioned when the founders first visited the site less than sixteen years before. And it was well on its way to becoming one of the miracles of nineteenth-century progress—not only as a bellwether industrial complex but as a social experiment as well.

FIVE. "STRUGGLING FORWARD TO WHAT WAS BEFORE US"

Congressman David Crockett, destined to die at the Alamo and to become one of America's most durable folk heroes, visited Lowell in 1834. "I wanted to see the power of machinery wielded by the keenest calculation of human skill," he wrote, and he was hardly disappointed with the display of industrial might that he saw on his tour, a tour that was on the itinerary of many a public figure of the day. Each age has its own symbols of national achievement and ambition, and at one time or another Presidents Jackson, Tyler, and Polk made pilgrimages to the Lowell textile complex in much the same spirit of wonder and pride that their twentieth-century successors would pay their respects to the nation's destiny at the space technology centers of Houston and Cape Kennedy. But Crockett, like legions of other visitors who flocked to Lowell, found more than mere machines to marvel at; he was also struck by the living and working conditions, the "character" and "morals" of those who tended them. "I could not help reflecting," he noted, "on the difference of these females, thus employed, and that of other populous countries where the female character is degraded to abject slavery."

In the beginning, at least, Lowell seemed a virtual paradise, far removed from the exploitive, sweatshop conditions that would later characterize much of American industry, including the textile mills of New England. Kirk Boott had carried out the vision of Francis Cabot Lowell to near perfection—Harriet Robinson, a mill girl during the 1840s, would write years later that the Lowell system of industrial organization included the novel idea that "corporations should have souls."

Benevolence, paternalism, soul—whatever it was, it was a quality almost dictated to the early corporations, no matter how high their motives, by economic necessity. Girls from the farms of New England would come to the mills in sufficient numbers only if living and working conditions were relatively attractive, a comfortable alternative to the tedium of feeding chickens, milking cows, and doing other rural chores. If they made a little money in the bargain, so much the better, but money alone would not draw them to the factories—even though wages for the mill girls, low as they were, were higher than women could earn at any other honest occupation, more even than was paid to country schoolmistresses at the time.

The hours of work were long, but not generally longer than the standard twelve-hour day of the period. And the work itself, for all the tedium, was not particularly strenuous; the machines, after all, just about ran themselves. The operative's job was merely to keep an eye on a couple of looms, watching for broken threads. There was plenty of time to daydream about the future, or even—though it was strictly forbidden during working hours—to read books, taken into the mill page by page, while sitting on a window recess minding the flying shuttles of the looms. Lucy Larcom, who worked in the Lowell mills in the 1840s, wrote forty years later that if the life there was not exactly "a paradise of work," there were compensations—not the least being that the girls always looked at their sojourn in Lowell as temporary. If their lot was sometimes hard, she said, "we had accepted its fatigues and discomforts as unavoidable, and could forget them in struggling forward to what was before us."

For many girls, the time spent at Lowell was more like going to a boarding school than working in a factory. There was an air of education and uplift in many of the boardinghouses; one, with just thirteen residents, subscribed regularly to fifteen newspapers and periodicals. There were also at Lowell numerous "Improvement Circles," groups of girls who got together regularly to discuss essays that they had written.

Perhaps more significantly, the mills offered women their first taste of real independence, gave them a feeling of solidarity with their sex that they had never had before. William Scoresby, a British clergyman who visited Lowell in 1844, noted that the girls called their fellow workers sisters, and that they exhibited an esprit, a pride in their class that he had not seen among their downtrodden British counterparts. On their way to the factories, the sisters often sang these lines from the "Song of the Spinners":

> Dependent on others we ne'er will be,
> So long as we're able to spin.

It was, perhaps, the first example of female consciousness-raising.

Lowell also spawned the first magazine edited and produced wholly by women. Dubbed the *Lowell Offering*, it sprang from one of the ubiquitous Improvement Circles, and while some detractors accused it of being a management mouthpiece, it did provide an outlet for the literary efforts of women who would otherwise have been condemned to lives of domestic drudgery. It was also a springboard to bigger things; by 1848, seven books had been published by contributors to the *Lowell Offering*, which Charles Dickens said would compare favorably with a good many British publications. Indeed, the magazine was regarded as so novel to Britishers, accustomed as they were to the ignorance and vulgarity of their own mill operatives, that a London publisher printed a book of selections from it, calling his book *Mind Among the Spindles*.

For a time it almost seemed that the utopian industrial vision of Francis Cabot Lowell had become reality. But it didn't last; it couldn't last, for paradises built on earth can never long endure. As early as 1836, still an idyllic time compared with what would come, there were signs of disaffection. Balking at a wage cut coupled with a boost in board payments, the mill girls went out on strike, an almost unheard-of act of defiance. But they'd had a taste of freedom, a dose of independence, and these New England farm girls were ready to stand up for their rights. Twelve hundred of them—clean, well dressed, and fresh faced—trooped through the streets of Lowell singing:

> Oh! isn't it a pity, such a pretty girl as I—
> Should be sent to the factory to pine away and die?
>> Oh! I cannot be a slave,
>> I will not be a slave,
>> For I'm so fond of liberty
>> That I cannot be a slave.

The strike was a failure, but the stage had been set for the eventual erosion of the unwritten social contract that had bound worker to capitalist. For the premise of Lowell's vision had been that both mill girl and mill magnate came from the same stock, shared the same values. And hadn't Nathan Appleton himself begun life as a poor New Hampshire farm boy? If not a blood relative, he was at least a spiritual father and brother, uncle and cousin to the early operatives, and felt a genuine responsibility for their well-being. The coming influx of foreign labor from Ireland and French Canada changed all this. As major stockholders withdrew from active management of their companies, turning operations over to men whose primary mission was to crank out regular dividends—and never mind how—wage exploitation became common. The new workers, after all, were driven to the mills by the goad of poverty, and should consider themselves lucky for whatever pittance they were paid. By the eve of the Civil War, general conditions in the mill towns had sunk so low that southern planters, damned for their support of the "peculiar institution" of slavery, could point to the lot of the North's mill operatives as being little better than bondage.

Revisiting Lowell in the 1890s, Harriet Robinson found scant evidence of the corporate soul that had guided the founding of the city. The hours may have been shorter, but the work was harder, and the mills were hot and dirty now. Boardinghouses once tenanted by transient farm girls bent on improving their minds while earning money in the mills had become the squalid warrens of a permanent working class too beaten down to do anything but trudge to the mill each day and return to recuperate from their labors. The esprit of old had long since vanished, and as Robinson surveyed what Lowell had become, she mourned for the 1840s as a "lost Eden."

SIX. "THE BREAD OF INDUSTRY AND QUIETNESS"

If the early days of cotton manufacturing in Lowell were a lost Eden to Harriett Robinson, they must have seemed a financial paradise to Amos and Abbott Lawrence, whose fortunes were among the largest to emerge from the heyday of the textile mills. And Amos, at least, would have savored Robinson's biblical turn of phrase. Early in his life he had a pocket book on which he had inked: "What shall it profit a man if he gain the whole world, and lose his own soul?" As it turned out, young Lawrence had little cause for apprehension—along with gaining a considerable fortune, he died with a sure and certain hope of glorious resurrection, though as a Congregationalist, and not through the rites of the Protestant Episcopal church of which his grandson would one day be a leading bishop. At the same time, his life would so exemplify this bit of scripture that the Lawrence qualities of charity, rectitude, and conservatism would become beacons for future generations of wealthy Bostonians.

Amos Lawrence was born on a farm in Groton, Massachusetts, in 1786. Tales of the American Revolution must have been common currency in the Lawrence household; Amos's father, Samuel, had fought at Bunker Hill, where he took a British musket ball through his hat. Perhaps prophetically, Lawrence's mother, like other country women of the time, used to spin thread and weave cloth by hand, often lulling Amos and his younger brother, Abbott, to sleep with the hum of the spinning wheel, the muffled click of the laborious hand loom.

When he was fourteen, Amos went to work as a clerk in a nearby country store. The owner was tiring of the business and within a year or two had turned day-to-day operations over to Lawrence. Some young men might have been satisfied with this responsibility and looked forward to a comfortable and respectable life as a rural storekeeper; Lawrence, however, had higher ambitions. In the spring of 1807, with twenty dollars in his pocket, he left for the headier atmosphere of Boston, where he proceeded to shell out two dollars to the obliging neighbor who had driven him to town by chaise. His stake now reduced to eighteen dollars, Lawrence got a job clerking in a small mercantile house that promptly went bankrupt. The defunct firm's creditors, possibly because there was no one else to handle the job, picked Lawrence to settle their affairs and were impressed with his abilities—it was said that he could add three columns of figures in his head as quickly as most men could add one column. On the strength of this performance, Lawrence was able by December to swing enough credit on his own to open a small store in Cornhill, the same section of town where the Appletons had set up shop just thirteen years before. Later, Lawrence would confess that he was "not worth a dollar" at the time of this maiden venture.

With a little help from home—his father mortgaged the family farm to lend the budding merchant $1,000—Lawrence prospered, doing so well that he didn't even put his father's loan into the business. Instead, he lent it out at interest, paying his father back as the mercantile business began making money, which it did from the start. In his first year, Lawrence made $1,500, and this with the hated embargo in effect, too. Also in the first year, he tapped the family farm for more help, in the person of his fifteen-year-old brother, Abbott, who came to Boston as his apprentice. In his second year, Lawrence made better than $4,000, and his fortune was fairly launched. Launched, too, was a firm and cautious principle that was to bind him throughout his career—years later, he recalled that

after just two years in business on his own he had decided "to
have property . . . to represent forty per cent. at least more than
I owed; that is, never to be in debt more than two and a half
times my capital. This caution," he said, "saved me from ever
getting embarassed. . . . Excessive credit is the rock on which so
many business men are broken."

In 1814—the same year that the Waltham mills went into
operation, and the year, too, that his son, Amos Adams Lawrence, was born—Lawrence was prosperous enough to put
$50,000 into a partnership with Abbott. The brothers styled
themselves A. & A. Lawrence, a firm name that was destined to
be one of the mightiest in the then-infant textile industry. But
the Lawrences were not yet ready to jump into untried enterprises; for the moment, at least, they preferred to stick to more
familiar channels of trade.

Abbott Lawrence sailed to Liverpool on a buying trip on
board the *Milo*, the first Boston ship to put out for England
after the conclusion of peace in 1815. William Ward, a Nathan
Appleton partner, also took passage on the ship, but Lawrence
beat Ward ashore and became the first passenger to leap to the
wharf when the *Milo* reached its moorings. With typical care
and caution, Amos Lawrence had advised his brother in his
letter of instruction that he should be upright in all his dealings,
and "In regard to your business transactions, let everything be
so registered in your books, that any person, without difficulty,
can understand the whole of your concerns. You may be cut off
in the midst of your pursuits," he had added gloomily.

For the return voyage, Abbott was nearly the last to board the
vessel and just barely missed being left behind. On the evening
before the vessel sailed for home, Abbott came alongside on a
lighter laden with goods for the store of A. & A. Lawrence, but
was told by the mate that there was no room for more cargo.
This wasn't what Amos had had in mind when warning Abbott
of the possibility of being cut off in the midst of his pursuits, but
to an ambitious Boston merchant, it was nearly as disastrous.
Leaving his lighter bobbing in the harbor, Abbott scrambled
aboard the *Milo* to check the hold for himself, and managed to
convince the mate that he could squeeze his goods aboard. Just

eighty-four days after he had left for England, Abbott was back in Boston, where his merchandise sold out in a week, at an enormous profit.

Much of A. & A. Lawrence's business was in cotton goods, so it was only natural that the firm should start handling the output of the Lowell mills, and eventually put money into the mills themselves. They had, after all, proved to be safe, sure investments, just the sort of steady enterprise to suit the Lawrence temperament. No need to scramble here, to wake up in the middle of the night fearing lost fortunes. Leave that to other men, in other cities. "When I see how people in other places are doing business," Amos wrote to Abbott while on a business trip to Philadelphia in 1819, "I feel that we have reason to thank God that we are not obliged to do as they do, but are following that regular and profitably safe business that allows us to sleep well o'nights, and eat the bread of industry and quietness. The more I see of the changes produced by violent speculations, the more satisfied I am that our maxims are the only true ones. . . ."

Amos Lawrence was not always able to practice what he preached. As early as 1818, he noted in a memo book that he kept through all his life that he was spending entirely too much time worrying about business affairs, and he vowed to change his ways. It was a short-lived promise. In 1826 he wrote of his business that "I now find myself so engrossed with its cares, as to occupy my thoughts, waking or sleeping, to a degree entirely disproportionate to its importance. Property acquired at such sacrifices as I have been obliged to make the past year," he said, "costs more than it's worth; and the anxiety in protecting it is the extreme of folly." The following year, he observed that he had indeed been able to slow down somewhat, though he was not entirely pleased with the results. "Our responsibilities and anxieties have greatly diminished," he wrote, "as also have the accustomed profits of business. . . ."

Single-minded pursuit of profits was a characteristic shared by many Boston businessmen of the early nineteenth century. William Appleton, the merchant and mill investor cousin of Samuel, Nathan, and Eben Appleton—and Amos Adams Lawrence's future father-in-law—confided to his diary in 1822 that "I feel that I am quite eaten up with business; while in Church, my mind with all the exertion I endeavored to make, was flying from City to City, from Ship to Ship and from Speculation to Speculation." Apparently, Appleton's fevered mind paused long enough to consider church business as well; little more than a week later, he noted that he had "Called on Dr. Jarvis and told him that until our Church could pay their expenses without borrowing money, I would give nothing to missionaries."

SEVEN. "MY PROPERTY IMPOSES UPON ME MANY DUTIES"

By 1830 the brothers Lawrence had become such powers in the cotton industry that one mill in which they invested heavily was named the Lawrence Company, with an authorized capital of $1,350,000. By 1837 the Lawrence firm had ceased to import foreign fabrics, and in addition to being a heavy investor in the mills was also the nation's leading selling house for domestic cloth.

The selling houses were keys to the prosperity of the textile mills, for they took from the manufacturers the burden of marketing their wares. Essentially, a selling house took cloth on consignment, collecting a commission—ranging from 1 to 2½ percent—on sales. In addition, as their profits mounted, the selling houses would often lend money to the mills during slack periods. A. & A. Lawrence was particularly active in this area, and interest on the loans often made up a considerable portion of the firm's yearly income.

As his fortune mounted, Amos Lawrence devoted more and more of his energies to charity and good works and less and less to business affairs. It was a course that was almost dictated by his health: on the first day of June, 1831, he took a hearty draft of cold water in his counting room and was struck with a violent digestive upset that plagued him for the rest of his life. From then on, he had to stick to a rigidly bland diet, eating alone in his room to avoid any excitement that might trigger his dyspepsia. It was an austere regimen for Lawrence, and he frequently grumbled about the thin gruel and tiny cuts of lean meat that were mainstays of his meals. But he was perhaps better prepared than most for such Spartan ways; a man of moderation in all things, Lawrence kept his desk drawer stocked with fine cigars which he frequently sniffed but never smoked.

Charity came easy to Lawrence, too. Not only did he have ample funds to give away, but he also felt a stern sense of responsibility for the less fortunate. "I have many things to reproach myself with," he once wrote in his ever-present memo book, "but among them is not idling away my time, or spending money for such things as are improper. My property imposes upon me many duties, which can only be known to my Maker. May a sense of these duties be constantly impressed upon my mind. . . ." To Lawrence, the duties of wealth were clear, and he discharged them in ways both large and small. He frequently gave clothes, books, and other goods to the needy, and had two rooms of his house set aside to store such materials. On rainy days he would while away his time sorting and packing these goods; on clear days he would frequently distribute books— mainly of religious or uplifting character—to passing strangers.

Though it was hard to be anonymous when handing out books on the street, Lawrence preferred to keep much of his largesse under wraps. As a rich man known for his generosity, he was constantly besieged for aid, and by the mid-1840s he had stopped seeing anyone seeking help unless he knew them or they were recommended by someone he knew. "The reputation of giving freely is a very bad reputation, so far as my personal comfort is concerned," he lamented. In 1845 Lawrence gave $10,000 to Williams College, and later gave the school an additional $5,000 to build a library, with the proviso that the president not disclose the source of the funds. Though most of his gifts were presented close to home, he also gave money to Wabash College, in distant Indiana, simply because its president, a New Englander, was a friend of his.

Perhaps inspired by his older brother's example, Abbott Lawrence, too, gave freely to worthy causes, his most notable gift being the $50,000 that he presented to Harvard in 1847 to establish the Lawrence Scientific School. Abbott had no way of knowing it at the time, but this gift would turn out to be a highly profitable investment for his and other wealthy Boston families. Louis Agassiz, the great Swiss naturalist, was offered the chair of zoology and geology at the school, and his son, Alexander, was later to develop Michigan's fabulous Calumet & Hecla copper mine, an enterprise that would do for latter-day Bostonians what the China trade and the textile industry had done for their fathers and grandfathers.

It 1852, the last year of his life, Amos Lawrence looked back over the preceding decade and reckoned that during that period his personal expenditures had come to a staggering $604,000, "more than five sixths of which have been applied in making other people happy...." At his death, it was estimated that he had given away a total of about $700,000 to various charities over the years, a sum that was believed to be the largest ever given by an individual up to that time. With his staunch religious faith, Lawrence must surely have been consoled in his last conscious moments with the firm belief that he would indeed be granted, as he had once written that he hoped for, "the happiness at last of hearing the joyful sound, 'Well done, good and faithful servant, enter thou into the joy of thy Lord!' Amen. Amen."

Lawrence fully expected that his charitable instincts would survive him in the person of his son, the textile merchant Amos Adams Lawrence. To that end, he advised the young man in 1832 to "divide your expenses into ten parts, nine of which may be termed for what is necessary, making a liberal calculation for such as your situation would render proper, and one part applied for the promotion of objects not directly or legally claiming your support...." It was an admonition that the younger Lawrence would take to heart, and in time he would outstrip even his father in the good works department. Another young man, too, would be inspired by the Lawrence example; in 1917, reminiscing about his boyhood, John D. Rockefeller recalled that at the age of sixteen he had read of Amos Lawrence's philanthropy and thought that "if I could manage it, some day I would give away crisp bills, too."

While Amos Lawrence was puttering about his rooms packing up books and clothes for the needy and winnowing the worthy causes from the numerous requests for aid that came his way, brother Abbott was minding the family store, though the cotton mill investments and the smoothly running selling house of A. & A. Lawrence required little of his direct attention. In 1834, having become a public figure of some note, he found the time to be elected to the United States Congress, succeeding his friend Nathan Appleton. He declined to run for a second term, but stood for election again in 1838, resigning early in 1840 when he came down with typhus. In the Congress, Lawrence served his constituents—and his own self-interest— by vigorously supporting a high protective tariff on imported cotton goods—an on-again, off-again measure that had first been instituted in 1815 after Francis Cabot Lowell had gone to Washington and convinced John C. Calhoun, among others, that the tariff would benefit the southern cotton growers as well as the northern manufacturers.

Lawrence was unsuccessful—in 1837, the lowered duty on cotton imports combined with the financial panic of that year to force most of the Lowell mills to pass their dividends—but this failure was made up for in 1842 with passage of a steep tariff bill that kicked off a four-year textile boom. The factories at Lowell were humming along at such a rapid clip, in fact, that the mill owners decided that more expansion was in order. Already, numĕrous new facilities had gone up around the original Lowell factories, and the banks of fast-flowing rivers and streams throughout New England were bristling with mills. At Lowell, the heart of Boston's vast investments in the cotton industry, so many mills were on stream that the corporations had been driven to buy water rights at the outflow of New Hampshire's Lake Winnipesaukee to insure a constant and sufficient supply of water to drive their majestically turning wheels. If growth were to continue along the Lowell pattern, a fresh site would have to be found, a new spot to establish another Lowell.

On the morning of March 20, 1845, the governor of Massachusetts signed an act incorporating the Essex Company, with an authorized capital of one million dollars. Later that same day a group of men set out by carriage from North Andover and soon arrived at a falls on the Merrimack River a few miles downstream from Lowell. Among those in the party were Abbott Lawrence and his brothers William and Samuel, both of whom were active in the cotton industry. (Another Lawrence brother, Luther, had been mayor of Lowell until one spring day in 1839, while touring one of the Middlesex Company mills, he fell into a seventeen-foot wheel pit, fractured his skull, and died.) Others included Francis Cabot Lowell, Jr., John Amory Lowell, William Sturgis, Charles S. Storrow, Nathan Appleton, and Patrick T. Jackson. Appleton and Jackson, at least, must have felt that they were reliving a similar trip of nearly a quarter of a century before.

Pacing along the shore, they gazed out over the swift-flowing rapids fed by water that just a short time before had been churning through the wheels of Lowell. And as they examined the lay of the land, imagining the mills and boardinghouses, the city that would soon be rising on the site, no one bothered to observe that the ground they walked on might one day boast tens of thousands inhabitants. That was a foregone conclusion; Lowell had long since pointed the way. Satisfied that they had picked a suitable location, the men reboarded their carriages and drove upriver to Lowell. After a leisurely dinner, Abbott Lawrence and John Amory Lowell, nephew of the first Francis Cabot Lowell and builder and treasurer of several of the larger Lowell mills, excused themselves and went into an adjoining room for a brief consultation. When they returned to the table, they offered Samuel Lawrence, president and treasurer of the Merrimack Water Power Association, $30,000 for land and water rights at the site they had inspected earlier in the day. In addition, Abbott agreed to lead off as an investor in the newly incorporated Essex Company. Samuel readily accepted the offer; it was, after all, a family matter as well as a business deal.

Two days later, Abbott Lawrence became the first and largest subscriber to stock in the Essex Company, taking a thousand shares at one hundred dollars each; he also became president of the company. Work on the new mill and the new city began in July, and there was never any doubt that the city would be named Lawrence. Other mills followed the Essex—the Atlantic in 1849, the Pacific in 1853. Abbott Lawrence, by now the acknowledged leader of the textile industry, was president of them both. Soon the city of Lawrence, built from nothing on the banks of the Merrimack, was rivaling Lowell as a cotton manufacturing center.

Cotton mill presidents were not concerned with the day-to-day affairs of their factories—their main duty was to preside at meetings of directors and stockholders—so Abbott still had plenty of time to spend on other interests. One of them was Whig politics; he came within a hair of the vice-presidential nomination in 1848, and after the winning ticket of Zachary Taylor and Millard Fillmore got to Washington, Taylor offered Lawrence the secretaryships of the navy or interior as consolation prizes. He turned both posts down, and in shunning the navy job, he was following in the footsteps of Thomas Handasyd Perkins. Asked by George Washington to become the nation's first secretary of the navy, Perkins graciously declined, pointing out that it would be more in the national interest for him to continue minding his own fleet of ships—which was larger at the time than the United States Navy.

Offered the ambassadorship to England, Lawrence gladly packed his bags and sailed for the Court of St. James's, where his great wealth gained him quite a reputation for lavish entertainments. While in London, Lawrence must have had some wistful thoughts about what might have been when he learned in 1850 that the death of Taylor had catapulted Fillmore into the White House.

Lawrence returned in 1852 to a Boston whose close-knit social fabric was beginning to strain at the first waves of Irish immigration, an influx that would also help bring to an end the idyllic industrial dreams in Lowell and Lawrence. He died three years later, leaving in his will $150,000 in public bequests—including another $50,000 to the Lawrence Scientific School, $10,000 to the Boston Public Library, and $50,000 for building model lodging houses for the poor.

EIGHT. "AMIDST ALL CHANGES OF OUR PUBLIC FORTUNES"

The city was in sore need of lodgings for its poor. Between 1825 and 1850, the population of Boston had leaped from 58,277 to 136,881, largely through immigration. Unlike earlier newcomers, who had for the most part arrived with the skills and resources either to make their way in Boston or move on to greener pastures, many in the new tide of immigrants stepped ashore with little more than the tattered clothing on their backs. From Ireland came the greatest numbers—whole families, as much in flight from the brutish poverty and famine of their homeland as in search of fresh opportunities in the New World. By 1850 Boston was home to some 35,000 Irish, most of whom had arrived in the past three years. Five years later, their number had swelled to 50,000, double the population of the whole town in 1800. Untrained for anything else, the newcomers worked as common laborers when they could find jobs at all, and tree-shaded streets that had in the past seen only the comings and goings of stolid Yankee burghers soon were thronged with lounging Irishmen with nothing to do and nowhere to go except possibly to Lowell or Lawrence, where their lot was to dig ditches and live in squalid shanties little better than those they had left behind in the poorest counties of Ireland.

The encroachment of tenements to house the growing immigrant population helped speed the already rapid exodus of the well-to-do to other quarters of the city. Development of Beacon Hill and other residential areas near the Boston Common and removed from the commercial center of town had long enticed those who could afford to live there; Lowells had lived along Colonnade Row, Charles Bulfinch's artful development abutting the Common on Tremont Street, since the second decade of the century, and the ever prosperous Thomas Handasyd Perkins moved nearby in 1831. The development of Beacon Hill got a strong push in 1832 when Patrick Tracy Jackson, not content with his income from the Lowell cotton mills, purchased as a speculation the easternmost of the three hills that had given Boston its earlier name of Trimountain. By the fall of 1835, Jackson had lopped off sixty-five feet of the hill—in the process tearing down the mansion that Peter Faneuil had inherited from his uncle nearly a century before—created more than four acres of filled-in land, and was ready to auction off twenty-five choice building lots in what would come to be known as Pemberton Square. Before it was destroyed in the 1880s to make room for a new courthouse, this would be one of Boston's most fashionable addresses, and those who lived there would include some of the town's mightiest merchants and manufacturers—among them Nathaniel Goddard, Robert Bennet Forbes, Amos Adams Lawrence, and John Amory Lowell.

Railroads, too, played a part in changing residential patterns in Boston. In the summer of 1835, three rail lines leading into the city were opened to passengers, and by 1847 Boston had seven separate railway terminals. The first commuter line, serving the town of Dedham ten and a half miles to the south of Boston, went into service in 1839, offering passengers a reduced fare. Others followed, and it is estimated that by 1848 a full 20 percent of Boston's businessmen lived in the suburbs and traveled to and from their jobs by rail via the eighty-odd commuter stations located within a fifteen-mile radius of the city. It was now possible, wrote Elias Hasket Derby, Jr., in 1850, for older residents to abandon the city to foreign laborers and flee to the suburbs, and he marveled that these urban refugees, the first in a long line, could "reach their stores and offices in the morning, and at night sleep with their wives and children in the suburbs. No time is lost, for they read the morning and evening journals as they go and return." And in their *Evening Transcripts* one day in 1855, these early-day commuters could read that the towns of Dedham, Milton, Quincy, Dorchester, Brighton, Newton, Medford, Woburn, Winchester, Somerville, West Cambridge, Melrose, and Malden had all become railroad suburbs of Boston. If they had had crystal balls, they would no doubt have been startled to see that they were enjoying better service than would be provided to their future fellow townsmen of the last quarter of the twentieth century.

In the main, however, these pioneer suburbanites were not the wealthy capitalists and traders, though the Forbeses—who later augmented their China trade fortunes with shrewd investments in railroads—moved quite early to Milton, where they have remained ever since. The titans of Boston trade, finance, and industry generally preferred to live within brisk walking distance of their counting rooms and offices, to sniff the salt air of the harbor whence their fortunes had sprung. If they moved beyond the city limits, it was frequently only to adjacent Brookline, where Thomas Handasyd Perkins had built a huge "summer house" as early as 1800. But even to live this short a remove from the heart of Boston's business district was sometimes disapproved of by friends and relatives. When young Amos Adams Lawrence determined in 1850 to leave Pemberton Square and build a home at Longwood, just two and a half miles west of Boston, he took William Appleton, his father-in-law, to view the ninety-acre plot he had purchased. Appleton, who had for years lived on Beacon Street, across from the Common, told Lawrence that it was "a poor business" and that he'd regret it. But then, Appleton was always somewhat acerbic, particularly when dealing with men who had married his daughters. Another son-in-law, the financier Thomas Jefferson Coolidge, recalled later that Appleton had made life miserable for him, and observed enigmatically that "I think I never knew him to do an unkind thing, and never heard him say a kind word."

Undeterred by his father-in-law's lack of enthusiasm, Lawrence went ahead and built a large stone house after the style of English country "cottages," and he lived there for the remainder of his life. Not being near a train line, he commuted to Boston on horseback.

Along with altering residential patterns, the great wave of immigration to Boston brought subtle and not-so-subtle changes to the city's social and intellectual character as well. Through its time of relatively static population, Boston had developed a spirit of homogeneity, based on the sharing by its citizens of common values and sensibilities. The old Puritan ideal of godly commonwealth had long since been discarded, but in its place had risen an equally lofty ideal of secular community. True enough, Boston's merchants and manufacturers were unrelenting in their quest for profits, but this feverish drive was tempered by a singular respect for education, for culture, for the life of the mind. As long ago as 1787, a correspondent for Philadelphia's *Columbian Magazine*, writing from Boston, had noted that "Arts and sciences seem to have made greater progress here, than in any part of America." And Charles Dickens, describing his American visit in 1842, observed that "The golden calf they worship at Boston is a pigmy compared with the giant effigies set up in other parts of that vast countinghouse which lies beyond the Atlantic, and the almighty dollar sinks into something comparatively insignificant amidst a whole Pantheon of better gods."

To be sure, devotion to higher callings was not universal among the city's men of means. Visiting Boston a few years before Dickens, the German aristocrat Francis J. Grund found that the growth of an aristocracy based on money threatened to produce a "vulgar oligarchy of calculating machines without poetry, without art, and without generosity." But even Grund, who unfavorably compared the moneyed aristocracy of Boston with the landed gentry of the southern states, conceded that this tendency was most evident among the newly rich. Those whose fortunes had their roots in the commerce of a generation or two before had presumably had the leisure to develop impulses transcending mere money-grubbing, and it was this class that set the tone and carved out the standards of achievement and service for much of nineteenth-century Boston. At the close of that century, looking back on his childhood in the 1820s and 1830s, the great preacher and orator Edward Everett Hale would recall that "There was plenty of money, and the rich men of Boston really meant that here should be a model and ideal city," a city where good sense, exemplary behavior, and elevated taste would be the norms. It was touching, really, this unshaken belief in the perfectibility of man, this pervasive respect for the value of culture. And if the merchant William Appleton cared so little for music that he stuffed his ears with cotton when he escorted his wife to a concert, he at least appreciated the fact that a man of his position owed it to the community to be seen at such high-toned musical events.

One representative example of this early nineteenth-century faith in culture is the Boston Athenaeum, even today one of the great libraries of the United States. At its beginning in 1807—it was an outgrowth of the Anthology Society, one of many reading and discussion groups that flourished at the time—the Athenaeum's founders well expressed the spirit that impelled them. Noting that in Boston "the class of persons enjoying easy circumstances, and possessing surplus wealth, is comparatively numerous," they suggested that inasmuch as national taxes are small, it behooved that class of persons to in effect tax themselves "for those institutions, which will be attended with lasting and extensive benefit, amidst all changes of our public fortunes and political affairs." By 1819 there were but three libraries in all the United States boasting more than ten thousand volumes: the city library of Philadelphia, the library of Harvard College —which was also heavily endowed with Boston money—and the Boston Athenaeum. Both James and Thomas Perkins were early backers of the Athenaeum; in 1822, James donated his house to the expanding institution, and Thomas served as its president from 1830 to 1832. From its inception, the Athenaeum has continuously been supported by Boston's wealthy.

Besides seeking to provide their fellows with the means to attain informed and healthy minds, the financial aristocrats of Boston paid equal attention to the health of their bodies. The Massachusetts General Hospital, now one of the world's foremost medical centers, was begun before 1820 with funds raised in a public subscription to which the brothers Perkins chipped in $5,000 apiece; the asylum for the insane which was the first order of business for the hospital builders has since become the renowned McLean Hospital. Later, in 1831, when he built his house near the Common, Thomas Perkins gave his old residence, valued at $25,000, to a new school for the blind. Now housed in much larger quarters in nearby Watertown, it is known as the Perkins School for the Blind.

NINE. "THE WANTS AND TASTE OF THE AGE"

Perhaps the crowning monument to the charitable and intellectual impulses of wealthy Bostonians of the early nineteenth century is the Lowell Institute, established in 1836 by John Lowell, son of Francis Cabot Lowell and both cousin and brother-in-law to mill magnate John Amory Lowell. (In approved Boston fashion, John Amory Lowell had married a first cousin, Susan Cabot Lowell, who was John Lowell's sister.) John, who for reasons best known to the family was called John, Jr., to distinguish him from his grandfather, the Old Judge, was born in 1799, and as a child accompanied his father on the latter's visit to Britain. After two unhappy years at Harvard, John cajoled his father into sending him to sea. Following two voyages to India, the young Lowell, with a substantial legacy received at the death of his father, set himself up as a Boston merchant, and later worked in the offices of the family mills at Waltham and Lowell. But John was a bookish, introspective man whose sights were trained on targets far beyond manufacturing and moneychanging. He was an avid reader, and took lessons on the flute; caught up in the educational fervor of his time and place, he was a founding member of the high-intentioned Boston Society for the Diffusion of Useful Knowledge, which sponsored public lectures by noteworthy speakers.

In 1833, following the deaths within a short year and a half of his wife and his two young daughters, Lowell determined to leave Boston to escape the scene of his grief and to make a grand tour to end all grand tours, a long and leisurely trip around the world. Mindful of his own ill health and the uncertainties of travel, he took care before he left to compose a will setting up a series of lecture courses that took the then-popular public-speaking circuit several steps further. What he proposed was that the speakers assembled under the auspices of his legacy would not deliver just a single talk but a comprehensive, cohesive sequence of lectures on "philosophy, natural history and the arts and sciences." Wary of putting such an enterprise into the hands of a committee of trustees, he stipulated that his lectures should be run by a single trustee, preferably a direct descendant—bearing the proud name of Lowell—of his grandfather and namesake, the Old Judge. He left his will, and the care of his business affairs, in the hands of cousin John Amory Lowell.

On the first leg of his journey, this wealthy and intellectual Bostonian took in the standard cultural sights and was able to

hobnob freely with the great and near great. Still thinking of
the source of his fortune, he found time while in England to
visit the cotton mills of Manchester and Birmingham, and to
inform his cousin of the latest refinements in their management and operation; like his father before him, he knew how to
mix business with pleasure. From Italy, after picking up a
young Swiss artist as a traveling companion, Lowell went to
Greece, sailing from there to Alexandria and up the Nile to
Cairo and Memphis where he busied himself calculating the
volume of the Pyramids. Moving on to Luxor, he wrote to John
Amory Lowell in Boston authorizing him to invest $100,000 in
a new cotton mill, and then set out to amass the largest assemblage of Egyptian artifacts yet put together by an American.
He also added a few refinements to what was to become the
Lowell Institute, displaying a keen sense of purpose as well as
an understanding that he was building not only for his own age
but for ages yet to come, ages whose interests and concerns he
could not dream of. From Luxor, feverish with dysentery,
Lowell wrote his cousin of his ambitious plan:

> As the prosperity of my native land, New England, which
> is sterile and unproductive, must depend hereafter, as it
> has heretofore depended, first, on the moral qualities, and
> secondly, on the intelligence and information of its inhabi-
> tants, I am desirous of trying to contribute towards this
> second object also;—and I wish courses of lectures to be
> established on physics and chemistry, with the application
> to the arts; also on botany, zoology, geology, and mineral-
> ogy, connected with their particular utility to man.
>   After the establishment of these courses of lectures,
> should disposable funds remain, or, in process of time, be
> accumulated, the trustee may appoint courses of lectures to
> be delivered on the literature and eloquence of our lan-
> guage, and even on those of foreign nations, if he see fit.
> He may also, from time to time, establish lectures on any
> subject that, in his opinion, the wants and taste of the age
> may demand.

In time, the wants and taste of a future age would see the
Lowell Institute, its wisely managed funds swelled to many millions of dollars above John Lowell's endowment of $250,000,

help spearhead and finance an educational radio and television station in Boston, all under the able direction of a direct descendant of the Old Judge. Even in the ancient and mysterious city of the Pharaohs, it was a wonder that could not be perceived.

Still ailing, John Lowell, Jr., traveled from Egypt to Ethiopia, then pressed on to India. When he arrived at last at Bombay aboard a British steamship, he was so weak that he had to be carried ashore. There, in a strange land far from home, his restless life's journey ended on March 4, 1836. Less than four years later, under the guidance of John Amory Lowell, the first of the Lowell Institute lectures began with a series of twelve talks on geology by Professor Benjamin Silliman of Yale, the most eminent scientist in the United States at the time. He was followed by equally respected speakers, and the Lowell Institute became almost immediately one of the prevailing winds in Boston's robust intellectual climate.

It is not recorded that Charles Dickens took in any of the Lowell Institute lectures on his visit to Boston in 1842, but he must surely have had their likes in mind when he wrote later that "Above all, I sincerely believe that the public institutions and charities of this capital of Massachusetts are as nearly perfect as the most considerate wisdom, benevolence, and humanity can make them. I never in my life was more affected."

Into this atmosphere, this air of unbridled optimism about the prospect of human improvement through culture and education ("Briefly," according to Edward Everett Hale, "there was the real impression that the kingdom of heaven was to be brought in by teaching people what were the relations of acids to alkalis, and what was the derivation of the word cordwainer.") came tens of thousands of Irish immigrants, beginning in the late 1840s. Poor almost past imagining, in the main ignorant beyond salvation except through tenacious faith in their fiercely parochial brand of Roman Catholicism, these swarms of newcomers cared little or nothing for such Boston enthusiasms. To the extent that the Boston brand of culture, education, and uplift seemed to smack of the ways of the hated

British, or worse, threaten the comforting grip of Mother Church on her children, the Irish actively opposed Boston's do-gooders and all their works. Even free, compulsory education, the benefit of which was an article of faith among Bostonians—the first public school in America had been founded in Boston in the seventeenth century—was hotly condemned by the Irish, who saw it as a devious Protestant plot to destroy their morals, faith, and families. Under the malign influence of public schools, railed the Irish Catholic *Boston Pilot* in 1852, "Our little boys scoff at their parents, call their fathers by the name Old Man, Boss, or Governor. The mother is the Old Woman. The little boys smoke, drink, blaspheme, talk about fornication, and so far as they are physically able, commit it. Our little girls read novels ... quarrel about their beaux, uphold Woman's Rights...." So much for acids and alkalis, the mysteries of cordwaining.

Earlier immigrant groups had eagerly embraced Boston's ways, sworn quick allegiance to its communal ideal. But the Irish were the insoluble lump of fat in the cultural melting pot of Boston. Despising what they saw as the godless intellectualism around them in their new home, they were in turn despised with varying degrees of intensity by many Bostonians, even including the city's minuscule black population. In time, as their numbers grew, the Irish formed their own culture, centered around their church and its schools. In time, too, still clinging to their communal dream even as they saw it slipping away, the old Bostonians, the wealthy class that had tried so hard to use its wealth to create a rational, ideal community, withdrew into the protective shell of their own institutions. They became strangers in a strange land, regarded by others and by themselves in much the same light as Americans abroad who seek to live in an American enclave in a foreign country. And their rock-hard faith in their own system of values often led them to project an air of smug superiority that was galling and infuriating to outsiders.

The seeds of this withdrawal, this extreme class consciousness, had been planted decades before the wave of Irish immigration gave them deep roots. The great trading families, and later the manufacturing families, shared common origins and experiences, and their members more often than not took care to marry into their own class. As new business opportunities arose, it was only natural that they were offered to relatives in preference to someone from outside the family, and this commercial incest created an esprit de corps, a feeling of apartness and homogeneity. And in the beginning, at least, when fortunes could be lost even more quickly than they were made, it sometimes created feelings of uncertainty and insecurity that were displayed in boorish, bullying behavior. Writing in 1839, Francis Grund observed that Boston's newly rich aristocrats frequently lacked the dignity and self-possession of Europe's men of rank, that they tended to be coarse and vulgar when dealing with their inferiors, in an effort to show that they were sufficiently independent not to care what others thought of them. Even among the wealthy, there were gradations of rank that, in the eyes of the merchants at least, placed those who had made their fortunes in trade a cut above those whose wealth came primarily from manufacturing. Cleveland Amory, in his *The Proper Bostonians*, tells of the day that merchant prince Thomas Handasyd Perkins, approached several times on a business matter by one of the well-known manufacturing Lawrence brothers, at last pointed a finger at Lawrence and said archly to a companion, "Who is that man who keeps following me around?"

Later, as Boston money was thrown into railroads, copper mines, and other diverse and distant enterprises, such fine distinctions would become blurred, but the great traders were for years considered to be aristocrats among aristocrats. Their serene sense of self-assurance as their wealth grew large beyond diminishing or loss would set a tone and establish a style of personal behavior that would long be cherished by Boston's moneyed men, and few would do more in this regard than the proud and prosperous Thomas Handasyd Perkins. Even at the height of his merchant powers, Perkins persisted in wearing his watch at the end of a cheap leather thong, until at last a Boston jeweler got up the courage to advise him that a man of his position should more properly sport a gold watch chain. "A man of my position," Perkins replied, "can wear his watch on a leather thong."

TEN. "THERE IS A CLASS OF CAUTIOUS CAPITALISTS"

Ironically, the tide of immigrants that engulfed and eventually destroyed Boston's old communal spirit was washed ashore as a direct result of the maritime prosperity that had made the achievement of ideal community seem possible. So significant had the port become that Samuel Cunard, when he began his regular transatlantic steamship service in 1839, chose Boston as the American terminus. Following the flag of a leader, other passenger lines favored Boston, too, and as Cunard's speedy, luxurious service began skimming off more well-to-do travelers, rival lines drove their fares down to levels that were within the limited means of even the poorest immigrants. By the 1850s, it was possible to make the Liverpool-to-Boston crossing for as low as seventeen dollars, a small price indeed to escape the crushing poverty of rural Ireland.

Flourishing as it was, the nature of Boston's seaborne commerce had changed, moving steadily away from foreign trade and coming to depend more and more on manufacturing. Ships still put out for distant ports—in 1843, William Appleton had three vessels voyaging to Canton—but as early as 1830, the number of Boston ships engaged in domestic trade was more than double those plying overseas routes. And many of the ships carried in their holds the fruits of the Lowell looms. Politically, the die was cast in favor of this shift in emphasis in 1830, when Nathan Appleton, the textile manufacturer and tariff advocate, was chosen over merchant and free trade man Henry Lee to represent Boston in the United States Congress. The voters of Boston saw clearly where their future lay.

In Washington, Appleton argued strenuously against charges by southern colleagues that the North's cotton mills made so much money that the protection of a tariff would only enable them to heap excess on top of excess, and it was in part through his efforts that a substantial tariff was enacted in 1833. But

Appleton was not cut out for politics, and he spurned a reelection bid in favor of returning to Boston—his place in Washington filled by fellow tariff stalwart Abbott Lawrence—to mind his family and business affairs.

His business career, however, had already been capped with its towering achievement. For Appleton, guided always by the "informing soul" of Francis Cabot Lowell and aided by Patrick Tracy Jackson and a handful of others—the Boston Associates, they called themselves—had not only helped introduce the factory system in the United States. He had also been instrumental in establishing for the first time a successful corporate industrial organization. On the foundations of a marginal paper mill on the banks of the Charles River, along the once-pastoral shores of the Merrimack, the Boston Associates had fathered American big business.

Prior to the formation of the first large Massachusetts cotton mills, there had been no mechanism or tradition for investing in the modern sense. With their substantial stock offerings, the Boston Associates provided a solid investment vehicle that offered a promise of continuity unheard of in previous industrial and commercial enterprises. Later, as the original group of large capitalists who had financed the mills began disposing of their shares, ownership in the corporations was dispersed among people of smaller means; Samuel Lawrence, treasurer of the Middlesex Company, noted as early as 1844 that 8 percent of the corporation's stock was in the hands of its mill operatives. The vaunted "people's capitalism" was on its way. By the eve of the Civil War, though great blocks of stock continued to be held by single individuals or trusts, the typical shareholding had dropped from the initial $25,000 to $100,000 per owner to about $3,000.

Management practices, too, took a new turn with the formation of the mills, and began to foreshadow the corporate organization that would become standard in most of America's big businesses. Previous enterprises, because of their relatively small size, had generally been operated and run by the same people who financed them; because of their scale, the mills made it both feasible and necessary to turn over much of their operation to nonowners, to men who in later times would be called professional managers. To be sure, nepotism was hardly unknown in mill management—though as long as relatives of major stockholders were competent, nepotism was not necessarily a bad thing. In the halcyon days when the Boston-backed mills had the market virtually to themselves, it was still possible to place an amiably bumbling son or nephew in an executive sinecure without damaging corporate dividends, but as competition increased and profits fell from their wonted high levels, managerial skills became the best ticket for entry into the executive ranks.

As early as the mid-1830s, the great burst of energy and innovation that had attended the founding of the textile industry had come to a halt, and mill operations had become routine. The interest of major stockholders in running their companies on a day-to-day basis had waned considerably; well capitalized and competently managed, a mill could turn a profit and pay out dividends with little help from shareowners. Unlike the still-active China merchants, whose prosperity hinged on constant wheeling and dealing in distant lands, the textile magnates were largely able to go about their business in leisurely fashion, secure in the knowledge that the sure and solid mills, those great brick hulks that could be seen and felt, were churning out dividends as well as cloth.

If they had a mind to, these heavy investors could go on a jaunt to Waltham or Lowell, and later, Lawrence, to inspect the headwaters of their ever flowing fortunes. Strolling through the neatly landscaped mill grounds, returning from time to time the respectful greetings of passing workers, they were the very lords of industrial creation, a new class of passive capitalists whose considerable incomes came, not from their current labors, but from their past investments, or the investments of their enterprising fathers. They were secure, a state of grace unknown to the more adventuresome. And their world seemed to be here to stay. Writing in 1846, probably the peak year of the cotton industry, Amos Adams Lawrence observed with no little satisfaction that whatever the future had in store, "the present impulse will at least have the effect of placing the manufacturing interest of the country on a basis from which it cannot easily be moved."

The mills had indeed become firmly established, both socially and economically. Boston's textile-rich capitalists could hold their heads up in the best of company, and no one could gainsay their considerable accomplishments, their contributions to their city and their country. But the textile boom was not fated to bloom quite so brightly as it had in its high summer of promise. Dividends, which had averaged 11.4 percent annually through 1836, edged down to an average of 9.7 percent over the next decade, and between 1847 and 1859 the payout dipped to 5.86 percent, a level that would not be much exceeded for the rest of the century.

It was an annoyance, this slippage of return, but not a matter of overwhelming moment. Some of the cotton capitalists had rounded out their holdings with investments in other fields that offered somewhat better profits, and besides, what was wrong with a safe and steady 5 or 6 percent? Why take risks? More speculative ventures with lures of fabulous returns had their place, but that place was not in the plans of the typical holders of large blocks of textile mill stock. Stick to what you know, to what has worked in the past—those were their watchwords— and leave the scrambling and the gambling to others, preferably to the coarse nouveaux of uncultured and unmannered New York. Boston's money—or at least a considerable portion of it—would be steered through well-charted channels, a course that was observed in 1847 by China merchant and railroad builder John Murray Forbes, who wrote of Boston that "There is a class of cautious capitalists who go for 5 or 6 per cent interest with security which they can see and know all about, and you cannot touch them at all at any rate of interest" for other types of investment.

It was a cautious tendency that would intensify with the passage of generations, and in time it would cripple and almost kill the old spirit of enterprise that had made Boston the cradle of American commerce and industry. But this venturesome spirit was yet far from dead. Quickened in the counting rooms of

Central Wharf, breathing the exotic fragrances of the Canton hongs, the spirit lived on in another generation of China traders, men born too late to ride the textile wave but too soon to be left on shore by the receding tide. A steady 5 percent was not for them; China's aureate sheen still glimmered on their horizon, and they would pursue it first with wooden ships and still later with iron rails that would reach across the American continent, binding the Atlantic to the Pacific and fulfilling the ancient quest for a Northwest Passage to the Orient.

Chapter Five

CHINA TRADERS,

OLD AND NEW

At the age of sixteen, I filled a man's place as third mate; at the age of twenty, I was promoted to a command; at the age of twenty-six, I commanded my own ship; at twenty-eight, I abandoned the sea as a profession; at thirty-six, I was at the head of the largest American house in China. . . . I had been blessed, by a kind Providence, with a fair amount of success.

—Robert Bennet Forbes

While Francis Cabot Lowell's Boston Associates were marveling at the success of their Waltham mill and laying the foundations of the great manufacturing city of Lowell, John Perkins Cushing remained in Canton tending the affairs of Perkins & Company. For the great China trader Thomas Handasyd Perkins, though he built a short-lived cotton mill of his own along the Charles River in Newton, just west of Boston, and later made some fairly substantial investments in the Lowell mills—he was even, for a time, president of the Appleton Company—remained first and foremost a merchant, far and away the leader of Boston's mercantile community. And when it came to weighing his merchant and manufacturing interests over the question of the protective tariff, Perkins chose the side of free trade without hesitation.

Cushing had returned home for a brief visit in April, 1807, setting sail again for China after just six weeks. Not yet twenty, he was a full and respected partner in the Perkins firm, one of the most successful trading houses in China. One reason for Cushing's outstanding performance was that he, like many Americans, approached the hong merchants and other Chinese with whom he dealt as equals and treated them with the respect that they thought was their due. This was in sharp contrast to rival European traders, who were accustomed to shouldering the white man's burden and asserting supremacy over people of darker races than their own. In Chinese eyes, Americans remained *Fan-Kwae*, foreign devils from beyond the borders of civilized society, but their honest and courteous bearing made them somewhat less devilish than *Fan-Kwae* from other Western lands.

Cushing managed to outdo most of his countrymen in gaining all-important respect from his counterparts in China. As late as 1815, it was widely believed by the Chinese merchants that the only truly reliable Americans in Canton were Cushing and Philip Ammidon, at the time representing another American firm, but later an agent for the Perkins interests. So noted was Cushing for his implacable honesty that an agreement by a hong merchant to supply an American supercargo with tea at the market price once specified that if quality and price could not be agreed upon he would be called in as an arbitrator, and "Mr. J. P. Cushing's opinion shall be binding."

By the 1820s Cushing was known as the most influential of all the foreigners in Canton. He was, according to young George W. Sturgis, who worked for him in the Perkins firm, "exclusively a *man of business* and in my opinion, as well calculated for one on a liberal scale as any I have ever met with; in manners the Gentleman, generous, intelligent, and independent, and deservedly esteemed and respected by all who know him."

Happily, Cushing had struck up a close business and personal relationship with the hong merchant Houqua, who at his death in 1843 was said to be the richest man in the world. Houqua had dealt with the Americans since the 1780s, and was as famed as Cushing for honest and upright conduct at a time when most Chinese merchants were noted for rascality and dishonesty in their dealings with foreigners. Indeed, Houqua at times displayed a streak of generosity that astounded his American clients. William C. Hunter, who in 1837 joined Russell & Company, the successor to Perkins & Company, recalled in his old age the experience of a merchant who had suffered considerable losses in Canton. To help the American recoup his losses, Houqua advanced him large sums of money, and after several years the two compared accounts and found that Houqua was out a total of $72,000. The hong merchant then took a promissory note for this amount and locked it away in his strongbox. Fortune continued to frown on the American trader, by now aching to return home but still hoping to repay his debt.

"You have been so long away from your own country, why do you not return?" Houqua asked one day. Told that only the unpaid $72,000 kept the American in Canton, Houqua called for his purser and asked for the note. "You and I are number one *olo flen*," he said to his debtor. "You belong honest man, only no got chance." With that, Houqua ripped the note into tiny pieces and tossed the fragments into his waste basket. "Just now have settee counter," he smiled, "alla finishee. You go, you please."

With a permanent branch office in Canton, with a virtual monopoly on the fur trade on the Northwest Coast, and with their substantial resources, the Perkins brothers were better able than most China traders to ride out the disruptions that came with the War of 1812. During a part of this period, in fact, they sat back and put their money out—at a goodly 18 percent interest—to other merchants in Canton. But as the fur trade paled and hard cash grew harder to come by, a search began for a substitute for the furs and specie that had been foundations of Boston's China trade. Opium seemed the ideal commodity to fill the gap, and during much of the 1820s, the drug was virtually the only profitable commodity in the China trade. The British, with their monopoly in opium-rich India, were far and away the heaviest dealers, but the Perkins interests, sparked first by Cushing and later by the brothers Robert Bennet Forbes and John Murray Forbes, ran a worthy second.

The British East India Company, whose corner on the tea

market had brought Boston's merchant tempers to a boil in 1773, had introduced opium to China in the same year. At first touted for its pain-dulling medicinal properties, the drug was soon found to dull pains of another sort, and it wasn't long before wretched Chinese peasants and coolies were turning to opium as a pleasant release from life's burdens. So widespread and devastating had opium smoking become—and so draining was it on China's balance of payments—that the emperor decreed in 1800 that the drug could no longer be brought in. The East India Company, not wanting to offend the emperor and jeopardize its favored position in the China trade, complied with the letter of the imperial edict while cheerfully flouting its spirit by auctioning off opium in India to independent British merchants who then smuggled the drug into China.

Having ready access only to the inferior grades of Turkish opium, American traders at first steered clear of the trade. But as the habit spread and addicts grew more interested in quantity than quality, a few American merchants began to dabble in the drug traffic, starting in about 1805. The first Perkins cargo of Turkish opium, on board the brigantine *Monkey*, arrived in China in 1816; when the transaction proved profitable, the firm dispatched an agent to Leghorn, Italy, to set up an opium-buying operation. It was the beginning of a thriving if illicit commerce for the house of Perkins and for the future of a number of other Boston fortunes.

Though they recognized the demoralizing effects of opium addiction, there is no evidence that these early drug dealers felt that they were engaged in an immoral enterprise. It hardly mattered to them that their goods were illegal and had to be smuggled to their destination; smuggling was a time-honored sideline among Bostonians. And the fact that they were giving the customer something that he wanted—and something that he would in any case get from British smugglers—seemed to bless their undertaking with enough commercial validity to overcome whatever moral qualms the merchants may have had. Years later, Robert Bennet Forbes, by then a pillar of his home community, would observe of his own deep involvement in the opium trade that it was engaged in by the prestigious East India

Company and was considered perfectly legitimate outside China. Besides, he said, he was only following the example of "the merchants to whom I had always been accustomed to look up [to] as exponents of all that was honorable in trade,—the Perkins's, the Peabodys, the Russells, and the Lows." Forbes also justified his activities by noting that the effects of opium were probably no more harmful than the ravages of "ardent spirits." A present-day Forbes has been heard more than once to wonder if today's drug dealers will in time be as honored as are his own forebears.

For all that, Western medical doctors of the nineteenth century freely prescribed opium for a variety of complaints, and while it is doubtful that many Bostons traders ever took up the drug in earnest, its use must certainly have been known to them. In 1837, William Appleton noted in his diary that his own mother, who had reached the ripe old age of eighty-one, had for the past two decades been using about four pounds of opium a year "without apparent bad effects." The elderly Appleton woman had begun taking the drug as a cure for chronic diarrhea, a condition that may or may not have been brought on by too-liberal consumption of the tea and rhubarb that the Chinese sold to the West in the belief that they were used as tonics to cure constipation. The Russell & Company partner William C. Hunter probably summed up the feelings of his colleagues when he wrote in later life that the opium trader's "sales were pleasantness and his remittances were peace. Transactions seemed to partake of the nature of the drug; they imparted a soothing frame of mind with three per cent commission on sales, one per cent on returns, and no bad debts."

Chinese officialdom did not view opium with such equanimity, and beginning around 1816 the imperial government launched a number of campaigns to enforce the ban on imports of the drug. By 1821 the crackdown was complete. Opium-carrying ships, which had previously slipped into the anchorage at Whampoa after payment of bribes to corrupt customs officials, were now barred from the anchorage. This time the Chinese meant business, and the ban was rigorously enforced. But the dope merchants were not about to let a little matter of law come between them and the profitable opium trade. They soon found ways to sneak their cargoes in and keep China's opium pipes burning.

Thomas Handasyd Perkins welcomed Chinese moves to halt the opium traffic, figuring that if China made things hot enough for drug dealers, the less venturesome traders would be scared out of the business, leaving a bigger share for the Perkins firm. It was a shrewd guess: rival merchants John Jacob Astor and Stephen Girard dropped the opium trade. For years, along with the Boston firm of Bryant & Sturgis—together, the Perkins firm and Bryant & Sturgis were frequently called the Boston Concern, and William Sturgis, scion of an old Cape Code seafaring family, was a Perkins nephew and erstwhile employee—the Perkins interests had a virtual monopoly on Turkish opium imports to China, sometimes buying as much as 75 percent of the some 150,000 pounds of opium produced annually in Turkey. In the coming century, this encouragement of opium-poppy cultivation in Turkey would yield a bitter harvest for American society, but the Boston Concern reaped lush profits from trade in the drug. Depending on market conditions, opium bought in Turkey for about $2.50 per pound sold for as much as $10 a pound in China.

Not only did the Chinese government oppose the drug trade; so did Houqua, the hong merchant upon whose good offices the Boston Concern's fortunes depended. For John Cushing, this posed a tricky problem; he didn't want to offend his Chinese associate, nor did he have any intention of missing out on so profitable a business. He solved his dilemma with a ruse that probably fooled no one, though it seems to have satisfied Houqua and has led some to claim that Cushing, bowing either to moral scruple or to Chinese law, withdrew from the opium trade. What he did was announce, on October 26, 1818, that the commission business of Perkins & Company would now be handled by a newly organized firm, James P. Sturgis & Company, whose head was William Sturgis's first cousin. On paper, this took Cushing out of direct involvement in the drug trade, since opium shipments from the Boston Concern would go through the Sturgis firm rather than Perkins & Company.

In fact, Cushing had hardly washed his hands of the opium traffic; not only was he related to the principals of James P. Sturgis & Company, but he was still a partner of the drug-dealing Perkins brothers, who also were Sturgis kinsmen. And even after he retired from active business and returned to Boston, he continued to invest in opium ventures.

To get around the strictly enforced Chinese ban on opium, the Bostonians followed the British lead and adopted the storeship system, or the Lintin system, as it was called in honor of the island downriver from Whampoa where opium ships would transfer their chests of drugs to a permanently anchored vessel that served as a floating warehouse and marketplace. The system had been worked out with methodical care. The Chinese smugglers, who handled whatever bribes may have been necessary, would pay cash for opium chits at a Canton countinghouse and make their buys aboard the storeship. In addition to paying the market price, they would also have to come up with a *cumsha* of five dollars per chest. (Each chest generally contained a picul, or about 133⅓ pounds.) The operator of the storeship charged sellers a commission on sales, and smaller dealers were charged a storage fee for their cargoes. For the Americans, it was a safe and pleasant, not to mention profitable, arrangement. The risks were taken by the Chinese smugglers who, to outrun government patrol boats, carried their cargoes ashore in wave-cutting galleys that sometimes had as many as thirty oars to a side. The Americans called these exotic vessels smug boats, or centipedes; to the Chinese, they were fast crabs or scrambling dragons.

The first Perkins storeship, the *Cadet*, anchored at the Lintin station in 1823, and was so successful that other dealers looked to Cushing to set the price of opium, which he was generally able to manipulate by parceling out the drug in quantities that would not drive prices down. On occasion, if a rival showed up with a large quantity of the drug, Cushing would start dumping his opium to move the price down, buy up his competitor's cargo at the lower tag, and then raise the price to its previous higher level. Between January, 1824, and July, 1825, the Boston Concern sent a total of 177,837 pounds of opium to China aboard six ships. In addition to dealing in their own cargoes of Turkish opium, the Perkins firm also handled the Indian product on a consignment basis, though a much larger share of Indian opium was brought in by another firm, Russell & Company, founded in 1824 with Cushing's encouragement. Later, Perkins & Company would be merged with the Russell firm, further consolidating the Boston Concern's interests in China.

TWO. "IF YOU MEET THE DEVIL
CUT HIM IN TWO"

On a fine spring day in 1830, twenty-five-year-old Robert Bennet Forbes, nearing Boston in a mail coach after a trip to New York, spotted a pair of coaches wheeling past him, headed south toward Providence. In the coaches, he recognized "the two individuals who held my fate in their hands," Thomas Handasyd Perkins and the captain-trader William Sturgis, leading principals in the Boston Concern's China ventures. Calling his coach to a halt at the first likely spot, Forbes rented a chaise and set out in hot pursuit. At Dedham, he was told that Perkins and Sturgis planned to pass the night at Fuller's halfway house in Walpole, and after buying a toothbrush and a fresh collar, Forbes dashed off once more, arriving just as the slower-moving Perkins-Sturgis party was alighting at the Fuller establishment.

Across the street at Polley's halfway house, Forbes cleaned himself up, buttoned on his sparkling white collar, and strolled nonchalantly into the dining room at Fuller's, where he found Perkins and Sturgis in high spirits and in the company of several young ladies. Forbes readily accepted a dinner invitation, and after the meal he took Sturgis aside and confessed that his presence there was more than a mere chance encounter. He was returning from New York, Forbes said, where he had inspected the ship *Milo*, which he intended to purchase in hopes that he would be given a chance to take it to the Lintin station as the Bryant & Sturgis storeship. This berth was currently occupied by the *Tartar*, under the command of a Sturgis nephew, but the elder Sturgis had long taken an interest in Forbes's seafaring career, and readily agreed to the young man's plan, advising him to forget about the *Milo* and buy a new ship instead. Later in the evening, Forbes cornered Perkins with his proposal, and when told that Sturgis had already approved of the scheme, Perkins said he had no objection to it. He, too, suggested a new vessel, and volunteered to advance Forbes the funds to buy it. The hour was now late, and Forbes decided to spend the night in Walpole before setting out once more for Boston. Sleep came easy, and never in his life, Forbes recalled later, had he been blessed "with more happy dreams of prosperity."

Forbes had been a long time in preparing for command of the Lintin storeship, which in addition to being the central cog of the Boston Concern's opium operations also did a thriving business in provisioning passing ships. And while he would later go on to bigger things, he had regarded the Lintin post as the height of his ambition, an ambition whose fulfillment was made possible by happy accident of birth. Like John Perkins Cushing, Forbes was a Perkins nephew. His father, Ralph Bennet Forbes, had married Margaret Perkins in 1799, and when the hapless Ralph Forbes's merchant ships seemed never to come in, young Bennet was taken under the generous Perkins wing, as were his brothers Thomas Tunno Forbes and John Murray Forbes.

In another time or another place, kinship to a princely merchant family might have bestowed more modest blessings, but the Forbes boys, born as they were in the first years of the new century, came into a world of great promise and prosperity. In the twilight of that century, the writer Julian R. Sturgis looked back wistfully at the generation of his merchant father, Russell Sturgis—born in 1805, and a nephew of the brothers Perkins as well as of their Sturgis associates—and remarked that Bostonians sired at that period "were exceptionally fortunate in the time of their birth." It was an age of energy, courage, and integrity, a time of boundless opportunity. Fortune was on the wing, ready to be brought down by those endowed with the will and ready to seize the way. No matter what their birthright, young people were expected to work, and work hard. There was no such thing, in Boston, at least, as the idle rich—"even the conception of a 'leisure class' was not yet," said Sturgis.

Robert Bennet Forbes entered this age of grace in 1804, the same year that his Cushing cousin was learning the ins and outs of the China trade, the same year that the first American opium ships were making their way to Canton. He got his first taste of the sea that would bear his fortune in 1811, when he and his older brother Thomas sailed with their mother for Marseilles, where Ralph Forbes had gone in search once more of his own elusive fortune. At Foster's Wharf on the bitter January day of their departure, young Forbes watched in wide-eyed wonder as the crew of the schooner *Midas*, which was heavy in the water with its mundane cargo of salt fish, beat ice from the canvas and rigging in preparation for setting sail. It was a rough passage, marred by the vessel's capture and brief detention by three British warships enforcing the blockade of French ports, but it was perhaps a fitting first voyage for a child fated for maritime adventure, and to bear the nickname of Black Ben Forbes.

The return trip, more than two years later, was no less eventful. On board the armed merchant ship *Orders in Council*, the Forbes family came under fire from a hostile British squadron—the War of 1812 was in full swing—and their Boston-bound schooner took refuge in a Spanish harbor. Boarding next the brig *Caroline*, the Forbeses fared no better; the *Caroline*, too, was bagged by a British frigate which towed the vessel to the mouth of the Tagus River. Eventually, mother, father, and children—another son, John Murray Forbes, had been born in Bordeaux—made it to Lisbon, where an obliging Sturgis cousin took them in and arranged for passage aboard a Baltimore ship bound for Newport. While waiting for the vessel to depart, the family did some sightseeing, and beneath an arch of an aqueduct near Cintra, the future Black Ben fired a pistol for the first time, and "heard the many reverberations resulting therefrom."

Back at home, which was now in Milton, just south of Boston, the Forbes boys enrolled at Milton Academy, where their fluent French and harum-scarum tales of sea fights and other worldly adventures made them the most curious of classmates, hardly the type to buckle down to studies and other such schoolboy concerns. So it was that in 1815, at the age of thirteen, Thomas Tunno Forbes was apprenticed at the Perkins countinghouse at Charles Bulfinch's monumental India Wharf. Bennet, too young to begin his mercantile career just yet, remained in school. But in 1816, just twelve years old, he became the first apprentice in a new firm formed by the junior Thomas and James Perkins along with Samuel Cabot, husband of the elder Thomas Handasyd Perkins's daughter Elizabeth. Boston business was ever a family affair.

Forbes's duties as a merchant apprentice were simple enough, but boring to one of his temperament. At the countinghouse of S. Cabot & J. & T. H. Perkins, Jr., on Foster's Wharf, the young man swept floors, laid fires on cold winter mornings, copied correspondence in letter books ("in a very indifferent manner," he confessed in his old age), and ran a variety of errands. He might have been satisfied to perform such lowly chores, confident in the knowledge that dutiful performance would surely lead to promotion and possible partnership. But Forbes had a touch of the sea in his blood, a tendency nourished by his doting uncle Thomas, with whom the young apprentice now lived. Dishing up heaping portions of pudding at dinnertime, Perkins would sometimes remark to his nephew that he would hardly be eating so high on the hog off the Cape of Good Hope, instilling in the young man the abiding notion, as he put it, that "I was *born to eat bad puddings off the Cape.*"

Perkins had marked Forbes's skill at sailing, the mysteries of which he had learned from his cousin James on Jamaica Pond. He must have noted, too, that Bennet often slipped away from Foster's Wharf to stroll along nearby Central Wharf, where the Perkins ships were fitted out for globe-girdling voyages to bring back the teas and silks of China. It was heady stuff for a young man, a boy, really, even one who had heard the roar of enemy guns and the drone of cannonballs passing overhead. Frequently, perhaps dreaming of distant lands, Forbes would scramble aloft on one of his uncles' safely moored vessels, surveying the city and the outer reaches of the harbor from his perch atop sturdy masts that had groaned at the beating of all the world's winds. No, a clerk's life was not for Bennet Forbes; boy that he was, he was summoned to the sea.

The call came in early October, 1817, when Forbes had just turned thirteen. On one of his regular jaunts to the Perkins ships, Forbes had gone aboard the *Canton Packet*, and it was there that his uncle Thomas found his nephew casting an eye at the rigging. "Well, Ben," said Perkins, waving at the forest of masts around them, "which of these ships do you intend to go in?" Without hesitation, Forbes replied, "I am ready to go in this one." Before three weeks had passed, Robert Bennet Forbes was on his way to China. Among other things, he took with him some seasickness remedies given to him by his mother and some advice from close family friend William Sturgis, who, in a pitched battle with Chinese pirates, had once prepared a keg of powder to blow up his ship rather than suffer capture. "Always go straight forward," Sturgis told the fledgling seafarer, "and if you meet the devil cut him in two, and go between the pieces; if any one imposes on you, tell him to whistle against a northwester, and to bottle up moonshine."

Forbes needed his mother's medicine long before he could heed any of Sturgis's words of wisdom, though neither her nostrums nor some pills given him by the captain prevailed against the severe bout of seasickness that kept him alternately throwing up over the side and moaning in his quarters for the first several weeks of the voyage. After his recovery, Forbes, whose youth and kinship to the *Canton Packet*'s owners made him a somewhat anomalous crew member, began volunteering for a number of shipboard duties. Thomas Handasyd Perkins, after all, had advised him that a key purpose of the voyage would be to help make him fit for future captaincy, and there is no better place to start than before the mast. Furling sails and standing watches, young Forbes learned the ways of the sea quickly, and when the mate informed him that once he had asked to keep the watch he would continue to do so when ordered, he learned something of discipline, too.

Arriving at Canton in March, 1818, Forbes was put up by his

cousin John Perkins Cushing in the foreigners' compound at
the edge of the walled city. And though he knew that the
natural order of things dictated that his older brother, Thomas,
was being groomed to come to China as a representative of the
Perkins & Company interests, he did a little grooming on his
own, clerking for his cousin, helping weigh teas and pack silks
for shipment home. Cushing was impressed with the boy and
asked him to stay on; Cushing, after all, had come to Canton at
sixteen, and knew that a boy could do a man's work in that
quarter of the globe. Forbes, bowing to his brother's claim to a
Canton post in the house of Perkins and heeding his own call to
the sea, declined, and in June he set out for home on the *Canton
Packet*. The ship put in at New York—already, that port was
rivaling Boston as a central distribution point for the teas and
silks of China—and after a brief visit with his family at Milton
he headed back to New York, where the ship was being prepared for another China voyage.

Before the sailing, Thomas Handasyd Perkins gave him a
box of dollars to invest as he saw fit on behalf of himself and his
brother, and advised him that he had instructed the captain to
teach him the mysteries of navigation. "You must bear in mind
that you have many duties to perform," Perkins wrote, "and
you must endeavor to conduct yourself in such manner as will
do you credit at home and abroad." It was still the keystone of
the Boston business philosophy. Do yourself credit at home and
abroad, do yourself credit for the sake of your friends and
close-knit family, no matter where they might be. For they had
put their trust in you, even as a boy, and your performance of
your duties was a reflection on them, a testing of their trust.
And if you can't trust your friends and kinsmen, whom *can* you
trust? It was the glue that bound the Boston commercial community together in a world of strangers.

In Canton once more, not two years since leaving Boston on
his first China voyage, Forbes again gave Cushing a hand in
minding the affairs of Perkins & Company and was again asked
to stay on as clerk. But Forbes had promised Perkins to stay by
his ship until he was fit to command it. Besides, he couldn't
stand in his brother's way, even on the road to sure fortune;

that's what trust was all about. Later, hot and dirty in his cramped quarters below decks on the *Canton Packet*, resting with his head on a splintery stick of wood, Forbes thought of the luxurious life he had left behind and consoled himself with the thought that "I was doing my duty,—doing what my mother and my uncles would approve."

While Forbes was in Canton on this second voyage, Cushing wrote to Thomas Handasyd Perkins about "our young friend, Bennet Forbes," suggesting that he be made a ship's officer on his return home. "He is," said Cushing of the fifteen-year-old Black Ben, "without exception, the finest lad I have ever known, and has already the stability of a man of thirty . . . he had profited so much by the little intercourse he has had with the Chinese, that he is now more competent to transact business than one half of the supercargoes sent out." But Cushing knew where Bennet's interests lay and wrote to Forbes's mother that "as he has set out to make a sailor it is best to let him persevere. . . ."

On the voyage out from Canton, the *Canton Packet* put in at Hamburg to sell its cargo, then sailed to London for refitting and a return voyage to China. It was a good season for trading, and there was no need for returning home. Before leaving London for Canton by way of Gibraltar, Bennet was made third mate and was addressed by the captain as Mr. Forbes. His seafaring career was well under way. Meanwhile, as planned all along, his older brother Thomas had left Boston for Canton to take up his post as principal aide to Cushing in Perkins & Company.

When he arrived again in China, Bennet's duties kept him close to his ship, and he had little time to spend ashore with friends and relatives. He was a man of the sea now, not a merchant or clerk. Before the *Canton Packet* left for Boston in February, 1821, Mr. Forbes, now sixteen, was promoted to second mate.

Forbes had little time, either, for family and friends in Boston. Arriving home in June, 1821, he left later in the summer on the *Canton Packet* for a year-long voyage that would take him to Manila, Canton, and Rotterdam. More voyages followed, and though he loved the sea, there were again times when Bennet envied his brother and his comfortable life in Canton. Already, Thomas Forbes was spoken of as Cushing's successor, and the succession seemed to be coming soon. With one brief visit home, Cushing had been in Canton for nearly two decades, and was ready to retire and lead the life of a Boston gentleman. Bennet Forbes still plowed the oceans, and with notable success for the Perkins concern. In the fall of 1824, Thomas Handasyd Perkins rewarded him with command of the *Levant*, and other captaincies followed.

But now Forbes was beginning to wonder where all his sea roving was getting him and where it would all end. His pay as a captain was a paltry fifty dollars a month, and while he was allotted space in the hold for small cargoes of his own, or to charge others for freight, he hardly seemed on the way to laying up a fortune, particularly when his progress was measured against his older brother's. He could top most men when it came to tales of travel and derring-do: he had outsailed pursuing pirates, seen much of the known world and some of the little-known, and helped put down incipient mutinies. But all this would profit him nothing in his old age, leave him little but memories of olden times and a stock of stories to spellbind wondering boys come to marvel at the tall masts of Boston Harbor. Forbes knew that he had to do more than sail other men's ships, hauling rich cargoes that were not his own.

THREE. "AN UPRIGHT & HONORABLE CONDUCT"

By the 1820s, the China trade had changed considerably from its earlier days of high adventure and romance. The rich fur trade on the Northwest Coast was no more, and ships seldom made the storm-tossed Cape Horn passage, stopping for water and provisions at exotic tropical isles. The eastern passage, the more direct route by way of the Cape of Good Hope, was becoming the rule for Canton-bound vessels; the trade that had begun as a constant scramble for goods had become a regular commerce, conducted, not by roving supercargoes, but by resident agents. Ginseng grubbed from the ground of New York

State, fragrant sandalwood chopped on lush Pacific islands, furs bartered for trinkets in Nootka Sound, all were giving way to the steady commodities of opium, hard cash, and cotton from the Lowell mills that had been built in large measure with the profits of earlier trading times.

As the New England textile mills began spinning out more fabric than the domestic market could absorb, it was only natural that sellers should turn to foreign shores for an outlet for their goods. As early as 1823, Boston's William Boardman sent out 3,400 yards of cotton sheeting on a ship "bound for Rio Janiero and a market," and in the following year he sent two more loads to Buenos Aires. Until Britain's opium war with China forced a humiliated Celestial Empire to fling open the doors of trade at numerous other ports than Canton, South America sopped up most of the exported American textiles, which had so thoroughly captured that market by the 1840s that British merchants seeking a piece of the South American action sometimes slapped such labels as "Appleton," "Boott," and "Suffolk" on their cheap cotton goods. The Near East, too, was a good early market for Boston's cloth, and even into the twentieth century cotton sheetings were still called cabots by the Turks.

But it was China, unindustrialized China with its teeming millions needing to be clothed, that was most highly prized as a consumer of American cottons. The first few shipments went out in the late 1820s and were so eagerly received that by 1830 John Perkins Cushing was advising the Boston Concern that if stock in a textile mill could be had at a "dog cheap" price, it would be worthwhile to buy out a factory for the sole purpose of turning out goods for China. It would not even be amiss, he added, to start a mill from scratch, so promising was the market. To textile king Patrick Tracy Jackson, Cushing wrote in the same year that "when you come to consider that the whole of the immense population of this country from the Emperor to the laborer are clad in cotton, you can form some idea of the extent of the consumption of cotton fabrics. . . ." And American cloth could be made at considerably less cost than the laboriously handwoven native Chinese article.

In time, China would become the most important single export market for American cottons, and when the so-called treaty ports were opened up in 1843, making possible much wider distribution in a huge country where interior transportation was poor, China's share of total U.S. cotton exports leaped to 34 percent, nearly triple the previous year's figure. By the late 1840s, the Lowell mills had become so dependent on the market in China that Nathan Appleton would chalk up the industry's depressing performance in that period to the sporadic rebellions and disturbances that upset trade in China. With the opening of still more ports in 1859, and the coming of stable conditions, China took nearly 56 percent of total American cotton exports. Oil for the lamps of China, indeed! There was more money to be made in clothing the country's coolies.

The China trade was changing, and so were the affairs of the house of Perkins. As early as 1821, James and Thomas Handasyd Perkins had decided that nearly thirty years in business was enough, and made plans for slow and orderly withdrawal. Hopefully, they brought their sons—who had previously set up a house of their own—into the senior firm, though it is likely that even pride of parenthood did not blind them from seeing the move as a vain gesture. Two generations of merchant genes had failed to fire the younger Perkinses: Thomas, Jr., much preferred the pleasures of wealthy Boston society to the hard-nosed rigors of commerce, and his cousin James, Jr., was an alcoholic who before the decade was out would be "daily disgracing himself." It would be left to other men's sons to carry on the Perkins interests and traditions, to nephews John Cushing and the Forbes boys, all sons of failed merchants whose setbacks would be more than made up for by the success of their offspring.

John Perkins Cushing returned to Boston from Canton, where he had spent nearly half his life, in 1828, leaving Perkins & Company's affairs in the able hands of Thomas Tunno Forbes. ("I had now become aware of his superiority over me," wrote Bennet Forbes of his older brother, "and was ready to look up to him as the head of the family.") Before his departure, he had written Forbes a lengthy letter, a distillate of all he had learned in his lengthy stay in the Orient. Always be punctual with the Chinese, he said, and never ask for credit from anyone but Houqua. "I need not again remind you," he reminded his protégé once more, "of the advantages that are derived in business concerns by pursuing on all occasions & with all persons with whom you have transactions an upright & honorable conduct. . . ."

The China trade had been good to Cushing—he had amassed a fortune of more than $600,000—and he was little inclined to leap into the hurly-burly of Boston business, which he found totally alien after so long an absence. Rejecting a proposal that he go into partnership with Samuel Cabot (a Perkins son-in-law) and Thomas Perkins, Jr.—Cabot was too unpopular, Cushing thought, and the junior Perkins would simply "not be a desirable partner in business"—Cushing also turned aside Perkins's offer to make him head of the Perkins firm, which since the death of James Perkins in 1822 had been run by Samuel Cabot and Thomas Handasyd Perkins with only the barest help from the disappointing sons of the founding partners. What Cushing had in mind was a life of ease, with an investment now and then in a China venture, but nothing that would keep his head spinning with business affairs. Not for him was the obsessive Boston concern for commercial matters, the "vortex of business" which the merchant William Appleton complained so engrossed his mind "that I can hardly free it when I return to my family or even on the Sabbath." Cushing didn't yet have a family, but he aimed to start one and live in well-earned peace.

His intended idyll came to an end almost before it started. In August, 1829, less than a year after Cushing had left his Canton business in the charge of Thomas Forbes, the ship *Mentor* anchored at the Lintin station. Learning at Macao that the vessel carried important letters from home—some of which, he thought, might have to do with the fate of the Perkins firms in both Boston and Canton—Forbes immediately set out for Lintin in his yacht, the *Haidee*. The evening was hot and humid, auguring a storm, but Forbes was sure that he could make the eighteen-mile journey in a couple of hours at most. His progress was slow, and when the boat was becalmed about seven miles upriver from Macao, Forbes threw out his anchor and awaited the wind. When it finally came, at about midnight, it was in the fitful gusts that herald a coming gale, and Forbes set his sails and steered back for the haven of Macao. By one in the morning, the *Haidee* was snugly anchored in the lee of the town—Forbes could have put ashore, but he didn't want to disturb his chief clerk, who was seasick in a bunk below deck.

Shortly before daylight the wind whipped in with hurricane force, churning the sea and killing all hopes of making shore. A cutter of the East India Company lay at anchor nearby, but its native crew either ignored or didn't understand the upside-down Stars and Stripes that a desperate Forbes ran up the mast as a plea for help. Soon after dawn, as the larger cutter got under way for the safety of the inner harbor, Forbes set out in its wake, but heavy winds and blinding sheets of rain soon forced him to haul in his sails and drop both anchors. As the winds increased, so did the danger; preparing for the worst, Forbes stripped off his clothes. It was a wise but futile move. First one anchor chain gave way, then the other snapped like a frail thread. At the mercy now of raging wind and water, the *Haidee* was hurled wildly through the waves, driven toward the sea. Running up a part of the foresail, Forbes fought for control, battled the rising tempest. Through driving rain he saw a small beach, but not the shoals that turned waves to crushing breakers as he steered for shore. One nearly swamped the fragile craft, but Forbes stayed at the helm; the next smashed the rudder, leaving the *Haidee* helplessly broadside and awash in the furious breakers. A native crewman, who lived to tell the tale, shoved a skylight to Forbes as a handhold, but Forbes leaped instead for the main shroud. For a few moments, he clung there, beaten by the waves, thinking, perhaps, of a packet of letters from home. Then his final wave came, and he was swept away. He was twenty-seven years old.

When calm came, Forbes's body was recovered and buried in the English cemetery at Macao, a grave far from home. "I have visited the spot," Bennet Forbes wrote to his mother in 1837, "and shall go again."

FOUR. "UNTIL MY NEW YORK AGENTS GO"

At twenty-five, Robert Bennet Forbes, almost constantly at sea for the past dozen years, was suddenly head of his family, a position that he had at long last granted without envy to his now-dead older brother. He could now expect to be offered his brother's post in Canton. But Forbes, lacking confidence in his mercantile abilities, feeling more at home in a captain's cabin than in a counting room, continued to pursue his less demanding ambition to head the Lintin storeship. He brushed aside the urgings of Cushing, Perkins, and other members of the Boston Concern that he represent their interests in China. It was a decision that was not made lightly, and one that would have a profound effect not only on the course of the Forbes family fortunes but on the eventual development of the American West.

John Cushing, persuaded by Perkins to join him in one last major speculation, was in London buying goods for shipment to China when he heard of the death of his cousin Thomas Forbes, who had prudently left behind instructions that Russell & Company should take over the Boston Concern's affairs if some mishap overtook him. Learning of Bennet's reluctance to go to Canton, and that Russell & Company principal Samuel Russell had a mind to return to Boston, Cushing himself left England for China in April, 1830, little more than a week after Ben Forbes had brushed his teeth and buttoned on a new collar in preparation for presenting Sturgis and Perkins with his scheme to take over the Lintin storeship operation. When he arrived in Canton in August, Cushing found that Russell had decided to remain in China after all, and though he stayed on for a time, selling off the cargo of English goods he had brought with him, Cushing sailed down the Pearl River for the South China Sea in March, 1831. He would not see China again, though he mirrored some of its exotic splendor in a $55,000 house that he bought on Summer Street. Later, at his estate in Watertown—it was called Belmont, and in time would give its name to a new town—Cushing became a virtual recluse, turning the management of his extensive investments over to Bryant & Sturgis for an annual fee of 2.5 percent of the income.

As his fortune grew through wise investments in a variety of domestic enterprises, Cushing enjoyed the life of an Oriental potentate, spending some $50,000 a year to maintain his household and pursue such avocations as horticulture and collecting music-box rolls. His library, his wine cellar, his extensive gardens with their banks of flowers, shrubs, and trees from Europe and China, all were tokens of his years of dealing in opium and furs, teas and silks. And he was, as William Sturgis had once described him, a generous man, on a liberal scale. It is said that the Watertown assessors, come respectfully to call on their most substantial fellow citizen to inquire what he thought his tax bill should be, were in turn asked what sum had to be raised. Informed of the total, minuscule by his munificent standards, Cushing advised the startled tax men to charge the entire amount to him.

Shortly before Cushing arrived at Canton for his last sojourn there, Captain Robert Bennet Forbes was setting out from Boston Harbor, bound for the same destination. His new ship—appropriately named the *Lintin*—had been launched from the Medford yards on June 17, 1830, to the echoes of a cannonade marking the fifty-fifth anniversary of the battle on nearby Bunker Hill, where Forbes's benefactor Thomas Handasyd Perkins was raising a commemorative monument. Less than three weeks later, the vessel, the first of many that Forbes would see launched in his name, slipped out of its moorings at Central Wharf and set a course for the Cape of Good Hope and the South China Sea. Among the passengers were Augustine Heard, a seasoned ship captain and supercargo who had been tapped to represent the Perkins interests as a partner in the revamped Russell & Company, and seventeen-year-old John Murray Forbes, whose upcoming clerkship in the firm was intended to prepare him for the partnership that Bennet had declined.

Nine years his brother Bennet's junior, John Murray Forbes

had been apprenticed at the age of fifteen in the countinghouse
of the Perkins firm near the end of Boston's Central Wharf.
Like his brothers before him, he had impressed his elder merchant kinsmen, and it was only natural that he should be eyed
as a prime candidate to fulfill the hope and trust that had been
placed in the deceased Thomas Tunno Forbes. When he arrived in Canton in November, Cushing introduced the young
Forbes to Houqua, and the venerable hong merchant immediately took to him as the successor to Cushing and Thomas
Forbes, even though Heard was actually in charge of the Boston Concern's interests in China. It was an understandable and
prescient error on Houqua's part: though affable and well liked
by all, Heard lacked countinghouse experience, and was slow
and plodding besides. Many of his duties soon fell to his young
clerk, who quickly showed a ready head for mercantile affairs.
Bennet, meanwhile, was busily running the storeship at Lintin,
provisioning other vessels, and doling out chests of opium—for
each of which he raked off a five-dollar *cumsha*—to Chinese
smugglers who hustled their contraband goods ashore in their
"scrambling dragons." It was hard and demanding work for
Black Ben Forbes, but it was far more profitable than his previous rovings on the high seas. Once he had consoled himself for
his hard lot with the thought that he was doing his family duty;
now his mind was eased by the prospect of "picking up 30m
[thousand] dolls per annum." Not a bad prospect at all for a
man whose salary as a ship captain had been just fifty dollars a
month.

In the spring of 1832, perhaps tiring even of anchor-bound
shipboard life, Bennet Forbes sold a half share of the *Lintin* to
Russell & Company for twenty thousand dollars, with the
agreement that 25 percent of the firm's proceeds from the
storeship operation were to go to his brother John. Bennet was
head of his family now, and he meant to look after his own.
With a tidy fortune, he sailed home to Boston, where he set up
in the offices of China merchant Daniel C. Bacon to handle
consignments from Russell & Company. Through the influence of John Murray Forbes in Canton—who managed transactions for Houqua as well as for the Boston Concern—the goods

readily came his way. For the two Forbeses, Houqua's business offered a double-barreled return: John picked up a percentage of the hong merchant's business in Canton, and Bennet got a commission on his shipments sold in Boston.

At the same time, Bennet began to build an expensive house on a hill in Milton—"I felt that I was carrying out my mother's wish to erect a fitting monument to the memory of my brother," Forbes said later. Family duty again, duty to those born and unborn. Bennet Forbes's descendants lived in this house until 1961; it is now the Museum of the American China Trade, under the curatorship of his great-grandson, Dr. H. A. Crosby Forbes, an expert on Chinese porcelain.

John Murray Forbes, his health broken from his labors, returned to Boston on doctor's orders in the summer of 1833. Together, the brothers Forbes must have made an odd pair as they strolled along the wharves: Bennet, with his deeply tanned face framed in a shock of once black hair gone gray, and John, not yet twenty-one but taken for thirty or more because of his advanced baldness and mature bearing. Both brothers married in the winter of 1834, and Bennet, the old sea rover, settled down and bought a house next door to the Thomas Handasyd Perkins mansion on Temple Place; John, his health restored and his eye on his fortune, shipped out just a month after his marriage as supercargo on Bryant & Sturgis's *Logan*, bound for Canton by way of Gibraltar.

John Murray Forbes had intended to return after the voyage and join the Perkins firm in Boston, but he arrived in Canton to find that Heard, fallen victim to exhaustion—an occupational hazard, it seems—was set to leave for home. Never one to dodge his duties, Forbes stepped in to fill Heard's place at Russell & Company; he would not see Boston again for nearly three years.

Forbes found the firm still deeply involved in the opium trade—"I have written and thought so much of opium," wrote Thomas Handasyd Perkins to John Cushing in 1827, "that it gives me an opiate to enter upon the subject." The previous year, to drum up even more business and make up for increased competition in the Turkish drug market, Russell &

Company had dispatched one of its clerks, Joseph Coolidge, to Bombay and Calcutta to arrange for more shipments of the higher-quality Indian article, sweetening the pot with an offer to forgo storage charges on lots of one hundred or more chests consigned to the storeship at Lintin. It was a concession that the firm could easily afford, since the storeship would still be skimming off its five-dollar bribe per chest, and Indian opium suppliers must not have seen it as much of a bargain—Coolidge was not very successful in his mission. Then again, he may have failed because of his notably abrasive manner.

Despite Coolidge's inability to get a grip on Indian opium supplies, and despite strong competition from the new firm of Russell, Sturgis & Company—formed in May, 1834, by relatives and former associates of the Boston Concern who, for reasons of their own, chose to plot an independent course—Russell & Company continued to prosper. And so did John Murray Forbes. When he returned to Boston in the spring of 1837, he brought with him a sizable fortune—including a half-million dollars of Houqua's own money which the hong merchant gave him to invest in American enterprise as he saw fit—and an agreement to get a three-sixteenths share of the firm's profits for three years, in exhange for looking after its interests in the United States.

Forbes got home just in time for the panic of 1837, and just in time, too, to help bail his brother out of some financial problems that would soon send Bennet Forbes packing back to China to recoup his lost fortune. By his own admission, Bennet had not learned to say no to a likely-looking business venture, and in what he later called a weak moment, he agreed to put a large sum of money into some Pennsylvania coal and iron mines whose output was to be used by a large nail works on which Forbes took a lien to secure his loan. How could he go wrong, he reasoned, when the nails could be made for three and a half cents per pound and sold for seven cents? A profit margin like that made nails look almost as good as opium. Unfortunately for Forbes, nearly everything went wrong. The iron ore and coal turned out to be inferior, the commercial crisis barred customers from paying for the nails they had bought, and Forbes was left holding the bag—which in this case held a trunk full of uncollectable bills, a nail factory, and an inventory of about twelve thousand kegs of nails. Not until Bennet had gone again to China was John Murray Forbes able to wind up the tangled nail works, at a loss of about $100,000.

The nail venture was bad enough, but it was only one of Bennet Forbes's sour speculations. Just before the crash, he and his associate, Daniel Bacon, sold a $100,000 shipment of Chinese silks, which they had bought on credit. Came the crisis, and buyers couldn't pay their bills; to maintain their own standing with the British house of Baring Brothers and with Russell & Company, which had advanced them credit, Forbes and Bacon had to dip into their own capital to make good. Once more, Forbes was left holding a bag, this time an empty one. It would not be the end of his troubles. At lunch one day in a Boston social club, conversation came around to the current rash of business failures and one of Forbes's tablemates rather tactlessly asked him how long he expected to hold out. Forbes replied, "Until my New York agents go," and before he left the table he heard that they had gone, owing him a considerable sum.

With Thomas Handasyd Perkins as cosigner, Forbes borrowed on promissory notes from his New York agents, but his finances had been struck a blow that could be salved only by a return to China. Leaving his tangled affairs in the abler hands of younger brother John, Forbes left in June, 1838, on board the *Mary Chilton*, loaded with goods consigned to him by sympathetic and well-wishing friends. And despite his failures at home, he was armed with John's power of attorney, entitling him to act in his stead as a partner in Russell & Company. It was a well-placed trust: Bennet Forbes was made chief of the firm on January 1, 1840, and manged to merge the competing house of Russell, Sturgis & Company into the older Russell concern.

FIVE. "THE EVEN TENOR OF OUR AFFAIRS"

Forbes arrived in China at a time of still more change. The imperial government, after decades of seeing its treasuries drained, its officials corrupted, and its populace demoralized by the opium trade, had determined at last to put an end to it. Most of the foreigners in Canton believed that this was just another bluff, that new ways would be found to bribe and smuggle, but they were disabused of this notion early in 1839 when the incorruptible Chinese "commissioner," Lin Tse-hsü, arrived in Canton. With few preliminaries, he demanded delivery of every chest of opium within Chinese waters; not even the Lintin storeships could save the trade now. Russell & Company, perhaps anticipating such a move and under strong pressure from Houqua to get out of the drug trade, had announced shortly before Lin's arrival that it would give up its opium business, but the move came too late. China was in earnest this time, and no mere announcement of good intentions could stay its hand.

Throwing a cordon of soldier-filled boats around the riverfront residences of the foreign merchants, Lin ordered all Chinese servants and cooks to leave the area. Trade was shut off, and the foreign community held hostage for its stores of opium, the "vile dirt used in smoking." Having little choice, the merchants agreed to comply with the order—the British more readily than the Americans, since the superintendent of British trade pledged that the crown would make up for its subjects' losses. While arrangements were made for delivery of the opium, which took about six weeks, the foreign contingent in Canton was virtually imprisoned in its narrow enclave. But according to Forbes, a jolly time was had by most, if not all. Left to fend for themselves, the Americans drew lots to see who would do what in the domestic chore department, and when Forbes flopped as a cook—"it was difficult to distinguish between eggs and ham: all bore the color and partook of the consistency of dirty sole-leather," he said of his first and last effort—he was transferred to caring for the glass- and silverware. Only the United States consul, P. W. Snow, seemed unable to enter into the spirit of things. "Is this not too bad, Mr. Forbes," he complained one day, "that a public official at my time of life, not owning a pound of opium, should be imprisoned and compelled to do chamber-maid's work?"

After the destruction of the confiscated opium—20,283

chests, worth some ten million dollars, were dumped into trenches, flooded with water, and left to rot—the British traders decided to retaliate by cutting off trade with the Chinese. The British had more to lose from a halt in the opium traffic than the Americans did: the drug accounted for about two-thirds of the value of all their imports to China, while American reliance on opium never reached such proportions. Shutting up their warehouses at Canton, the Englishmen withdrew downriver to Macao, sure that the Chinese would quickly repent of their folly. They begged Forbes, now head of Russell & Company, to join in their boycott, but he refused. Later, Forbes said that he told the British superintendent that "I had not come to China for health or pleasure, and that I should remain at my post as long as I could sell a yard of goods or buy a pound of tea." It was business as usual for the Bostonians, and the British were soon evading their own boycott by sending goods to Canton on American ships, which returned to the British anchorages in the South China Sea laden with teas and silks. It was a profitable sideline, this windfall ferrying trade, and British merchants paid dearly for it. According to Forbes, it was not at all unusual to charge as much as seven dollars for carrying a single bale of cotton on the ninety-mile voyage upriver to Canton. Forbes was well on his way to making up for his bad speculations at home.

The British, meanwhile, were biding their time, certain that their queen, who by the grace of God and the Royal Navy held dominion over a global empire, had more than mere boycott in store for the Chinese. In June, 1840, British warships blockaded Canton and other Chinese ports, and by the following year troops of the thin red line were slashing at will through China. Canton fell to the British, and so did the imperial capital of Peking. In Chinese eyes, the despised *Fan-Kwae* had more than lived up to their reputation, and the victors imposed a harsh peace. The hong system of trade monopoly was abolished, and Amoy, Foochow, Ningpo, and Shanghai, the so-called treaty ports, were opened to foreign trade. No longer would Canton be the only Western entry to the vast Chinese interior. In the bargain, the British took over Hong Kong and slapped China with an indemnity of twenty-one million dollars. The Chinese Empire, which in the words of former President John Quincy Adams had held itself to be "the center of the terraqueous globe, equal to the heavenly host," had been humbled beyond recall, reduced to near vassalage by the claims of a more powerful commercial empire. To the Chinese, it was a bitter outrage that would not soon be forgotten, and it is perhaps more than mere coincidence that Western businessmen seeking to buy or sell goods in the People's Republic of China must now go to . . . Canton.

Bennet Forbes, driven to exhaustion, left China for Boston shortly after the British blockade of Canton. He arrived home in December and was pleased to note that he had made up his losses and had a "handsome balance" besides. "I had worked hard," he said, "and had earned my reward by acting in very hazardous times with good judgment and decision." After working through the 1840s with his brother as a dealer in China goods, he returned to Canton once more in 1849. (Not yet done with derring-do, he leaped into the sea to help save a number of passengers when the British ship on which he had booked passage collided with another vessel; for his heroism, he was presented with medals by the Liverpool Shipwreck and Humane Society, Lloyd's Shipwreck Society, and the Humane Society of Massachusetts.) But the China trade was now totally different from the hazardous and heroic times past. The old hong system was dead, and so was Houqua, whose patronage had so benefited the Boston Concern. So regular and steady had commerce with China become that Forbes remarked in later life that the "even tenor of our affairs" had been marred during his two-year stay only by an illness so severe that he had ordered his coffin to be made from the mainmast of his first ship, the *Lintin*.

New York was rapidly surpassing Boston as a port of entry for the teas of China, due both to its more central location and better access to transport to the interior and to an action by the Massachusetts state legislature, which was as ready then as it is today to slap new and ingenious taxes on the business community. Over the objections of Boston's merchants, the legislature had imposed a tax of 1 percent on all goods sold at auction, which the merchants claimed would surely drive the tea market to New York. When this prediction began coming true, the tax was reduced, in 1849, to .25 percent, and repealed altogether in 1852. But the move to New York was unstoppable, and by 1857, only six China ships arrived in Boston Harbor; of the forty-one that docked in New York, twenty were Boston owned.

To be sure, there were still profits to be made in the China trade, though they were not quite so heady as the spectacular results of some individual voyages might suggest. William Appleton, for example, cleared a cool $200,000 from the cargo of a single Canton ship that docked in New York in the fall of 1840. Writing of his own profits in the trade, John Murray Forbes observed in the early 1840s that with the exception of a couple of lucky speculations, his earnings from China ventures had not topped 6 percent—that magic figure so beloved by the mill magnates—since he returned from Canton in 1837. And he firmly believed that the average return on all the capital invested in the China trade during the previous two decades had probably not passed the 6 percent mark.

For venturesome Bostonians, China was losing much of its allure, though few doubted that its importance as a market would continue to grow. As late as 1855, Russell & Company partner Edward E. Cunningham observed that along with one or two countries in Europe, "China will become, in the course of time, our most important commercial connection, if no untoward event intervenes." But now there were new and fresher frontiers to be found closer to home, on the broad midwestern prairies and beyond. And the China merchants with their friends and kin, with their great stores of capital resources and their sharply honed entrepreneurial instincts, were well equipped to cross them.

Chapter Six

THE YEARS OF BUILDING

Whenever any coal mines are to made accessible, or ill managed Rail
Roads made available, or indeed any scheme that requires Capital &
intelligence they come to Boston for help & those that take hold do it
on such terms that they play with sure cards.

—John Murray Forbes

When he arrived back in Boston in 1837, John Murray Forbes
had every reason to be satisfied with the outcome of his stay in
China. Starting with nothing but his own willing ambition and a
blood bond to the powerful Perkins interests, he had, at the age
of just twenty-four, put together a considerable fortune, which
his continued ties to Russell & Company would surely increase.
Many of his contemporaries were still serving countinghouse
clerkships, but Forbes was already a wealthy man, a figure to be
reckoned with in the Boston commercial community.

Forbes brought with him more than treasure from Canton.
He carried, too, a set of firmly held values, attitudes, and traditions, and ideas about the conduct of business affairs that
would stand him and his associates in good stead during the
years and decades to come. Operating far from home, Forbes
and his colleagues in the China trade had assumed great responsibility, often at an early age. Unlike managers of the Lowell mills, who could consult at will with their directors, the men
who managed cargoes in the Far East had been left to their own
devices and had made major decisions based on their own as-
sessments of constantly changing conditions. It was a business

that called for cool confidence, a readiness to take decisive action—and to take credit or blame for the consequences. It was an often lonely life, requiring a measure of individual initiative seldom demanded by other sorts of enterprise. "In these days of steam and telegraph," wrote Forbes in his old age, "it is difficult to imagine the state of isolation in which we lived. When a ship arrived she often brought news five or six months old from home." Such a life was not for the timid or the dependent soul.

Bred to such a time and place, the men of the China trade had developed drives that were distinctly different from those that had come to motivate many of their elders—and their contemporaries, too—in the close-to-home textile industry. The cotton manufacturers avidly grouped themselves together in large combines to build more and bigger mills; the China merchants leaned more toward individual action, the lone pursuit of profits. It was an understandable spirit for men whose capital had been their cargoes and their reputations, whose productive equipment had been world-roving wooden ships. And it was a spirit not likely to be fulfilled in Lowell or Lawrence—which had, in any case, already been staked out as virtually the private preserves of the original promoters and their families, though some of these men were to make frequent investments in other fields. Many of the China merchants had ties of both family and friendship to the cotton mill capitalists—the small compass of Boston's mercantile and manufacturing aristocracy had seen to that—but their common experiences in Asian commerce with all its distant risks and dangers had made them almost a separate breed, drawn them together in a community within a community. They remained Bostonians, loyal to the city's rich heritage of traditions, but the scope of their vision ranged far beyond Boston and Massachusetts.

TWO. "THE CURSED NIGHTMARE OF A RAILROAD *HORSE* RIDING *ME*"

Bostonians were among the first to see the value of railroads, if not as an immediately profitable investment, then as an efficient way to haul freight and passengers. Along with Amos Lawrence and other Boston business community leaders, Thomas Handasyd Perkins had, in the 1820s, spearheaded construction of the Granite Railway to transport stone from the quarries at Quincy to the site of the Bunker Hill monument. This was a horse-drawn affair, and the founding at about the same time of the Baltimore & Ohio's steam-driven line between Baltimore and Ellicott's Mills robs the Granite's claim to have been the nation's first true railway. But the line's success was nonetheless an early demonstration of the advantages of iron rails over roadways and watercourses. It was not long before Boston was looking for more ambitious projects.

The Erie Canal, completed in 1825, had been an insistent spur to such developments. Linking the Hudson River to the Great Lakes by water, the canal had turned the immense western hinterland into a tributary of New York City, making it more economical even for the produce of western Massachusetts to be shipped coastward by way of New York rather than through Boston. Already benefiting from its more central seaboard location, New York was now bidding to engross the growing trade with the expansive western frontier, leaving Boston as a mere outpost of regional distribution. Mountainous terrain separating Boston from the Hudson barred a water link between the two points; rails were soon seen as the only competitive solution. But first, the more immediate needs of the cotton magnates would be served.

In January, 1830, a group of prominent Boston capitalists, including the ubiquitous Thomas Handasyd Perkins, met at the home of Patrick Tracy Jackson to discuss the building of a railroad line to Lowell. The Middlesex Canal, so high on the list of selling points when the Lowell mills had been projected nearly a decade before, was inadequate to the demands of the growing manufacturing complex on the shores of the Merrimack; a railroad seemed the obvious answer to the seasonal freezing that closed the canal and made it necessary to ship goods over more costly overland routes. By 1835, financed by the likes of Perkins and Jackson, Amos and Abbott Lawrence, and John Amory Lowell, the single-track Boston & Lowell Railroad was in full operation; at about the same time, a rail link was opened between Boston and Providence to the south. This line was soon followed by the westward-running Boston & Worcester and Western railroads, and by 1841 the port of Boston was served by rail lines running as far inland as Albany, New York. A matrix of rails had been laid down in Massachusetts, but it was not to live up to the dreams of its promoters; the arterial Hudson, once probed as a gateway to the fabled Northwest Passage, was still the cheapest way to ship western produce to coastal markets. It soon became apparent to some investors that if money were to be made from railroads it would come from financing the roads themselves rather than from any benefits that they might bring to the city and port of Boston. Boston was to become not a railhead, but a fount of railroad capital, and later, a pool of managerial talent.

Among the first to recognize this coming role were the China-rich John Perkins Cushing and his investment managers, John Bryant and William Sturgis of the firm of Bryant & Sturgis. Sooner than most, they began injecting their capital into railroads outside of Massachusetts—first in New York, later in Pennsylvania. As early as 1839, Cushing held three hundred shares in the Utica & Schenectady Railroad; by 1843, Sturgis was a director of the Attica & Buffalo. John Murray Forbes, too, saw great possibilities in railroads, though his enthusiasm came only after a period of strong misgiving. Writing to Bennet Forbes from Canton in early 1836, no doubt aware of his older brother's tendency to leap feet first into any plausible investment possibility that came along, Forbes minced no words in his advice to be more than wary of the infant railroad enterprises. "My dear Bennet," he said. "The principal object of the present is to request that you will by no means invest any funds of mine in railway stocks, and to advise you to keep clear of them. I have good reasons to believe, from all I can learn of the English railways, that ours will prove a failure after the first few years; the wear and tear proves ruinous. At any rate, keep clear of them. . . ." Nearly a half century later, John Forbes would steadfastly maintain that this judgment had been a sound one; in the meantime, his judgment of the conditions and prospects of the nation's railroads had changed considerably.

Long before Horace Greeley advised his enterprising young countrymen to go west, the western frontier of the United States was a powerful magnet, drawing fortune seekers first toward the banks of the northern Mississippi River and later to the beaches of the Pacific. Sweeping stands of timber, limitless expanses of rich prairie land unbroken by the plow, dreams of precious metals locked in the fastness of the Rockies and the Sierra Nevada or tumbling freely down rapid mountain streams—all combined to form an irresistible vision of national riches waiting only to be tapped by the ambitious. But it was not enough merely to fell trees, plant wheat, or raise livestock, to mine silver, gold, and copper. The treasures of the West had to be moved to market before they had any value, and the markets were in the settled East. Providentially, mid-continental America was blessed with a natural system of waterways which, augmented by canals where nature had not foreseen the needs of civilized man, made extensive water transport possible, if by slow and circuitous means. But not even the coming of steamboats, with their much greater speed and carrying capacity, was enough to make the Mississippi and Ohio rivers equal to the transportation needs of a growing nation, particularly as the frontier was edged across prairies unserved by navigable rivers. Shorter, faster, and more direct east-west routes were required, and they could be provided only by rail.

Haltingly at first, then with growing momentum, the first tendrils of America's great railway system began lacing through the countryside. And Boston capitalists were in the advance guard of this development. By 1845, it would be estimated that of some $130,000,000 invested in all U.S. railroad enterprises, a full $30,000,000 had come from Boston, and in the same year railway analyst J. J. Stackpole wrote to Reading Railroad President John Tucker that "The Boston people are certainly the only Community who understand Rail Roads. At the present time they have more money than they know what to do with."

The Forbes brothers, John and Bennet, made their first leap into railroad finance in 1843 when, at the urging of William Sturgis, they put a total of $5,000 into the Attica & Buffalo. It was a small beginning, but the Forbes interest in railroads was to become much enlarged in the years to come, and would take John Murray Forbes far beyond the eastern seaboard and its immediate hinterland.

One of the western states where railroad fever ran high during the 1830s was Michigan, which planned to build three rail lines with public funds. The panic of 1837 stymied these projects, and by the mid-1840s it was plain that the only solution was to sell the partially built roads to private investors. The Michigan Central, already laid along a 145-mile route between Detroit and Kalamazoo, seemed most attractive as an investment, and in 1845 John W. Brooks, the young superintendent of New York's Auburn & Rochester Railroad, went to Detroit to look into the possibility of a sale. Brooks, who had cut his railway teeth on the Boston & Maine, had numerous contacts in the Boston capitalist community, and in the winter of 1845–46, he went to both Boston and New York to line up backing for a scheme to buy the Michigan Central, which, when completed, would form a key link between the East and Chicago. Eventually, he found his way to John Murray Forbes, whose interest was quickly whetted. Not only had Forbes already made some relatively small railroad investments, but several ventures in steamship building—though they didn't work out quite as planned—had given him a firsthand look at the value of steam locomotion. Besides, thought Forbes, a major investment in the Michigan Central might give him a chance to install his brother as the road's president, which Forbes believed would be a mere figurehead position. And Bennet Forbes, whose years at sea had ill-prepared him for a land-based business career, was in sore need of such a sinecure.

The charter for a privately owned Michigan Central Railroad was drawn up by Daniel Webster, and included among its incorporaters the Forbes brothers, Thomas Handasyd Perkins, William Sturgis, and John Bryant, all of whom owed their fortunes to the China trade. The Michigan legislature approved the sale—at a price of two million dollars—in March, 1846, though one member objected that the act might just as well be titled "a bill to transfer the sovereignty of the State of Michigan to a company of Yankee speculators." Terms of the sale called for payment of $500,000 in six months, and John Forbes himself took the lead, chipping in $200,000; through connections with his wife's family, the Hathaways of New Bedford, he also managed to bring some Massachusetts whaling money into the enterprise, though he would find most of the initial funding in New York. Meanwhile, to give the venture more credibility among potential investors who were somewhat leery of western railroads, John Forbes had thought better of his plans for Bennet, and took on the presidency himself. It would be a heavy burden, but it was a burden that Forbes was prepared to shoulder with willing grace. Years later, seeking to explain why Forbes had turned with such gusto to railroad-building, an associate would say that "Mr. Forbes never seemed to me a man of acquisitiveness, but very definitely one of constructiveness. His wealth was only an incident. I have seen many occasions when much more money might have been made by him in some business transaction but for this dominant passion for building up things. . . ."

The Michigan Central certainly needed building up. Not only had it failed to reach its intended goal on the shores of Lake Michigan, but years of financial famine had left the roadbed in shoddy shape, and travelers on the line were sometimes attacked by "snake heads"—flimsy rails that would spring loose from their wooden ties and lash through the bottoms of the cars. Such were the conditions that Forbes found when he first visited his railroad in the spring of 1847, a trip on which he also passed up what would have been the crowning investment opportunity of his life. Staying at a hotel in Chicago, which then had a population of about 15,000, Forbes was approached by a land agent who offered him property near the hotel at the bargain-basement price of $1.25 an acre. He could well afford to, but Forbes declined to make the purchase, and it was with no little misgiving that he wrote thirty-five years later that "My hotel bill of one hundred and twenty-five dollars would have bought one hundred acres now worth $8,000,000 to $12,000,000."

Though Forbes's original intent in getting into the Michigan Central was primarily speculative—he was looking for a respectable return on his investment, with hopes of disposing of his shares at a profit at some later date—his position as president and his own large financial stake in the road soon changed him from mere speculator to railroad builder. Indeed, freewheeling, opportunistic speculation of the type engaged in later by the railroad tycoons of New York was something that a self-respecting Bostonian undertook at his peril. For the Boston entrepreneur, unlike his rootless counterparts in other cities, was constantly answerable to his family and his friends, who frowned on raw speculation because it undermined their cherished belief that financial success was the reward of diligence and virtue. Bostonians still coveted riches, to be sure, and would go to great lengths in their pursuit. But they were not ready to jettison the old values and put their trust in lucky gambles. The Forbes "passion for building up" was more than a personal quirk; it was an integral part of the Boston ethos. For Forbes to have bought cheap land in Chicago would have shown foresight and faith in the future growth of the city, and any gain from later sales would be a well-deserved reward for a man of constructive vision. But to buy a bundle of railroad stocks and then unload them at the first whiff of profits would have marked him as a fickle opportunist whose gains were somehow ill-gotten. Such attitudes would later lead many a Bostonian to be outdone by less scrupulous men from other cities, and in time would harden into an unwillingness to take any risks at all. But in an age of national development Boston's constructive drive would serve America well.

With John Brooks as superintendent on the scene in Michigan, work on refurbishing and expanding the line proceeded under full steam. By the spring of 1849 rails had been laid as far west as New Buffalo, Michigan, on the very shore of Lake Michigan. The roundabout, three-day lake voyage from Detroit to Chicago had been trimmed to a mere fifteen hours, though passengers and freight still had to cross the tip of Lake Michigan by boat. Within a few months. plans were being made to drive the line around the lake toward Chicago, with Michigan City, Indiana, as the first goal. After a series of missteps— Forbes developed a case of financial cold feet and rejected a proposal by Brooks that the Michigan Central buy right-of-way that would have carried the line from Michigan City as far as the Illinois border—the Michigan Central teamed up with the Illinois Central to lay rails to Chicago, and the first Michigan Central train chugged into that city in May, 1852. Detroit to the east and Chicago to the west were bound together by iron rails. Meanwhile, Forbes had even more ambitious plans in mind.

In his 1850 annual report, Forbes had told Michigan Central stockholders that "We are bound to use every exertion to make our road a link in the great chain of communication between the East and the West." But Detroit was linked to the East, not by rail, but by water; travelers and goods crossed Lake Erie by steamer, considerably slowing their passage in the best of weather and halting it altogether in the icebound winters. To Forbes and his associates the answer was clear: the shortest eastward route ran along the north shore of the lake, through terrain that had already been staked out by Canada's Great Western Railroad. But the Canadians had had problems raising sufficient capital, so Forbes set out to sell American investors enough Great Western stock to take up the slack. It was a difficult task, but Forbes came through with the needed one million dollars; by 1855 the Great Western had reached Niagara Falls, tying Chicago to the East Coast by rail.

Forbes had gone into the western railroads primarily as an investor, but he had now become a full-fledged developer, committed to a vision of a West made richer—indeed, of a nation made richer—by his efforts. If his railroads made money in the process, so much the better; it was fitting reward for hard work and enterprise, for foresight and faith in the future. Writing to his cousin Paul S. Forbes in Canton, Forbes made plain the sense of mission that had gripped him. "The Rail Way in our Western prairies is the most economical labor saving machine ever invented," he said, "for it doubles and often trebles the value to the farmers, of the coarser grains, by bringing them within reach of water carriage & by bringing customers to their doors.... The richness & depth of the soil ... furnishes business for the R. Road, and renders it impossible to transport the rich products of the soil to the market by any *other* mode."

And if he had been able to, Forbes might even have carried his vision to the country where he had made his first fortune: "I should like to build the first Rail Road in China!!!" he once told his cousin.

But Forbes was too busy in the American West to do any railroad work in the Far East, and his next goal was the Mississippi, that great spinal river swarming with traffic bound for the eastern seaboard and points in between. It was a goal that had been early foreseen by at least one great Boston capitalist, even as John Forbes was in Canton mulling over the budding U.S. rail system and hoping that the amenable Bennet would have sense enough not to invest in some harebrained and ruinous railroad scheme. At a meeting held in 1835 in Faneuil Hall, the eighteenth-century merchant Peter Faneuil's enduring legacy to his city, textile magnate Abbott Lawrence had urged the assembled merchants and manufacturers to invest in railroads for the benefit of Boston as well as for whatever financial gains might be forthcoming. Edward Everett, the Unitarian orator and educator who moved easily in the world of commerce, also addressed the meeting, and as he finished his speech and resumed his seat behind the podium, Lawrence turned to him and smiled. "Mr. Everett," he said, "we shall live to see the banks of the upper Mississippi connected by iron bands with State Street." Indeed, Everett did live so long, though the ultimate beneficiary was to be Wall Street rather than Boston's own financial thoroughfare.

Forbes and the men he had mobilized around him in the Michigan Central had been scouting for a direct route across Illinois to the Mississippi since early 1852, when their first train steamed into Chicago from Detroit. They soon found three existing charters that looked promising, and quietly went to work—there was no need at this point to let competitors know what they were up to. By June, they had met with representatives of the proposed lines—who had eagerly sought the Bostonians' financial aid—and Forbes had begun to raise capital for the Chicago & Aurora Railroad, the first link in his chain of rails to the Mississippi. However, to avoid alerting rival railroad men, and possibly to avoid upsetting potential investors who might have balked at the ambitiousness of the plan, Forbes steadfastly maintained that the intent of the new line was merely to move far enough west to hook up with the north-south Illinois Central, then abuilding. This road, financed largely by Boston capitalist Augustine Heard and other former China traders from both Boston and New York, was intended to split Illinois in two, connecting with the Mississippi at the north and south of the state. Both John and Bennet Forbes owned shares in the Illinois Central, but did not take an active hand in its management.

Soon the cat was out of the bag. Shortly after the Chicago & Aurora had been authorized to build to a junction with the Illinois Central at Mendota, it sought and gained legislative permission to buy into a road running northeasterly from Quincy, on the banks of the Mississippi, to Galesburg. And it just happened that John Brooks, superintendent of the Michigan Central, where the Bostonians had got their start in western railroading, was also president of the road that proposed to link Galesburg with Mendota, the alleged end of the line for the Chicago & Aurora. On paper, at least, the Forbes group had deftly assembled a rail line from Chicago to the Mississippi. And more was yet to come. In 1854, little more than two years after they had begun their march out of Chicago, the Forbes interests bought still another road which ran from Burlington, on the Mississippi north of Quincy, to Peoria by way of Galesburg. By 1856, the system had been completed, and was consolidated and renamed the Chicago, Burlington & Quincy Railroad. Among its directors were John and Bennet Forbes.

John Forbes, meanwhile, had been driving himself so hard to scratch up capital for the emerging Chicago, Burlington & Quincy—at one point, he sold $100,000 worth of manufacturing stock at a loss to make a loan to one of the roads—that he came down with exhaustion, that old chronic complaint of the China traders. In 1855, while retaining his directorship and financial interest, he resigned as president of the Michigan Central, turning the post over to John Brooks. But this partial withdrawal didn't offer enough relaxation, and his doctor soon advised him to take a trip to England and leave his business cares behind. Forbes tried this prescription, but he doubted at first that it would turn out to be what the doctor had ordered. When he returned, Forbes wrote that "On my outward passage to England I found the railroads had made such inroads upon my brain that the moment I got to sleep I was harder at work upon them than when here; and until I got on shore and amid new scenes I could not get rid of the cursed nightmare of a railroad *horse* riding *me*."

To further recuperate, Forbes spent the summer of 1857 on Naushon, an island off Cape Cod which he had bought as a retreat for his family. While there, according to a biographer, Forbes occupied himself with "eating, sleeping, talking and wearing out old clothes." He was well suited for the latter pastime. Noted for his indifference to dress, Forbes generally wore his suits until long after most men would have discarded them; his clothes, it was said, seemed in time to become almost a part of his body, and his daughter once recalled a hat that appeared, after just a few days' wearing, to have been virtually molded on her father's head.

Forbes's frequently rumpled appearance may have belied his growing wealth, but it was not enough to discourage the inevitable stream of alms-seekers drawn to his door. One, an elderly widow with an improvident grown son, called at Forbes's office one day to say that she thought it might be nice if she and her son could buy a house of their own, and asked Forbes if he could be of any help. After listening patiently, Forbes reached for a stack of papers on his desk. "Madam," he said, "I'll think about it," and went back to his work.

Pausing in the doorway on her way out, the woman turned to Forbes once more. "I'm afraid you won't do it," she said.

Forbes looked up briefly from his papers and smiled. "I'm afraid I shan't," he replied.

Another woman, the recent mother of twin boys, had been misinformed that the Forbes of J. M. Forbes & Company was named John Malcolm. For only five hundred dollars, she wrote to John Murray Forbes, she would honor him by naming her sons John Malcolm and Malcolm John. Forbes got a good chuckle out of that one, but the mother did not get her money; presumably, the twins were given different names.

With those he deemed deserving, however, Forbes could be more generous, and he often said that he would rather spend his money while he was alive than have it tied up in trusts after his death. But he was not one to make a big production of his largesse: a young relative, given the gift of a house by Forbes, marveled that he "handed me the deed as if it had been a ticket to the opera." Considering the hazards that he sometimes took with his fortune, such offhanded generosity is somewhat peculiar on Forbes's part. Like the less venturesome Amos Lawrence, he was wary of debt, and made it a policy never to borrow more than he could repay by selling off all his property—at one point, he mortgaged both his Milton home and his beloved Naushon Island retreat to raise money for railroad ventures.

Forbes's summer of beating about on Naushon, luxuriating in well-worn clothes, had come at a propitious time. His railroads were hard hit by the fall panic of 1857, and the Michigan Central hovered near bankruptcy that was averted only when Forbes went to England and, using financial contacts made in his China trade days, managed to raise enough money to pull the line through. The Britishers, though cool on American railway stocks, had faith in Forbes, a faith that was strengthened when they learned that he was putting $250,000 of his own into a bond issue floated to save the road.

The increasingly complex affairs of the Michigan Central and the Chicago, Burlington & Quincy were not Forbes's only concerns in the 1850s. For reaching the Mississippi, ambitious though it was, was just a part of his grand design in the West. There was yet another river—the Missouri—to reach by rail, and Forbes had determined as early as 1852 to press for that goal. His main chance came in 1853 when local backers of the proposed Hannibal & St. Joseph Railroad, in desperate need of funds, appealed to Forbes for help. He readily obliged, and by the following year the Forbes brothers and three other Boston capitalists had been named directors of the line. John Forbes, with the additional job of fiscal agent, set out to raise capital for the unbuilt railroad, which was completed from Hannibal, on the Mississippi, to the Missouri River at St. Joseph, in early 1859. The Forbes-backed rail system now stretched from Detroit all the way to the Kansas border. And more was yet to come.

Robert Bennet Forbes, though never placed in the railroad presidency that his brother had once planned for him, was still active as a director and investor in a number of roads in the West. On a visit to Iowa in early 1853, he found that promoters of the newly chartered Burlington & Missouri River Railroad needed capital, and told John Forbes that the line looked like a good investment. The younger Forbes, with more faith now in his brother's judgment, agreed, and threw his own capital and influence into the road. Work proceeded slowly, and was interrupted by the Civil War, but the line was destined to span Iowa and approach Omaha, Nebraska, in early 1870. It would be just in time to connect with the transcontinental system made possible by the Union Pacific, a monumental railroad built largely by Bostonians who would reap little gain and less glory for their enterprising boldness.

THREE. "YOU COWARDS, WILL YOU DESERT US NOW?"

As the nation lurched with looming certainty toward civil war, Boston's commercial and industrial community had changed considerably from previous decades. The great textile man Patrick Tracy Jackson had died in 1847. Amos Lawrence, the poor boy from New Hampshire who had made a fortune in trade and magnified it in cotton, died in 1852; his brother Abbott survived him by only three years. Nathan and William Appleton would not live long after the war's first guns, though William, on a business trip to the South, would observe the shelling of Fort Sumter and examine the shattered stronghold a few days after its surrender to the insurgent South Carolinians. Thomas Handasyd Perkins, progenitor of some of Boston's greatest fortunes, died in 1854, praised by all for his munificence and sung to rest by a choir that included sightless students from the Perkins School for the Blind, as ships in the harbor flew their colors at half mast. John Perkins Cushing, protégé of Thomas Handasyd Perkins and in turn mentor of the Forbes brothers, died in 1862, his fortune increased through wise investments to more than triple the some $600,000 he had amassed in the China trade. The old guard, the pioneers of trade and textiles who had shown Boston the way to wealth and enterprise for better than two generations, had passed away.

New men, if not new blood, had come forward to fill the thinning ranks of the city's economic and social elite. Some, like John Murray Forbes, were essentially self-made, though helped mightily by family connections. Others, including John Amory Lowell and his cousin Francis Cabot Lowell, Jr., Amos Adams Lawrence, and Thomas Jefferson Coolidge, were second- and even third-generation members of Boston's establishment of wealth, which already had begun to solidify into a tight community grounded on past achievement. Still more, among them the likes of Charles Francis Adams, Jr., Henry Lee Higginson, William Hathaway Forbes, and Charles Russell Lowell, Jr., were sprung from goodly heritages but were yet too young to have proved themselves worthy of their promise, too young to have been tested against the trust of friends and family. For many, that first test would come, not in the countinghouse or the cotton mill, but on distant battlefields of the South, from which not all would be returning.

Wittingly or not, Boston had done much of the spadework leading up to the War Between the States. The Massachusetts cotton mills had not only led to irreparable cleavage between an industrial North and an agrarian South, but they had also created a huge market for cotton, a demand that could be met—or so it seemed to southerners at the time—only with more slaves, and by the extension of slavery into new lands of the expanding West. That peculiar institution of human bondage, which had been on the wane even below the Mason-Dixon line, was given fresh impetus by the cotton-consuming mills on the Merrimack.

At the same time, beginning in the 1830s, a great reformist spirit swept much of the nation, inspired in no small measure by the Boston belief in the dignity and perfectibility of man—all men, including even black bondsmen. It was inevitable that the compulsion to reform prisons, insane asylums, and school systems, to urge the benefits of uplift and temperance on the working classes, would soon turn to that greatest of evil indignities, slavery itself. Boston was a hotbed of the abolitionist movement, the home of William Lloyd Garrison's tocsin, the *Liberator*—which in addition to being against slavery, also opposed tobacco, another southern cash crop that depended on slave labor for its cultivation. Garrison was not always honored as a prophet in his chosen city; he was once dragged through the streets by an angry mob who saw him as a dangerous agitator. But Bostonians were, in the main, heartily against slavery, and the same Faneuil Hall walls that had once heard demands for freedom from English colonial rule frequently rang with calls to break the chains that held blacks to their southern masters.

In 1851, one such meeting had spilled into the streets to the Court House, where an escaped slave was being held for return to his owner. Inflamed by Faneuil Hall rhetoric, the crowd battered down the Court House door, and in the melee that followed a deputy marshal was shot dead. The rescue attempt was unsuccessful, though spirited. As the crowd was driven out of the Court House, Thomas Wentworth Higginson, clergyman, author, and member of a prominent merchant family, pushed to the door, shouting to his fleeing comrades, "You cowards, will you desert us now?" Cowards or not, they did, and the hapless black was later hustled down State Street by a troop of militiamen and put aboard a ship to carry him back to Virginia. But it was the first time that blood had been shed in an effort to free a fugitive slave, and it happened in Boston. The South was enraged by the incident, seeing in it just one more example of the North's undying hostility toward southern tradition and law.

John Murray Forbes, as one of the nation's premier railroad builders, was hardly the type to go crashing through doors to liberate runaway slaves. In his own way, he was vigorously anti-slavery, but his motives were more political than humanitarian. Explaining his position to the British merchant William Evans in 1864, Forbes confessed that "The fact is, I am not good enough to be an abolitionist, which demands a certain spirit of martyrdom, or least self-sacrifice, and devotion to abstract principle, which I am not yet up to.

"I am," Forbes added, "essentially a conservative; have rather a prejudice against philanthropists, and have been anti-slavery more because slavery is anti-republican, anti-peace, anti-material progress, anti-civilization than upon the higher and purer ground that it is wicked and unjust to the slave! I have no special love for the African, any more than for the low-class Irish, but don't want to see either imposed upon. You cannot steal one man's labor or any part of it by law without threatening to steal, when you get strong enough, every man's labor, and property and life! Hence to be anti-slavery is to be conservative."

Forbes's conservatism did not keep him from associating with the radical fringe of the abolitionist movement, however, and when John Brown came to Boston in 1859 seeking support for his cause, Forbes invited the border firebrand out to his Milton home for tea. After Brown had regaled the assembled company with tales of heroics and conflict, Forbes gave him $100 to help carry on with his work, though he didn't know that his contribution was to be used months later to draw blood at Harpers Ferry. Forbes's interest in Brown's mission was not entirely selfless, however. At immediate issue was the question of slavery in Kansas and Missouri, and a nonslave Missouri would presumably increase the state's free and white population and better the prospects of the new Hannibal & St. Joseph Railroad. Still, Forbes was taking no chances: one night after he harbored John Brown, he entertained the proslavery governor of Missouri, who had a $3,000 bounty out for Brown's head.

FOUR. "I WANT A GREAT DEAL OF MONEY TO USE"

Another Bostonian of means who got caught up in the Kansas-Missouri question was Amos Adams Lawrence, son of textile man Amos Lawrence and nephew of the towering Abbott Lawrence. Born in 1814, just a year after John Murray

Forbes, Lawrence's life had been set on a course far different from those charted by Forbes and others of their generation who sought wealth in the China trade. Not for him was the lowly clerkship at a young age, sweeping floors, building fires, running menial errands, all in preparation for voyages to distant ports and lonely tours of merchant duty far from home. As the scion of an already richly endowed Boston family, Lawrence's life would be one of easier opportunity, of less demanding tests of mettle and ability. While John and Bennet Forbes were proving themselves in China, Lawrence was a student at Harvard. Already, he saw his life spread out before him, knew that he was destined to be a creature of heritage.

"My present design," he wrote shortly before his graduation in 1835, "is to be a merchant, not a plodding, narrow-minded one pent up in a city, with my mind always in my counting-room, but (if there be such a thing possible) I would be at the same time a literary man in some measure and a farmer.... My advantages for becoming rich are great: if I have mercantile tact enough to carry on the immense though safe machine which my father and uncle have put in operation, it will turn out gold to me as fast as I could wish: and to be rich would be my delight.... If any one has any love for his fellow creatures, any love of the worthy respect of his neighborhood, he will be willing and glad to be rich. They say riches are a burden that harass the soul and lead into temptation: so they are to the miser who is in constant fear of losing his acquisition, and to the profligate who receives an inheritance merely to squander it on his passions. A good man will willingly endure the labor of taking care of his property for the sake of others whom he can do so much benefit by it...."

The charitable and responsible impulses of the father had found a ready home in the bosom of the son, who knew full well that there would be few surprises in his life.

Just days after leaving Harvard, young Lawrence was studying the operation of the family mills in Lowell, a princeling of industry inspecting his birthright. A short time later, he took a job in a textile selling house to learn that end of the business, and in 1837 he felt he knew the ropes well enough to open up his own establishment, dealing in broadcloths, cassimers, and silks. He was already a solid citizen, and within two years, if not by virtue of achievement then of inheritance, Lawrence was made a director of the Suffolk Bank and a member of the corporation of the Provident Institution for Savings. It was a comfortable time for the young man treading quietly in his family's footsteps, and by late 1839 he was ready to try something new; he closed up his business and went on a leisurely tour of Europe, where he spent part of his time traveling with William Appleton and his son Warren. Back in Boston the following year, Lawrence once again took up a business career, and became a frequent visitor at the Appleton home on Beacon Street. But it was not the merchant William that he came to see—it was his nineteen-year-old daughter, Sarah Elizabeth, whose engagement to Lawrence was soon announced. "He is a young man of good common sense, with business habits, a very safe man to trust a daughter with," wrote Appleton of his prospective son-in-law. The two were married in early 1842, and settled down in a house in Pemberton Square.

In 1843 Lawrence went into partnership with Robert Mason and became selling agent for the Cocheco Company, a manufacturer of printed cotton cloth. Lawrence saw great promise ahead, and ever mindful of his responsibilities, he wrote in his journal that if success should come, he hoped that "I may not forget my duty in using it, not for my own aggrandizement, but for the advancement of Christ's kingdom on earth." Success did come, and more was to follow. Soon, Lawrence bought the Salmon Falls Company, and later became treasurer of that company and president of Cocheco. By 1850, he could record that among other duties he was a director of ten corporations, in charge of his ailing father's property, and manager of his own extensive properties, "including lands in the West, the building of a seminary and a town [Appleton] in Wisconsin. . . ."

Lawrence's lands in Wisconsin, though they eventually proved immensely profitable, had hardly been acquired through wise investment. They had almost literally fallen into his unwitting hands, through the unlikely agency of one Eleazar Williams, who claimed to be the lost dauphin of France, the son of Marie Antoinette. Williams, who had long since given up on making good any kingly claims, was a Protestant Episcopal missionary working among the Indians near Green Bay, Wisconsin. He came to Boston in 1845 to raise funds on five thousand acres of land he owned in the Fox River Valley, and was soon put in touch with the elder Amos Lawrence, that noted philanthropist whose generosity was later to inspire John D. Rockefeller. Lawrence was intrigued by the missionary, but because of his own ailing health referred him to young Amos. He, too, was taken with the prospect of doing good works with sure collateral, and put up money for the Reverend Mr. Williams. The fortunes of the alleged dauphin soon waned, however, leaving Lawrence the unwilling and somewhat mystified owner of five thousand acres in Wisconsin. Making the best of what must have been a somewhat uncomfortable situation, Lawrence gave ten thousand dollars for construction of a seminary—which later became Lawrence University—in the new town of Appleton, which was named, not for father-in-law William, but for his childless cousin Samuel.

Lawrence, at least, was left with something to show for his transaction with an enigmatic stranger. During the War of 1812, the usually astute brothers Perkins had entrusted the delivery to England of forty thousand dollars in gold coin to a man they knew as Charles Sandos, who spoke with a heavy Dutch or German accent and seemed every inch an honorable gentleman. The gold never arrived at its destination, and despite a diligent search that took their agents—among them Ralph Bennet Forbes—to England, France, and Germany, no trace was ever found of either the Perkins gold or the wily Sandos. It was not the last time that Bostonians were to be gulled by smooth-talking foreigners, as Charles Ponzi and Ivar Kreuger would prove so spectacularly in the coming century.

The immense machine of wealth that his father and uncle had set in motion continued to produce more riches for Amos Adams Lawrence, to his frequent amazement. By 1870 he could note that his total property, worth $290,000 in 1858, had grown to $474,000, and during that period he had spent, given away, or lost a total of $805,000. "That is," he commented wonderingly, "with a property of $290,000, I spent $805,000 in 12 years: and had $474,000 left. Verily this is like the 7 loaves among 5000 people. It is the hand of the Lord that has done it."

It had been more than that, of course. When the elder Lawrence died in 1852, he left $215,000 to his son—"He had been liberal to me always," Lawrence observed—and the younger Lawrence was not content to sit back and wait for divine intervention to keep his money machines running smoothly. In 1860, he moved into a different branch of the textile field, buying a knit-goods mill in Ipswich. Customer preference for French and British wares worked against him for a time, and by January, 1868, the hand of the Lord had been so cool to Lawrence that he could record a loss of not less than $100 a day for the previous eight hundred days. "I feel the loss very much," he lamented, "for I want a great deal of money to use." In the long run, though, it proved to be a wise investment; the mill prospered, and Lawrence later bought two more in New Hampshire, making him the largest knit-goods manufacturer in the country. All things come to those who wait, and Lawrence was in no hurry. "Losses are made in a day," he later told his son, "while profits are a long time accumulating."

Like his father, Lawrence was not the type to chance sleepless nights worrying about the outcome of highly speculative investments, though it's likely that few business problems would ever have disturbed his rest. He had a peculiar ability to doze off at any time, under any circumstances, and could rouse himself at will. He fell asleep, in fact, during his oral examination for admission to Harvard, and woke up just as he heard the professor say "sufficient" to the boy sitting next to him.

While watching the slow and sure buildup of his profits, enjoying the "bread of industry and quiet" that had been relished, too, by his father, Lawrence had plenty of time for other concerns. One of them was the slavery question, which since the Compromise of 1850 had again begun to greatly agitate the northern states. In 1854, he became treasurer of the New England Emigrant Aid Company, whose goal was to raise money to send northern settlers to Kansas and insure its admission to the Union as a free state. Lawrence spent considerable money on this enterprise, which all told staked some 1,300 emigrants to the western trek. Once settled, many of these new Kansans were armed with weapons which the aid company shipped to them in casks labeled "Books." In gratitude, the citizens of Wakarusa, Kansas, renamed their town Lawrence, and Lawrence, in recognition of this honor, contributed $10,000 for the founding of an "academy," which became the nucleus of the University of Kansas.

John Brown, too, had reason to be grateful to Amos Adams Lawrence. From time to time, Lawrence gave financial help to Brown, and it was with this money, and with firearms so obligingly provided by the Emigrant Aid Company under the guise of books, that Brown was able to mount his raid at Harpers Ferry.

Lawrence, of course, did not approve of Brown's violent methods, but he was heartily in favor of his goals. The same feelings were shared by numerous prominent Bostonians, even after Brown's cruel and bloody massacre of five proslavery settlers at Pottawatomie, Kansas, in the spring of 1856. Two years later, when the messianic Brown staged a "convention" of Negroes and whites in Canada, and quixotically set up a provisional United States government with himself as commander in chief, he gained still more support in Boston from, among others, the respected clergymen Theodore Parker and Thomas Wentworth Higginson. The twentieth century can claim no monopoly on parlor radicals and guerrillas.

John Brown's crusading days came to an abrupt end in December, 1859, when he was hanged after being subdued at Harpers Ferry by federal troops under the command of Robert E. Lee. But his soul went marching on, and in the aftermath of the abortive uprising Amos Adams Lawrence was damned by southern politicians as a Yankee "cotton speculator" who had hired Brown to do his work.

FIVE. "ALL THAT THEY HAD OR HOPED FOR"

One of the men that John Murray Forbes had hired to help do his work on the western railroads was Charles Russell Lowell,

Jr., grandson of Patrick Tracy Jackson, kin to the Cabots and distant cousin of the textile Lowells. Born in 1835, graduated first in his class at Harvard in 1854, Lowell was perhaps the most promising member of his Boston generation. Forbes, a self-described "practical, unsentimental, and perhaps hard" man, would write later that Lowell had magnetized him at first sight, and that "I came home and told my wife that I had fallen in love." Small wonder that Lowell became a protégé of the great China trader turned railroad builder.

Shortly after his graduation from Harvard, Lowell went to work in Forbes's Boston office, then humming with plans for western railroad construction. He "penetrated the mysteries rapidly," Forbes said, but after six months he was on to something new, signing on as a workman at the Ames Company, a metalworking concern in Chicopee, Massachusetts. He liked the work, but growing restless again he moved on to Trenton, New Jersey, to take a job in a steel-rolling mill, where he soon came down with tuberculosis. Under the patronage of Forbes, Lowell went on a two-year trip to Europe where, among other things, he did a lot of horseback riding, took fencing lessons, and traveled for a time with his friend and contemporary, Henry Lee Higginson.

Back in Boston in the summer of 1858, Lowell spent a month on Forbes's Naushon Island, sailing, riding, fishing, and tutoring young William Hathaway Forbes in algebra and history. Forbes was plainly worried about his son's prospects, wondering if he would prove worthy of his heritage. Already, William's performance at Harvard, where he was a member of the class of 1861, had been disappointing, and earlier in the year Forbes had written to him: "Consider what a miserable thing it will be to begin life as a failure! What a bad auguring for your future fortunes!" The steadying influence of Lowell seemed to be just what William Forbes needed to help set himself straight.

By the end of that summer, Forbes had offered Lowell the job of assistant treasurer of the Burlington & Missouri River Railroad, and Lowell readily accepted the post. For Forbes, the offer had echoes of the China trade days, when merchants relied on men they knew, men they trusted, to act wisely far from home. "I think the mistake we have made on our R. Rd.

lines," he once wrote to a friend, "was in not bringing up youngsters we know something about as foremast hands, for the chance of picking our good mates and captains just as the old-fashioned shipowners used to do in taking green hands at six dollars a month." Forbes certainly knew something about Lowell, who had already proved himself as a green hand in Forbes's Boston office and now seemed on his way to becoming a good mate and captain.

By September, Lowell was on the banks of the Mississippi at Burlington, Iowa, where, in addition to his considerable financial duties, he was soon put in charge of the railroad's 300,000-acre land grant, given by the government as an incentive to build the road. He was a hard worker, well deserving the trust placed in him, and often stayed at his desk until midnight. Forbes was pleased with his protégé's progress and in the fall of 1860 offered him still another job, this time as ironmaster of the Mount Savage Iron Company, near Cumberland, Maryland, which Forbes and his associates had bought as a source of rails. Lowell's stay in Maryland was short-lived; John Brown, bankrolled in part by John Murray Forbes and Amos Adams Lawrence, had done his work all too well, and the guns of Harpers Ferry were soon echoed in Charleston Harbor, though William Appleton, viewing the shambles of fallen Fort Sumter, still believed that war would not come.

When it did, Charles Russell Lowell made his way through hostile territory to Washington, where he sought out Massachusetts Senator Charles Sumner and requested a commission in the Union army. "I am twenty-six years of age," he wrote, "and believe that I possess more or less that moral courage about taking responsibility which seems at present to be found only in Southern officers." Before long, wearing the uniform of a captain in the Third United States Cavalry, Lowell was riding at the head of a squadron of troopers ranging through Tidewater Virginia from Yorktown, where Cornwallis had surrendered to Washington, to Williamsburg, where another generation of Virginians had joined their Boston brothers in revolt against the British crown. "He laughed at us for dodging when we heard the shells whistle past," his orderly recalled. "He said there was no use to dodge after we heard it whistle. . . ."

William Hathaway Forbes, Lowell's pupil of just a few summers before, had also put on the Union uniform. Under the tutelage of Lowell, Forbes had applied himself to his Harvard studies for a time, but soon was in trouble of another kind. During a college prank he had clubbed a watchman on the head, and the watchman had fired a shot at him. Forbes was expelled, and not even his father's wealth and influence could save him from criminal prosecution. Despite a sizable payoff to the watchman, the case came to trial, and young Forbes was fined $50 and costs. John Murray Forbes, perhaps wondering how he had failed as a father—or more likely, how William had failed as a son—put his boy to work as a clerk in the Boston office of the Chicago, Burlington & Quincy Railroad, and the war came just in time for young Forbes to prove himself as he had never been able to do in Boston.

Commissioned a lieutenant in the First Massachusetts Cavalry, Forbes saw action at Antietam, and in January, 1863, was made a captain in the Second Massachusetts Cavalry, newly raised under the command of Colonel Charles Russell Lowell. Six months later, risen now to major, Forbes was skirmishing through Maryland and northern Virginia on the trail of the legendary Confederate John Singleton Mosby. Forbes's big moment came in July of the following year when he caught up with Mosby and his men near Aldie, Virginia. In the bitter hand-to-hand combat that followed, a southern soldier later wrote, "Major Forbes occupied the center of the action, standing in his stirrups with sabre drawn, fighting desperately." Mosby himself, wheeling through the billowing Virginia dust, took quick aim and shot Forbes's horse from under him. On foot now, shaken by his fall, Forbes had no choice but surrender, and after giving up his fine boots to an ill-shod Confederate, he was shipped by boxcar to a southern prison camp. Recaptured after an escape attempt, he was finally exchanged in December, and soon rejoined his regiment as a lieutenant colonel. But there were to be only a few more battles for Forbes; in April, at a small brick farmhouse in Appomattox, he would look on as Robert E. Lee gave up his Army of Northern Virginia to Ulysses S. Grant.

Charles Russell Lowell, meanwhile, avoided wounds and capture, and as William Forbes was rolling south in a boxcar, Lowell stood with Sheridan's army at Harpers Ferry, poised for the great sweep through the Shenandoah Valley to Winchester. "I don't want to be shot till I've had a chance to come home," he wrote to his new wife in early October, 1864. "I have no idea that I shall be hit, but I *want* so much not to now, that sometimes it frightens me."

By mid-October, Lowell was camped along Cedar Creek, near the village of Middletown. On the morning of the nineteenth, under heavy fire from Jubal Early's artillery, he was ordered to throw his brigade into a gap that had opened up in the Union lines. General William Dwight, who watched the troops as they galloped out for their new position, wrote later that "Lowell got by me before I could speak, but I looked after him for a long distance. Exquisitely mounted, the picture of a soldier, erect, confident, defiant, he moved at the head of the finest body of cavalry that today scorns the earth it treads."

At Middletown, Lowell put part of his brigade behind a stone wall, then led two mounted charges against the enemy lines. Later in the day, as the front seemed to have stabilized, he rode out to reconnoiter, wearing, as always, his crimson officer's sash. "It is good for the men to have me wear it," he said. It made a good target for Confederate sharpshooters, too, and soon a bullet smashed his arm and struck him on the chest, collapsing his lung. Back behind his own lines, bleeding from the mouth and unable to speak above a whisper, Lowell lay on the ground until midafternoon. Before him, an enemy battery continued to lob shells into his position, and against the orders of his divisional commander, Lowell reformed his men, had himself lifted into the saddle, and led a charge for the Confederate guns. He was waving his saber with his one good arm when a bullet plowed through him from shoulder to shoulder and severed his spinal cord.

Beside him in the makeshift hospital where he died, one of his junior officers, racked by pain that paralysis had mercifully spared Lowell, lay dying too. "I have always been able to count on you," Lowell whispered, "you were always brave. Now you must meet this as you have the other trials—be steady—I count on you." Then the bright star of promise that had so bewitched, John Murray Forbes, that could have had all the world that Boston offered, slipped away. A day or two later, a courier from Washington arrived at Cedar Creek with a commission promoting Charles Russell Lowell to the rank of brigadier general. Abraham Lincoln had signed it as Lowell made his final charge.

Six weeks before he died, Lowell had written to his friend Henry Lee Higginson, who was himself wounded in the war and would proudly carry to his grave the scar of a saber gash on his right cheek. "I wonder," said Lowell, "whether I shall ever see you again." The two did not meet again, but Higginson would cherish the memory of Lowell and other members of their generation who fell in battle. A quarter of a century after the war, grown to be one of Boston's richest and most influential men, Higginson gave Soldiers Field to Harvard in memory of Lowell and five others who had died during the Civil War. They were, said Higginson, "... dear friends... who gave freely and eagerly all that they had or hoped for...."

SIX. "BEYOND THE WILDEST DREAMS OF COPPER MEN"

Amidst all the tragedy and loss of the Civil War years, commercial life went on in Boston. For the textile industry, it was a time of boom and bustle, and mill magnates such as Amos Adams Lawrence, John Amory Lowell, and his son Augustus served their country and their fortunes well, churning out miles of blankets and cloth for uniforms. For some, it was a time of high speculation. Thomas Jefferson Coolidge, great-grandson of Thomas Jefferson and son of China trader Joseph Coolidge, made a tidy fortune buying and selling large lots of commodities such as coffee, pepper, and iron. It was a profitable business indeed for a man who, at the insistence of his father-in-law, William Appleton, had abandoned a mercantile business of his own after the panic of 1857 to take a steadier job as the salaried treasurer of a textile mill; in his first year as a wartime speculator, Coolidge cleared $100,000.

John Murray Forbes, with two richly rewarding business careers already behind him, all but withdrew from business affairs, choosing instead to support avidly at home the war that his son and his doomed protégé were fighting in the hills and valleys of northern Virginia. Among other things, Forbes contributed money for the relief of Union prisoners and helped raise funds for the Sanitary Commission, forerunner of the Red Cross. He was also active in encouraging the formation of regiments of black soliders, and as an adviser to the Navy Department he went to England on a purchasing expedition. Closer to home, when he and other staunchly Unionist members of the exclusive Somerset Club became upset over some of their fellow clubmen's less-than-enthusiastic support of the Lincoln administration, Forbes led a walkout to form the Union Club, which occupied Abbott Lawrence's old house on Park Street and later expanded to take over the John Amory Lowell mansion next door. The Union Club still occupies the same quarters, and it is sometimes said that its membership roll is heavily laced with lawyers who mind the financial affairs of more affluent members of the Somerset Club.

Bennet Forbes, too, turned his attention to the war. Still an incurable romantic and man of the sea, he organized a short-lived private "coast guard" and built ships for the Union navy. As seemed to be his frequent habit, he lost money on these ventures, though he was able to soothe his financial wounds with the thought that he had acted out of patriotic motives. "I still love the Stars and Stripes," he said later, "and I doubt not, if any similar emergency should arise, I should repeat the folly of sacrificing something to serve my country." Unintentionally, Forbes had put into practice a theory that he had toyed with early in the war, that every capitalist should give as much as one half of his property to the government to insure a speedy quelling of the rebellion.

While Bostonians were fighting and dying, losing and making money during the Civil War, Edwin J. Hulbert, a surveyor and sometime copper prospector, was staking out state roadways on Michigan's northern Keweenaw Peninsula. Hulbert knew that the area was rich in copper deposits; Indians had been digging the metal out of the ground for centuries, crudely smelting it to hammer out arrowheads, utensils, and ornaments. Since the 1840s, white men, too, had opened mining operations in the region, though not all companies were successful. Those that prospered, however, paid off spectacularly. An investor lucky enough to have picked up five hundred shares of the Cliff Mine in 1845, for example, would have paid just a shade over $9,000 for his block of stock. By 1859, he would have received $88,000 in dividends; sale of the shares at that year's high would have brought $167,000, working out to a total return of 200 percent a year. No wonder that Hulbert, even while minding his plumb line and peering through his transit, kept an eye out for telltale outcroppings that might signal the presence of rich red metal.

One day in 1864 his search paid off. Near the roadway that he was laying out, Hulbert spotted the overgrown entrance to a pit in the ground, and several hundred feet away found a large block of conglomerate—copper nodules imbedded in rock. Precisely what Hulbert believed he had found remains unclear. By his own account, written in a bitter old age, he knew from the beginning that the pit had been dug by Indians as a cache for copper found nearby. But the Bostonians who later reaped fortunes from his find would maintain that the naive Hulbert had taken the storage pit for a mine shaft and had foolishly begun blasting away at the bottom in a feverish attempt to uncover a lode of copper.

Whatever Hulbert thought he had found, he tried to keep it under wraps. With the help of some minor Boston capitalists who had taken a previous interest in the Michigan copper country—one of the few places in the world where copper appeared naturally in pure form—he set himself up as the Hulbert Mining Company and quietly tried to buy up the land where he had found the pit and copper-bearing boulder. Unfortunately, the property was priced too high for his meager resources, so Hulbert had to settle for a tract to the north. Marking a straight line from the pit to the boulder to the nearest point on his own property, he began sinking a shaft, and by mid-September was into a rich vein of copper. Almost immediately, he shipped some ore samples back to Boston in a barrel, and before long Hulbert was in Boston himself, seeking funds to finance his promising mining operation.

While in Boston, Hulbert met with Quincy Adams Shaw, son of the successful merchant and real estate owner Robert Gould Shaw and grandnephew of Samuel Shaw, who had sailed as supercargo on board the *Empress of China*, the first American ship to reach Canton. Wealthy by inheritance, Quincy Shaw had shown little interest in business. After his graduation from Harvard in 1845, he toured the West with the historian Francis Parkman, who dedicated his monumental work, *The Oregon Trail*, to his traveling companion. Later, Shaw had spent considerable time in Europe, living for seven years in Paris, where he befriended Jean Millet and developed a lifelong passion for art. But Shaw was a practical man, too, and had already made some investments in Michigan copper properties. He readily agreed to Hulbert's proposal that Shaw and some of his Boston friends buy a controlling interest in the Hulbert company and set up a new corporation, to be known as the Calumet Mining Company. It was Hulbert's understanding that he would receive, in exchange for certain lands turned over to the Calumet company, 10,833 shares in Calumet, and with $16,800 borrowed from Shaw to buy still more property, he headed back to the Keweenaw Peninsula. Later, he would claim that "Quincy A. Shaw of Boston, dishonorably, and by repeated false pretenses," cheated him out of his share of what was to become the fabulously productive Calumet & Hecla copper mine. But first, he would run afoul of Shaw's brother-in-law, Alexander Agassiz.

Agassiz had come to Boston as a child when his father, the renowned Swiss naturalist Louis Agassiz, accepted a professorship at the scientific school established at Harvard by the textile magnate Abbott Lawrence, and he had a smattering of mining experience. A biologist by training, he had been managing his father's museum at Harvard when John Murray Forbes, learning that the young Agassiz was not making enough money, got him a job as president of some coal mines in Pennsylvania.

Later, back at the museum once more, Agassiz decided in the summer of 1866 to take a vacation trip to Michigan and inspect Shaw's mining operation. Shaw was married to one of Agassiz's sisters, and it was only family duty for Agassiz to wonder if his brother-in-law had made a wise investment.

Agassiz had strong misgivings about the way Hulbert was managing things on the scene, but he was impressed with the extent and probable richness of the lode. He was particularly optimistic about prospects for lands south of the Calumet mine, the very spot where Hulbert had come upon the old Indian copper storage pit two years before. Back in Boston, Agassiz persuaded Shaw and his associates to buy the property and organize the Hecla Mining Company to exploit it. As an earnest of his optimism, Agassiz, who at the time had little money of his own, borrowed from Shaw and bought into the company himself. In the bargain, Agassiz was made treasurer of both Calumet and Hecla.

By December, dissatisfaction with Hulbert was running high in Boston. From the beginning, the mine manager had barraged his Boston financial backers with glowing progress reports, but had produced little to show for the money that had been pumped into the enterprise. It was obvious to the Bostonians that they would have to take closer control of their copper venture, and Agassiz was dispatched to Michigan to put the mines on a paying basis. He found the works in a shambles. Hulbert, it seemed, had been systematic only in deceiving the investors, and Agassiz promptly fired him and took over direction of the mine himself. Before long, he also fired Hulbert's brother, John, who had been equally lax as manager of the nearby Hecla mine.

Still bristling over Hulbert's "systematic deception," Agassiz kept his faith in the mines. In early 1867 he was confident enough to assure his brother-in-law and fellow copper investor Henry Lee Higginson (like Shaw, Higginson had married one of Agassiz's sisters) that "The value of the mines, both Hecla and Calumet, are beyond the wildest dreams of copper men...." It was encouraging news to Higginson, who was in the process of losing his shirt in an ill-conceived southern cotton-growing scheme, and he was confident that Shaw and Agassiz would be more successful at copper than he had been at cotton. "I know that coppers are very risky," he wrote to his stockbroker father, "but a mine of such promise, well managed, should be good property.... Quin and Alex, with their knowledge of just this business, with their ability, honesty, industry, nerve, and power (in the way of money), and with their complete control of these mines, give me faith in them as an investment." Once again, business was a matter of faith in trusted kinsmen, though Agassiz had nagging fears that this faith might be misplaced. He had put every cent of his own into the two mines, he said, but "I hate to advise anybody about such precarious things as mines."

Working hard through the summer, resented by some of the older hands as an intruder from the outside, Agassiz struggled to set up and fine-tune the heavy equipment needed for mining and processing the rich copper lode that was now under his complete control. By fall, the new machinery—much of it ordered to replace the inadequate equipment purchased by Hulbert—was in place, and Agassiz began building a rail line to serve the mine sites. Unfortunately, he knew more about mining than railroads, and in setting the gauge of his tracks Agassiz used a measurement taken from the inside rather than the outside of the locomotive wheels. Not until the tracks had been laid did he discover, to his overwhelming embarrassment, that they were a critical one inch too narrow for his engine and ore cars. Hulbert would never have been forgiven for such an outrageous error, but Agassiz was, though by March, 1868, he was all but admitting failure. Unless conditions improved substantially, he advised the investors back in Boston, they should "sell out the whole thing in a block, if it can be done and let somebody else try their hand at it."

As it turned out, such a drastic move was uncalled for. After another slight problem with the disgruntled Hulbert—a dam at the Calumet mine flooded some property that Hulbert was working nearby, and he brought suit; later, according to Agassiz, Hulbert destroyed a portion of the offending dam—things were at last put right at the Calumet and Hecla mines, and

Agassiz was confident enough to leave day-to-day operations to a superintendent and return to Boston.

He had done his work well. The Hecla mine, which just happened to lie beneath the old Indian copper storage pit discovered by Edwin Hulbert in 1864, turned out to be rich beyond all imagining. In December, 1869, the Hecla paid a $5 dividend on shares that had sold for just $5 only three years before. The Calumet followed with a $5 payout (its shares had been quoted at as low as $1 in 1866) the following August, and in the spring of 1871 the two properties were merged along with two smaller mines to form the Calumet & Hecla Mining Company, which before long was accounting for a full 50 percent of all U.S. copper production.

Located in supposedly worthless territory that had been given to the state of Michigan in compensation for the loss of disputed lands in Ohio, the Calumet & Hecla became a financial bonanza of staggering proportions, one that far outstripped the China trade, the textile mills, or the railroads. As late as 1868 shares of either of the two premerger companies could have been purchased for $30 each. Over the next three decades, a 100-share, $3,000 investment in Calumet or Hecla would have paid out cash dividends of $131,250; stock dividends over the same period would have swelled a 100-share portfolio to 250 shares, worth $132,500 at the 1898 price of $530 per share.

Calumet & Hecla had begun as a Boston family affair, and it remained so for at least two generations. Though not a native, Alexander Agassiz had served his adopted city's traditions well, and when Quincy Shaw retired as president soon after the merger, he turned the reins over to Agassiz. By 1875, Calumet & Hecla's 80,000 authorized shares were tightly held by about eight hundred predominantly Boston stockholders, thirteen of whom owned 34,000 of the total. By family, Shaws had 14,000 shares, and 7,802 shares were owned by the Agassiz clan. The Higginsons held 4,574 shares; the Cabots, 525. For decades, the Shaws alone were reaping a steady annual dividend of nearly $300,000 from Calumet & Hecla.

Not all who put their money in Calumet & Hecla did so out of any deep conviction that it was a sound venture. There were other considerations, too, and John P. Marquand, that peerless observer of the Boston mind, expressed them well when he had Thomas Apley, father of the late George, explain to his brother the purchase of a large block of stock in "young Agassiz's copper mine." Wrote Apley: "This was partly out of friendship to the family of the great naturalist—for, as you know, I do not think much of mining speculation. However, it has elements which might interest you." In real life, Dr. Samuel Cabot, son of the merchant Samuel Cabot and father of the future fortune builder Godfrey Lowell Cabot, bought Calumet & Hecla shares largely out of extended family duty—a Cabot cousin was the stepmother of Alexander Agassiz.

Then too, there were those who missed out altogether on Calumet & Hecla's high tide, to their everlasting regret. Years later, Charles Francis Adams moaned that an investment in the mines had been almost forced upon him in the salad days of 1868, but that he chose instead to put his money in "some wretched Michigan lumber railroads." In time, Adams did buy stock in the company, and collected good dividends, but he failed to sell at the high-water mark. "I have missed a great coup in Calumet," he wrote. "I feel bad."

But those who trusted Agassiz and Shaw from the start were to see their richest dreams fulfilled. By 1898, their mines had paid out dividends totaling nearly $53 million; in the boom year of 1899 alone the payout was $10 million, or $100 per authorized share. Once again, the Boston instinct for building up, for taking risks in new and untried fields, had yielded fabulous rewards, rewards that were payable in more than money. Because they had been based from the start on ties of kinship among Boston's already established mercantile and manufacturing families, investments in Calumet & Hecla became not only a mark of financial success but a badge of social prestige as well. To have been let in on the ground floor of this great copper lode was unalloyed proof of good standing in the slowly closing circle of Boston's economic and social elite.

And what of Edwin Hulbert, the surveyor-prospector whose discovery had made this cornucopia possible? According to the

Boston version, his find had been mere accident, and it was only coincidence that the Hecla lode was uncovered at the _ _ of Hulbert's Indian copper storage pit. Indeed, it would become part of Boston folklore that Alexander Agassiz, during his Michigan vacation in the summer of 1866, had been out hunting for geological specimens to take back to his father's museum when he chanced upon an amiable prospector— presumably Hulbert—who showed him a copper nugget that he had found nearby. According to this story, the prospector obligingly directed Agassiz to the spot where he had discovered the nugget, and Agassiz promptly staked out a claim for the Hecla mine and rushed back to Boston to raise money from his friends and family. In any event, it seemed plain—in Boston, at least—that such a lush store of metal was too important to be left in the care of outlanders, that it could be properly exploited only by richer and more sophisticated Bostonians.

Hulbert continued to insist that he was a lot smarter than his erstwhile Boston associates said he was, though it appears that when given his option to pick up the Calumet shares promised to him, he chose instead to exchange them for an interest in another mine that never panned out. Quincy Shaw, perhaps out of charity, perhaps out of shame, later "practically gave" one thousand shares of Calumet & Hecla to Hulbert, who lived his last years as a comfortable exile in Italy. But he was not nearly so comfortable as he would have been with what he believed to be his fair share of the mines, and he neither forgot nor forgave his alleged ill-treatment at the hands of Calumet & Hecla's Boston owners. "In my younger days," he wrote scornfully, "I became strangely, confidently, and I may add, foolishly, impressed, [with] the significance of an oft quoted phrase, which read, in this way, 'The solid men of Boston.'"

SEVEN. "MY INSANE DESIRE TO TURN HUNDREDS TO THOUSANDS, THOUSANDS TO MILLIONS"

Even as most of Boston's solid men had been shifting away from trade and rallying to textile mills, railroads, and copper mines as sources of wealth, there were those who hewed to the old ways of seaborne commerce or struck out in new directions of their own. Thomas Handasyd Perkins, of course, though not above dabbling in other fields, had remained primarily a mercantile man, as did his contemporary Nathaniel Goddard. Goddard, in fact, was such a traditionalist that he wore knee britches into the fourth decade of the nineteenth century, winning for himself the lonely distinction of being the last Bostonian to appear publicly in such attire. With such an attachment to the old ways, it is hardly surprising that Goddard preferred to stick mainly to the coastal, European, and Indies trade that had served him so well in his youth. Even at that, he tended to plot an independent course, and in 1819 he wrote to one of his captains, about to embark on a voyage to India, that "I think our prospect good, for many people are discouraged about India voyages, therefore I am encouraged; I like the gloomiest times best for fitting out."

Goddard's most notable venture outside his field proved only that he was probably right in clinging to what he knew best. In 1833 he bought Constitution Wharf for $25,000, and after making numerous improvements on the property, sold it in 1848 for a substantial $200,000. But he then invested most of the proceeds in a steam-powered textile mill that turned out to be a near-total loss to his heirs. Had he lived to see it, Goddard most certainly would have taken this misadventure in stride—in 1840, writing to one of his debtors, he confided that he could well understand the man's problems. In the past dozen years, Goddard confessed, he had himself lost more than $350,000 through various misfortunes and failures. Nonetheless, this farmer's son—whose father had strongly opposed his son's choice of a merchant career—lived to see his own children marry into some of Boston's most prominent families.

Goddard was a man of infinite patience, even when dealing with his hired help. Once, preparing to set out on an errand, he summoned a literal-minded servant, one Michael Larkin, and said, "Michael, won't you put the horse in the chaise and bring him round to the door?"

"I can't do it, sir," said Michael.

"Why not, Michael?" asked Goddard.

"Because he is too heavy, sir," Michael replied.

"Michael," said Goddard evenly, "won't you be good enough to attach the horse to the chaise and lead him round to the door?"

Larkin might have been better off in the household of China merchant Russell Sturgis, well known as a great purist when it came to language. Whenever he heard anyone use the term "fellow countrymen," he would intone "Friends, Romans, countrymen," and observe that what was good enough for Shakespeare was good enough for Americans. As for the phrase "quite a number of persons," Sturgis would counter by asking what number was *not* quite a number.

Augustus Hemenway, too, went about his business with little concern about what others in Boston were doing, which may be one reason why imports of one of his staple commodities, Chilean copper ore, were so hard hit by the Calumet & Hecla lode. But Hemenway must have been only dimly aware of the impending threat of competition from the Michigan mines, for during the early development of Calumet & Hecla he was confined in a Connecticut sanitarium, the self-confessed casualty of Boston's overweening zeal in the pursuit of riches.

Born in that charmed year of 1805, Hemenway was the son of a dissolute physician who seldom supported his family, and at the age of thirteen he went to work in a Boston dry goods store at a salary of $60 per year plus room and board. The store soon went bankrupt, and Hemenway then worked for a series of other merchants, all the while sending small lots of cloth and sewing materials for his mother, who had moved to Steuben, Maine, to sell to her friends and neighbors. This sideline expanded considerably, and by the time he was nineteen, Hemenway had branched out and begun to send goods to South America. Before long, he was shipping fish and lard to Cuba and St. Thomas, and by 1829 he was exporting large quantities of kerosene, lumber, sugar, lard, turpentine, nails, cotton goods, and agricultural and woodworking machinery to Chile, bringing back wool, hides, and copper ore in return. By 1842 he had invested $50,000 in a Cuban sugar plantation.

Hemenway was a stickler for detail, and his unwillingness to delegate responsibility to others extended even to the loading of his ships, which he insisted on supervising in person. He urged his wife—the daughter of a prominent New York merchant—to live a life of luxury in his spacious Beacon Hill home, though he himself was content with a Spartan existence of all business and no social life or recreation. In time, this relentless work schedule took its toll on Hemenway's nerves, and in 1860, turning over his power of attorney to his brother, his father-in-law, and the merchant Francis Bacon, he entered a mental sanitarium in Litchfield, Connecticut. After a few months of rest, he felt recovered enough to take a trip to England with his wife and one of his daughters, but his dark depression quickly caught up with him. From England he wrote back to his brother that he had lost all his "strength and courage." When he got back to Boston, Hemenway went once more to the sanitarium for what he would later call a "Rip Van Winkle sleep" of a dozen years.

In his office on Long Wharf again after this long absence, Hemenway nonchalantly hung his hat on the same old peg and went to work, his ardor for business affairs somewhat cooled. "I have been thoroughly cured of my insane desire to turn hundreds to thousands, thousands to millions and so on 'ad infinitum,'" he wrote to his partner in England, "and shall hope to live in future, not for myself only but for others, especially the poor and needy."

Despite this resolve, Hemenway was soon up to his old tricks. By June, 1874, he was in England supervising the building and testing of equipment for his Cuban sugar operation, and from England he sailed to Cuba to see first hand how things were getting along. While there, he was captured and held for ransom by a band of insurgents, who must have been startled to find that this wealthy Bostonian would not pay a price that he thought too high even for his own life—for a whole night, Hemenway sat placidly on a log, smoking Havana cigars and beating down the ransom demand.

After a brief time back in Boston, Hemenway was off to England once more, and by the spring of 1876 had returned to Cuba again, where he died in June. When his body was put on board a ship for home, all the vessels in the harbor had their flags at half-staff.

In his will, Hemenway left $10,000 to the director of the sanitarium where he had spent more than a decade of his life, and instructed his executors to distribute $100,000 to worthy charities, preferably those that would not "make two paupers where there was but one before." He left the remainder of his estate to his widow and children, who in spite of their father's indifference to Boston society managed to marry into leading families. His daughter Amy married Louis Cabot, son of Thomas Handasyd Perkins's partner and son-in-law Samuel Cabot; his son, Augustus, Jr., married Harriet Lawrence, daughter of Amos Adams Lawrence, the textile king.

EIGHT. "I HAVE RISKED REPUTATION, FORTUNE, EVERYTHING"

While Augustus Hemenway was trying with limited success to cure himself of raging commercial fever, the spearhead of Boston's constructive drive was still pointed at the western frontier, a frontier that was becoming more thickly settled and in need of expanded rail service. Indeed, the admission of California to the Union in 1850 had given the nation an irrevocable continental view of itself, making it only a matter of time before the Atlantic was joined to the Pacific by a thoroughfare of steel.

Such an undertaking, requiring as it did the crossing of vast stretches of barren prairie—in some cases inhabited by hostile Indians—and a breach of the forbidding Rocky Mountains, was far beyond the abilities of private capital to achieve, and it was soon apparent that some sort of federal assistance would be needed to spur construction of a transcontinental rail line. This aid came in 1862, with passage of the Pacific Railroad Act chartering the Union Pacific Railroad Company and giving it a sizable land grant plus the loan of government bonds totaling some $60 million. But even this was not enough to pull sufficient private funds into the enterprise, and it was no easy task to scrape up the minimal commitment required to qualify for government aid. Thomas C. Durant, the Massachusetts native and seasoned midwestern railroad builder charged with raising the private capital, could drum up little interest in this bold project; in many cases, he had to lend money to friends before they would buy in. John Murray Forbes and most of his associates, their hands full with existing lines, and almost wedded to a careful policy of driving westward a state at a time, steered clear of the Union Pacific, feeling that so lengthy a road was somewhat premature at best, and far too risky at worst. Years before, after all, Forbes had observed that he and other Boston investors, when they plunged into railroad schemes, did so "on such terms that they play with sure cards." The government, claiming first call on all the Union Pacific's assets in the event of failure, left private investors facing a stacked deck; Forbes may have been a bold capitalist, but he was not a gambler, especially when the odds were against him.

Besieged by Durant and others with an interest in the Union Pacific, Congress soon altered the terms for federal aid to the line. Among other things, the government's claim on assets was dropped, and the land grant was doubled. President Abraham Lincoln signed the new Pacific Railroad Act in July, 1864, making the Union Pacific somewhat more attractive to private investors. Durant, meanwhile, had made a fateful move. Three months before, he had bought the charter of the Pennsylvania Fiscal Agency, set up originally to finance construction of railroads in the South and West. Deciding that the corporate title sounded a bit too parochial for what he had in mind, he renamed the company the Crédit Mobilier of America. In time, it would be joined by Teapot Dome and Watergate in the annals of national scandal.

The idea behind Crédit Mobilier was simple enough. The Union Pacific charter specified that stockholder liability for the company's debts was not limited only to the amount of individual investment in the line, but was extended to the total resources of each investor. Conceivably, failure of the Union Pacific could cost a backer not only the sum that he had put in the railroad but a considerable portion of his other properties as well. Men of means were understandably reluctant to commit themselves to an enterprise that could wipe out totally unrelated holdings. The renamed Pennsylvania Fiscal Agency had no such sweeping provisions in its charter, and by making Crédit Mobilier the contractor for construction of the Union Pacific, the stumbling block of total financial responsibility was removed from the path of prospective investors in the railroad. As a sweetener, Union Pacific stockholders would also own Crédit Mobilier, assuring themselves a share of the rich profits to be reaped from construction contracts. By the spring of 1865, the initial Union Pacific contract had been assigned to Crédit Mobilier, which set out to raise funds to finance construction. The search soon led to Boston, and to the brothers Oakes and Oliver Ames.

Their father, the original Oliver Ames, had founded the family firm, Oliver Ames & Sons, in North Easton, Massachusetts, early in the century. Its principal products were shovels and other tools that were in great demand during the period of frenzied canal-, highway-, and railroad-building, and the company had become large and prosperous. Oakes and Oliver Ames were partners in the company, and in addition had invested in a number of western railroads, doubling at times as construction contractors. Oakes Ames knew of railroading in another connection, too; in 1862 he had been elected to Congress, where he served on the committee that helped frame legislation to build the Union Pacific. Just a decade later, Ames would be a broken, ruined man, lamenting that "it would have been better that I had never heard of the Union Pacific Railroad."

The Ameses were intrigued by the possibilities of Crédit Mobilier, as well they might be. Owned in common by stockholders of the Union Pacific—Crédit Mobilier investors were to be given Union Pacific bonds as a bonus for purchasing shares in the contracting company, which in turn distributed its profits in the form of Union Pacific shares—Crédit Mobilier's profitability hinged on a sizable spread between actual construction costs and the price contracted for; in effect, the Union Pacific's owners would be making construction agreements with themselves, inflating the contracts to assure a healthy return on the highly risky investment. Within a year, the Ames brothers had put more than $400,000 of their own funds into Crédit Mobilier and had rounded up a like amount from other Boston investors. By the fall of 1866, with 247 miles of rails laid westward from Omaha, Nebraska, the Union Pacific's directors elected Oliver Ames to the presidency.

Following a series of squabbles with some of the railroad's original promoters who resented their growing influence, the Ames investors were able in late 1867 to get stockholder approval for a new contract to continue construction of the Union Pacific to link with the Central Pacific being built from California. The contract called for the building and equipping with necessary support buildings of 667 miles of track, at a total cost of $49,915,000. Happily for the contractor, the agreement included 138 miles of track that had already been built. Because of factional bickering, however, the deal was not made directly with Crédit Mobilier; instead, it was with Congressman Oakes Ames, and was administered by trustees representing both sides of the dispute. But this was a somewhat meaningless compromise between the old and the new Union Pacific–Crédit Mobilier promoters—though Ames was not then an officer or director of either company, the trustees' job was to divide the profits among the stockholders of Crédit Mobilier.

Construction under the so-called Oakes Ames contract proceeded at a furious—and profitable—pace. The agreed-upon price had been set so high because of the supposed difficulties in building through the Rockies; instead, as insiders must have known all along, the Continental Divide was crossed through the great Evans Pass, at considerable savings over the blasting and tunneling that had been assumed in the estimates. On May 10, 1869, what Horace Greeley had called "the grandest and noblest enterprise of our age" was completed. At Promontory, Utah, the last symbolic spike linked the Union Pacific with the Central Pacific. The continent had been bridged by rail.

But Crédit Mobilier's bubble had already been punctured beyond all patching. Stockholders, wanting to keep a good thing to themselves, had tried to exclude outsiders from their gravy train, but they hadn't reckoned with the wheeler-dealer Jim Fisk. Barred from buying into Crédit Mobilier, Fisk went to court in the summer of 1868 to charge, among other things, that his interests as a Union Pacific stockholder—he owned six shares—had been damaged by high payments made under terms of the Ames–Crédit Mobilier contract. An obliging state judge threw Crédit Mobilier into receivership and enjoined Union Pacific from issuing any further bonds or conducting business of any kind. Company officers ignored the ban, and after fleeing New York for New Jersey to escape a sheriff come to enforce the injunction, they moved their headquarters to Boston. Public confidence in Union Pacific plummeted, and so did the value of its stock; as the road's problems continued to simmer, backers of the Pennsylvania Railroad stepped in to save it, but they were soon ousted by the Vanderbilt interests, who were in turn displaced by the railroad speculator Jay Gould.

Crédit Mobilier, meanwhile, had become a national scandal, and Oakes Ames a broken man. Congressional investigations found that he had improperly sold the construction company's stock at a discount to federal officials—among them Vice-President Schuyler Colfax and Congressman James A. Garfield—in order to dispose them favorably to Union Pacific's cause, and Ames was censured by the House of Representatives. A short time later, in May, 1873, he died at his home in North Easton.

Little more than two months before, rising on the floor of Congress, Ames had delivered a ringing defense of his conduct. His offense, he said, was this: "that I have risked reputation, fortune, everything, in an enterprise of incalculable benefit to the government, from which the capital of the world shrank. . . ." Indeed, Ames had risked all, and lost all—including even his life—to build the Union Pacific Railroad. The scandal that brought him down cannot erase this towering achievement, and for all that, given the business standards of the day, Crédit Mobilier was not a particularly unusual mechanism for the construction of a railroad, especially one so ambitious as the Union Pacific. If profits to the promoters were high—and they were not so high as was alleged at the time—so were the risks, and it is hardly reasonable to expect that private capitalists would have hazarded their fortunes on such a project without an assurance of gain. And the Union Pacific, though financed largely with private funds, had all the trappings of a great national adventure, an expression of the national will that was probably unmatched until the days of the space program. Albert D. Richardson, as he watched a locomotive inching slowly westward in the wake of workmen who sometimes laid as many as two and a half miles of track a day, saw more than a mere construction job, saw more than rails spiked to crossties to make way for trains laden with passengers and goods. Said he: "It was Civilization pressing westward—the Conquest of Nature moving toward the Pacific."

It was that, and more. It was, finally, the long-sought Northwest Passage come true, a dream of centuries realized at last. Bret Harte, moved to verse by the ultimate joining of rails at Promontory Point, saw this clearly when he posed an imaginary conversation between nose-to-nose locomotives from East and West. The western engine, unimpressed by its eastern brother's bragging of the civilized wonders brought west in its train, replies:

> You brag of the East. *You* do?
> Why, I bring the East to *you*!
> All the Orient, all Cathay
> Find through me the shortest way . . .

Oakes Ames's misfortune was that at a time when no one else was willing or able to do so he had made possible the building of that great thoroughfare from East to West, from West to East. That he was dragged down to disgrace for his troubles may be as great a scandal as Crédit Mobilier ever was, a possibility that was recognized by some of his contemporaries. Learning of Ames's death, Congressman Henry L. Dawes thundered to his colleagues that "A grateful nation will yet rear his monument; and its inscription will be, THE BUILDER OF THE UNION PACIFIC RAILROAD."

The nation does not easily forgive its malefactors—justly or unjustly accused—and the perfidy of Oakes Ames and Crédit

Mobilier remains snugly imbedded in the American consciousness. But both he and his brother are memorialized in a monument erected by the Union Pacific itself. Capping a summit at Sherman, Wyoming, the highest point above sea level reached by the railroad in its drive across the Continental Divide, the hulking stone monument stands sixty feet tall and bears bas-reliefs of the Ames brothers looking out over the land that they conquered to join East to West. The inscription tells nothing of their heartbreak or their sorrows, but reads simply, "In memory of Oakes Ames and Oliver Ames."

NINE. "VANDERBILT OR GOULD HAVE A GREAT ADVANTAGE OVER US"

John Murray Forbes, while steering clear of the Union Pacific, had already done considerable work in making an Atlantic to Pacific railroad link possible. Since his first venture into western railroads in the 1840s, Forbes had driven his system from Detroit across Michigan, Indiana, and Missouri, and at the time the Union Pacific was chartered, he stood poised on the banks of the Missouri River at St. Joseph, some 125 miles south of the Union Pacific's starting point in Omaha. But his Burlington & Missouri River Railroad, the most logical through route to Omaha, was stalled at Ottumwa, Iowa, 175 miles to the east. This shortfall was soon remedied, however, and by 1870 the line had been pushed through Iowa to Council Bluffs, where it connected across the Missouri with Omaha and the West. A short time later this link was further strengthened with the formation of the Burlington & Missouri River Railroad in Nebraska, which paralleled the Union Pacific tracks through that state and joined them in the south-central city of Kearney.

Meanwhile, a group of Forbes's western associates had been striking out in new directions of their own, motivated in part by real estate and other investments in Kansas City. Led by James F. Joy, a former Detroit lawyer who had been deeply involved with the Forbes railroad ventures since the old Michigan Central days, and who was now president of the Chicago, Burlington &

Quincy, they plumped for a Union Pacific connection with the Hannibal & St. Joseph Railroad via Kansas City, with a north-south road to be built up the west bank of the Missouri River to Omaha. Forbes, somewhat reluctantly but not wishing to cause friction among colleagues who had worked so well together for so long, agreed to this scheme, even though it ran counter to his long-held view that sequential east-west construction was the best way to go about railroad expansion.

Forbes's misgivings turned out to be well founded, and it would be years before the Kansas City–centered system—which was also built as far south as the Kansas border—carried its own weight. But a break had been made in his careful policy of east-to-west development, and it was not long before this led to open conflict between Forbes and his associates, between the circumspection of Boston and the more flamboyant spirit of the West.

Seeking still more expansion to the north, James Joy teamed up in 1870 with a businessman from Dubuque, Iowa, to build the River Roads, two back-to-back lines that would link Clinton, Iowa, with Minneapolis and St. Paul, Minnesota, presumably feeding traffic from this region into the Chicago, Burlington & Quincy's main line to Chicago. Along with several other Burlington directors who had been involved in his Kansas City system, Joy set up a construction company to build the lines under terms strikingly similar to the Crédit Mobilier of America. And in their capacity also of directors of the Burlington, Joy and friends saw to it that the line supported the River Roads through purchase of bonds.

Forbes, unaware of his fellow directors' stake in the construction company, went along with the deal, though he soon had reason to regret it. Returning to Boston after a lengthy vacation tour that had taken him to the Azores and to California, he found the financial affairs of the River Roads in total disorder. Worse, he discovered that in his absence the directors of the Burlington had dipped into company funds to pay interest on the River Roads' bonds—some of which he held in his own portfolio.

Forbes's first impulse was to return his interest payments to

the Burlington's treasury. Dissuaded from this course by a fellow director, Forbes fumed that "while I can guess at many
good reasons for paying out such a large sum to outsiders, I am
utterly at a loss for reasons justifying our voting it to ourselves."
Besides, he said, "That it will eventually come out and be challenged is as sure as that we live, and now is the time for any of
us who were not responsible for the transaction to take their
ground." Schooled in upright and honorable conduct by the
old China traders, John Murray Forbes was determined to do
the right thing, and he wasn't about to become entangled in a
net woven by men who had betrayed the trust he placed in
them.

On a western trip after the panic of September, 1873, almost
brought the River Roads down completely, Forbes discovered
that the situation was even worse than he had imagined, and
learned for the first time of the directors' involvement with the
construction company. He was outraged by this display of bad
faith and tried hard to convince the errant directors that some
sort of restitution was in order. Using all of his persuasive powers, Forbes would grip a colleague's right arm with his left hand
and forcefully walk him up and down, punctuating his remarks
with a jabbing right forefinger. He was good at getting his
points across, and perhaps better at drawing out other people's
ideas. Once, on a western jaunt with a friend from Concord, he
was collared on his train by a newspaper reporter who wanted
to get the great railroad builder's impressions of the West.
Forbes asked *him* questions—about his job, his life, his
ambitions—and the bemused journalist stumbled to the plat-
form without discovering Forbes's views on anything, or that
his silent traveling companion was Ralph Waldo Emerson.

But Forbes could score few points with the Burlington directors, so he determined in early 1875 to oust the offenders
from the board and replace them with a clean slate. With the
help of his son, who had returned from the Civil War to go into
business with his father, and John N. A. Griswold, an old China
trader turned railroad man, Forbes was able to round up
enough proxies to succeed at this move, and by the following
year he firmed up his control by naming a protégé and cousin,

Charles E. Perkins, to the key post of operating vice-president. Forbes himself took over the presidency of the Burlington in 1878, giving up the reins in 1881 to Perkins.

Perkins was one of the "foremast hands" that Forbes had brought into railroading at an early age. A grandson of Forbes's uncle, the merchant Samuel Perkins, Charles Perkins had been raised, not in Boston, but in Cincinnati. At the urging of both Forbes and Charles Russell Lowell, he had gone to work in 1859 as Lowell's clerk—at a salary of thirty dollars a month—on the Burlington & Missouri River Railroad. At the time, Forbes had written to the eighteen-year-old Perkins that "if you can make yourself useful there, you would certainly stand a good chance of having your services recognized by pay and promotion when the proper opening comes." Young Perkins learned his lessons well and in time became Forbes's most trusted adviser on western railroad affairs, and one of the nation's foremost railroad executives.

Building on the base laid down by Forbes, Perkins led the Chicago, Burlington & Quincy through the great period of western expansion. By 1890 the system could boast more than five thousand miles of track, up from a little more than one thousand miles in 1874. The railroad that had once aimed for the Mississippi River now stretched far beyond that great waterway, its tracks knifing as far west as Denver and Cheyenne. It was, indeed, one of the nation's largest railroads, and it remained a Boston concern (Bostonians owned nearly 486,000 shares in 1890; New Yorkers held a shade over 269,000 shares), paying stockholders a steady dividend of 8 percent before increased competition and government regulations trimmed the payout to a more conservative 4 and 5 percent.

Through it all, too, it was an enterprise whose backers were, in the main, propelled by a passion for building rather than for speculation, guided by principles laid down—if not always honored—by two generations of China traders and manufacturers. Not yet had this spirit been tempered with the hesitant caution and conservatism that would later leave Bostonians ill-matched in conflict with new and more venturesome—if less scrupulous—competitors from other cities, and Boston's days of financial pioneering were far from over. But changes were in the wind, and in the end Boston's traditions would not prevail against them. John Murray Forbes may have foreseen this in 1880, when the freewheeling William Vanderbilt bought ten thousand shares of Chicago, Burlington & Quincy stock as a quick speculation. "Vanderbilt or Gould," he wrote to his friend John N. A. Griswold, "have a great advantage over us in these stock operations—they can buy and sell millions of company stock as if it were their own." Such speculation was sometimes tempting even to him, Forbes said, but added that "I fear the effect of it, especially as I know how such operations have always been looked upon in Boston."

Financial freebootery may have been frowned upon in Boston, but the pursuit of profits was still an honorable profession—provided, of course, that it was undertaken in the "right" way, with the sensibilities of friends and family borne always in mind. For a rising generation of younger Bostonians, those too young to have been China merchants, factory builders, or railroad pioneers, the quest for riches continued to be a virtual compulsion, a duty imposed by their heritage and demanded by their place and time. Looking around him after his graduation from Harvard in 1850, Thomas Jefferson Coolidge observed that "Everybody was at work trying to make money, and money was becoming the only real avenue to power and success both socially and in the regard of your fellow-men. I was ambitious," added this son of a moderately successful China merchant, "and decided to devote myself to the acquisition of wealth."

So, too, did many of his contemporaries, goaded by ambition, necessity, or a craving to prove themselves to their fathers. Not all of them would go about their tasks with the same single-minded gusto of preceding generations; indeed, they would find that in a world grown more complex and even predatory there was a shrinking market for the indelible Boston values that had served so well in the past. In response, some would tend to husband their wealth and profits, caring more for steady, present gain than for future growth and development. Others, encouraged by a Boston intellectual climate made possible only by the city's great wealth, would grow to despise their own callings and turn away from business enterprise. Meanwhile, an expanding nation could still call on Boston's capital resources, and the city's financiers remained willing to accept new challenges, could still summon up some of the spirit of their forefathers.

Chapter Seven

THE FINANCIERS

In the year 1848 Mr. John C. Lee, of Salem, and Mr. George Higginson, of Boston, who were cousins by marriage, joined hands in making a stock-brokerage house, and established themselves in State Street. . . .

—Henry Lee Higginson

Gusty winds stirred the rain and whipped bright yellow leaves from the elm trees of Harvard Yard on that late October day in 1864 when a group of soldiers carried a flag-draped coffin to the Appleton Chapel, built in 1853 with a bequest from the merchant Samuel Appleton. The scabbard of the sword topping the coffin was scarred and battered; the cap and gauntlets that lay beside it were grimy with the dust and sweat of battle. Charles Russell Lowell, his promise broken by Confederate gunfire, was coming home, and as pallbearer Henry Lee Higginson helped ease the coffin down at the altar, he must have pondered the advice that he had received from his friend not long before he fell mortally wounded on a Virginia battlefield. "I hope you have outgrown all foolish ambitions and are now content to become a 'useful citizen,'" Lowell had written. "Don't grow rich; if you once begin, you will find it much more difficult to become a useful citizen. The useful citizen is a mighty unpretending hero. But we are not going to have any country very long unless such heroism is developed."

Higginson was probably flattered by Lowell's admonitions. Almost thirty, he had shown few signs of becoming either rich or particularly useful as a citizen, and it would be several more years before he was launched on the career that would make him one of Boston's wealthiest men and most generous benefactors.

George Higginson, Henry's father, had been born in 1804, but the rich promise of his generation had long eluded him. While his contemporaries were laying up fortunes in trade and textiles, George was floundering as a marginal merchant, and not even his extensive family connections were enough to bring success his way. Seeking a fresh start, he abandoned Boston for New York—where Henry was born in 1834—but returned after being wiped out in the panic of 1837, the same upheaval that sent Robert Bennet Forbes back to China to make up for his own considerable losses. In Boston, George Higginson set himself up in a small way as a commission merchant on India Wharf, and it may have been only out of desperation that he finally, in 1848, formed a brokerage operation in partnership with his wife's cousin, John C. Lee. Neither partner showed much initiative or enterprise, and for the first five years business was so sparse that they got by without so much as a clerk. The pace quickened as Boston became a central market for western railroad stocks, and by the early 1850s several additional partners—Lee family members all—were taken in, and the firm began styling itself Lee, Higginson & Company, a name that would grow mighty in the world of finance..

Henry Lee Higginson, however, had little interest in his father's business. Known to his friends as Higgy or Bully Hig, young Henry entered Harvard's class of 1855, along with Alexander Agassiz, his future brother-in-law, but dropped out after a few months because of failing eyesight. A European trip seemed in order, and in the spring of 1852 Higginson sailed for England. He later made his way to France, Italy, and Germany, where he spent most of his time attending operas and concerts. Back in Boston a year and a half later, Higginson balked at returning to Harvard—he was too worldly now, he thought, to start anew as a freshman—and chose instead to be privately tutored. It was an agreeable life, but in time his father began to wonder what it was all leading to, how his son would ever make a living for himself. In the spring of 1855, shortly before his class graduated from Harvard, Henry Higginson was put to work in the countinghouse of the merchants Samuel and Edward Austin on India Wharf, where he served as clerk and bookkeeper, handling monthly shipments coming in from Australia, Calcutta, Java, and Manila. His performance was satisfactory enough, but his heart wasn't in it, and when Edward Austin asked him one day what kind of work he wanted to do, Higginson answered that he didn't know for sure but that the job in the countinghouse didn't really give him a chance to use his mind. "I guess when you have some notes to pay, you will find that your mind is busy enough," Austin muttered.

Through it all, Higginson kept up with the Harvard crowd, talking into the night with his friend Charles Russell Lowell about the state of the world and the slavery question, wondering what a young man could do to set things right. With the proceeds from a venture in indigo, Higginson tried to do his part by financing the settlement of an antislavery Irishman and his family in Kansas, but the gesture proved a failure, the first of many for Henry Higginson—the man got only as far as Albany, where he deserted his family and disappeared.

With less than two years of his lackluster business career behind him, Higginson decided in the fall of 1856 to head for Europe again, a trip made possible by a $13,000 inheritance from a well-to-do uncle. This time he stayed for four years, visiting for a while with Charles Russell Lowell in Italy, traveling the continent taking in operas and studying music, trying to master the mysteries of harmony and composition. And if George Higginson had worried about his son's future while he was at home, it concerned him even more during this long period abroad. "I have heard two or three times from our countrymen who have seen you in Vienna," he wrote at one point, "that your street dress is rather peculiar and shabby. If such is the truth, let me request you to consider more favorably what the personal appearance of one of your class should be. . . ." By the spring of 1859 the exasperated father was writing that "You should return to this country in the autumn, decide on a pursuit, and take it up in earnest." A short time later, he was asking plaintively, "Can't you come home and get musical instruction here?" Finally, he strongly advised his son to "Come back and begin to *earn*!" When Henry demurred, his father could only say that he was making a "misjudgment, a serious error."

Early in the following year, George Higginson was at it again. "Your place is *here*—in readiness for *work*," he wrote. "Have you anything in prospect for me, daddy dear?" Henry replied later. It was hardly the kind of question that Bostonians of an earlier time would have thought to ask. Nathaniel Goddard, for one, was often scolded by his mother for his impatience at making money. "Something will turn up by and by," she would say. "Perhaps so, ma'am," he would answer, "but not until I turn it up."

At long last Henry Higginson did return from his European interlude, arriving in Boston in December, 1860. But prospects were slim for a young man who had spent the past four years studying music in Europe, and even his own father couldn't see his way clear to offer him a job at Lee, Higginson. Living at his father's small rented house, Henry marked time, hoping that something would turn up by and by, consoled by Charles Russell Lowell's advice that unless he felt himself becoming a disreputable loafer, he should "be in no hurry to plunge into trade." The times were uncertain, after all, and who could tell where the mounting conflict between North and South would lead?

When it led to war, Higginson joined his generation and was commissioned in the Second Massachusetts Infantry, but soon transferred to the First Massachusetts Cavalry, with the rank of captain. Among his fellow officers was Charles Francis Adams, Jr., who was to become a lifelong friend. Promoted to major, Higginson was severely wounded in June, 1863, near Aldie, Virginia, not far from the spot where William Hathaway Forbes was captured by Mosby's men a year later. During his long convalescence in Boston, he married Ida Agassiz, sister of his Harvard classmate, and after a brief return to his troops resigned from the army because of failing health.

With a wife to support, Higginson decided at last to give up hopes for a musical career and turn his mind to business. If nothing else, his first ventures must have shown his father the wisdom of not offering him a job with Lee, Higginson. Sent to Ohio by a group of Bostonians who had raised $25,000 to form the Buckeye Oil Company and exploit the state's newly discovered oil fields, Higginson rapidly proceeded to demonstrate, in the words of even a doting biographer, that "His ignorance of his duties was absolute." Expenses far surpassed any hopes of return, and Higginson's bookkeeping methods left much to be desired; at one point, he wrote to his father seeking guidance, asking him which side of his account book was for credits and which was for debits. It was as if Robert Bennet Forbes had written home from the Cape of Good Hope to ask which side of his ship was starboard, which was port.

Buckeye's Boston backers soon had second thoughts about their agent, and within a few months were warning him that he was rapidly running through their capital resources. Higginson persisted in his prodigal ways, and by July, 1865, just six months after his arrival in Ohio, it was all over for Henry Lee Higginson and the Buckeye Oil Company.

His next venture was even more disastrous than the first. With two Boston friends, Higginson bought—for $30,000—a five thousand-acre Georgia plantation called Cottonham, where the trio planned an idyllic Lowell-like operation to make their fortunes while uplifting their newly freed black workers. It seemed like a sure thing, and Higginson confidently assured his doubting father that his calculations indicated a first-year profit of $5,633 per partner, with only four hundred acres under cultivation. Unfortunately, Higginson's figures were wide of the mark, and when he toted up his accounts in January, 1867, he found that cotton that had cost more than $20,000 to produce had sold for just $10,000. "I am at present rather looking forward to leaving this place in the summer for good," he wrote to George Higginson, adding in his next letter that "I should have done better to enter your office in '64 as a paid clerk...."

Conditions at Cottonham continued to worsen, and the capper came when the partners discovered that the previous "owner" of the plantation had in fact owned only half of the five thousand acres he sold them. Their title to the rest was as worthless as the dreams of riches that had sent them south. In May, 1867, Higginson packed his bags and returned to Boston with yet another failure under his belt. By the end of the year, the second crop had been wiped out by caterpillars, and the disheartened Boston cotton men sold their plantation for a piddling $5,000. The whole venture, they figured, had cost them about $65,000.

Meanwhile, Higginson's prospects in Boston had taken a turn for the better. His mother's father had died, leaving sizable sums in trust for his grandchildren, and Higginson had invested part of the proceeds in the Michigan copper properties being developed by his brothers-in-law, Alexander Agassiz and Quincy Shaw. Flightiness and failure seemingly behind him, Higginson at last found his way into the family firm of Lee, Higginson, where he was taken on as a partner in January, 1868. It was, he said later, "a matter of charity, to keep me out of the poorhouse; I had been in the War, had been planting cotton at the South, and lost all I had, and more too."

Now his days of loss were over, and if he was to disobey Charles Russell Lowell's injunction not to grow rich, he would also become a useful citizen. But it was to be a laborious grind, unleavened by the consuming passion for commercial affairs that had sustained past generations. Higginson would spend more than fifty years at Lee, Higginson, becoming the very personification of the firm. But in his later life, he confessed to a close kinsman that he had never walked into his office at 44 State Street without wanting to sit down on the doorstep and weep for the vanished dreams of his youth.

TWO. "A RATHER LOW INSTINCT"

When his private railroad car rolled into Fort Worth, Texas, one day in 1889, Charles Francis Adams, Jr., was hardly surprised to find a throng of prominent citizens gathered to meet him at the station. And he took it all in stride when he was given a tour of the town, winding up at the stockyards where he was served a lunch complete with that Boston delicacy, oysters. For

Adams was, after all, more than just the grandson and great-grandson of United States presidents, more than the son of the distinguished Civil War ambassador to England. He was president of the Union Pacific and was known throughout the West as a ready investor in stockyards, real estate, and other promising properties. It was an odd distinction for a Bostonian who referred to "that great, fat, uninteresting West," and who had once faulted Boston's early railroad builders for "exploiting in the far West" while their home city's railway service was deteriorating.

Unlike Henry Higginson, his close friend and former comrade-in-arms, Adams had had little doubt about his life's work. "I endeavored, " he wrote later, "to strike out on a new path, and fastened myself not, as Mr. Emerson recommends, to a star but to the locomotive engine. I made for myself what might be called a speciality in connection with the development of the railroad system." While Higginson was agonizing over the failure of Cottonham, then learning the ropes at the family brokerage house—and trying vainly to interest Adams in Calumet & Hecla shares—Adams was busying himself at breaking into the railroad business. And with the independent streak so typical of his family, he chose to do so by a rather round-about means: instead of going to work for a railroad, he chose to enter the field by way of journalism.

In 1867 and 1868, Adams published in the prestigious *North American Review* three articles on railroads, a subject that the imminent prospect of an Atlantic to Pacific rail link had spotlighted in the national mind. In the first article, he called for better management and more coordination between systems; in the next two, he focused on Boston's own situation, observing that the city's railroad magnates had "built great railroads throughout the West, and managed them with incomparable skill, but those roads did not lead to Boston." To prevent Boston from being left behind in the railroad sweepstakes, said Adams, Massachusetts needed a plan, a goal to be worked out by a high-level committee of experts. Readers needed little imagination to judge that Adams considered himself just such an expert.

In 1869, prodded in part by Adams's *North American Review* articles, the state created a railroad commission to oversee its rail system; Adams, with his considerable family influence, became a member. Throwing himself wholeheartedly into his work, freely using his great talents as a speaker and writer, Adams soon began attracting national attention. After three years he was made chairman of the commission, and when he declined another term in 1879—it was time to move on to something else, he thought—he was quickly tapped to serve on an industry committee working to standardize rates between the Midwest and the East. He had become a man to reckon with in the railroad community.

Meanwhile, Adams had also become an avid investor, part of the informal group gathered around Nathaniel Thayer, a Boston banker and an associate of John Murray Forbes in a number of western railroad ventures. Possible conflicts of interest barred him from putting money into Massachusetts railroads, so he turned to the West. Largely through Henry Higginson, he bought shares in the Chicago, Burlington & Quincy and the Atchison, Topeka & Santa Fe—which, like the Burlington and the Union Pacific, had been built with Boston capital. Railroads were not his only western interest; by the early 1870s, he owned seven hundred shares in the Kansas City Stockyards, and in 1875 became president, a post he would hold for nearly four decades. The "fat, uninteresting West" had proved a fertile field for Adams's capital, and for twenty years he toured the western states at least once a year, sometimes spending several months, and sometimes in the company of Boston friends such as Henry Higginson. Not yet was he afflicted with the misgivings that had assailed Higginson on a trip to Burlington, Iowa, to check out western investment possibilities and visit railroad man Charles Perkins—"Money, money, success in material pursuits!" Higginson wrote. "It is injuring our generation, but perhaps the next may be the better for it. More good and educated men and women may strive for the welfare and civilization of America."

Adams frequently had to borrow money for his numerous investments, a practice that would not have sat well with his maternal grandfather, Peter Chardon Brooks, whose daughter's marriage to Charles Francis Adams, Sr., had brought considerable wealth to a family that had for generations been devoted to public service rather than to moneymaking. Brooks, said to have been Boston's first millionaire, had made his fortune in marine insurance, retiring in 1803 at the age of thirty-six. He had made enough money, he said, "to turn any man's head." But it hardly turned Brooks's head. He was an extremely cautious man who never in his life sought credit, and who stubbornly refused to invest in the many railroad opportunities that cropped up before his death in 1849. "To him," his Adams son-in-law wrote, "extravagant profits were no temptation to enter into hazardous enterprises." Once, when he did venture to speculate, Brooks backed out before his investment bore fruit, selling for little more than what he had paid a large parcel of Ohio land that later became part of the city of Cleveland. The naming of Chardon, Ohio, after Brooks was small consolation to his heirs.

Brooks's grandson was untroubled by such cautious scruples, and while he railed against Wall Street speculators as "jockeys and gamblers," some of his own ventures were little more than gambles. He never, however, went quite as far as his contemporary Thomas Jefferson Coolidge, who on a visit to Virginia City, Nevada, was told of a supposedly rich silver mine that had been discovered nearby. Fortified with champagne cocktails, Coolidge flipped a coin to determine whether or not to buy stock in the lode. "Unfortunately," he recalled, "heads turned up; we bought Sierra Nevada, and for my part before I could reach New York and sell, the stock had cost me twenty thousand dollars." At the time, the coin-flipping Coolidge was, among other things, a director of the Chicago, Burlington & Quincy Railroad and head of Amoskeag Mills, the nation's largest textile producer.

Adams's western investments were generally more solid than Coolidge's Nevada silver mine, though he was from time to time burned in mining ventures that would temporarily sour him on stocks of any kind. In the main, Adams stuck to land, buying property at promising but undeveloped points, improving it, and then selling. In 1879, already heavily into the Kansas

City Stockyards, he began buying land across the Missouri River in Kansas City, Kansas, where prices were running to only $150 to $200 per acre, compared with some $1,000 on the Missouri side. His Kaw Valley Town Site & Bridge Company bought up more than $300,000 worth of land, then put up a bridge that soon led to a boom. For the year ending in June, 1885, the company paid its investors a 40 percent dividend; in 1886 the payout was 10 percent a month, and by 1912 the company had paid out 400 percent on its capital.

In the mid-1880s Adams moved still farther west, buying the Denver Stockyards and considerable land in the Colorado city. Later, he bought property in San Antonio, Salt Lake City, Portland, Spokane, and Seattle, as well as in a number of smaller cities. While he was fairly sophisticated in choosing his western acreage—he would study the resources and potential of an area, then climb to some neighboring high point to look over the land and assess where things were likely to expand—Adams made an occasional mistake. In 1896, checking on a tract that he had bought earlier in Spokane, he learned that the nine-hundred-acre parcel of land he owned was not the same one that he'd had in mind buying.

Through all his western land speculations—and land speculation, based as it was on long-term faith in future development, was a perfectly acceptable occupation for a proper Bostonian—Adams remained a railroad man. Indeed, the prosperity of his western properties depended on rail service and the growth that followed it. And it was not long before his interests in the West drew him into the Union Pacific, first as an investor, then as a director, and then as president.

Following the Crédit Mobilier scandal, control of the Union Pacific had passed to stock market manipulator Jay Gould, who by 1878 owned 200,000 of the line's 370,000 shares. In a brilliant series of market maneuvers, Gould managed in 1880 to merge the Union Pacific with the competitive Kansas Pacific, which he also controlled, to form the Union Pacific Railway Company. Charles Francis Adams, meanwhile, had been appointed a government director of the line, and in the fall of 1882 spent two weeks inspecting the system. He liked what he saw and began buying stock. More than that, he also urged other Bostonians to do likewise, to wrest control of the Union Pacific from the New York speculators who owned the major interest.

Adams, who at times toyed with the idea of becoming a sort of national railroad czar, and who did not suffer fools gladly—while serving on the industry rate-stabilization board, he had referred to one of his fellow members as a "thick witted lunkhead"—was elected a private director of the Union Pacific in 1883. The following year, he was named president, and the line's headquarters moved once more from New York to Boston. As it had been in the beginning, the Union Pacific was again a Boston railroad, and Adams set out to put its tangled affairs straight.

Topping the list of things for the new president to do was settlement of the government loans made during the days of construction. At the mercy of rate-cutting competitors whose trackage had been built more cheaply than the Union Pacific's, the road's revenues had fallen and left the Union Pacific delinquent in repayment to the federal government. But Adams, who had been placed in the presidency with the assumption that his influence in Washington would help ease the way to accommodation with federal officials, was unable to live down the sour aftertaste of Crédit Mobilier and the manipulations of Jay Gould. Congress declined to lighten the Union Pacific's crushing burden of debt. A bond issue, floated to buy branch lines in the Northwest and bolster sagging revenues, failed to sell; the stock market crash of 1890 drove Adams to seek outside help to cover his railroad's debts. Desperate now, he offered control of the line to anyone who would come to his aid. Only Jay Gould, seen by John Murray Forbes as the nemesis of tradition-bound Bostonians, took Adams up on his plea; reluctantly, but having no other choice, Adams resigned and turned the reins over to Gould and his New York associates.

Whipped by the superior forces of Wall Street, Adams withdrew to the womb of Boston, bitter and disillusioned with the world of big business that had been born in his home city. In his younger days, Adams had snickered at what he saw as the

dusty, backward-looking pretensions of the Massachusetts Historical Society; it was, he said, "a cross of the genealogical tree
with the female prig." Now, he became the society's president, a
keeper of the family flame. He kept up with his western
properties—some of his Kansas City land was sold in 1905 as
the site of the giant Union Station—and numerous other investments, but wanted no more active part of the corporate
enterprise that had come to hallmark American business.

In 1869, still on the threshold of his railroad career, Adams
had told the American Social Science Association that its field's
most important lesson must be that "the accumulation of wealth
is not the loftiest end of human effort." It was a lesson that he
himself was a long time learning, and shortly before he died in
1915, he wrote that his own experience had convinced him that
what he termed "money-getting" springs from "a rather low
instinct." As for those he had rubbed shoulders with in his own
years of money-getting, said Adams, "I have known, and
known tolerably well, a good many 'successful' men—'big'
financially—men famous during the last half-century; and a
less interesting crowd I do not care to encounter. Not one that I
have ever known would I care to meet again, either in this
world or the next. . . ."

THREE. "AN ANXIOUS MOB
OF RESPECTABLE CAPITALISTS"

When he became president of the Union Pacific in 1884,
Charles Francis Adams quickly found that his obligations as
chief executive of a major corporation required a house in
town, a place to entertain. It just wouldn't do to drag visiting
railroad men and investors out to the ancestral town of Quincy
where Adams had previously built a new house on President's
Hill. Beacon Hill was one possibility—Adams had grown up
there, in a Mount Vernon Street house given to his mother by
her father, Peter Chardon Brooks. But he chose instead a
newer part of Boston, the Back Bay. Toward the end of 1884,
he moved to a rented house on Fairfield Street, where he lived

while building a huge, three-story brick house at the corner of Gloucester Street and Commonwealth Avenue, not far from his friend Henry Lee Higginson's home at 191 Commonwealth Avenue.

When Adams and Higginson were boys, the Back Bay had been a six-hundred-acre expanse of tidal flats, enclosed by the Mill Dam built in 1821 with the encouragement of Thomas Handasyd Perkins and other leading merchants of the day. Through a cut in the dam, water from the tidal Charles River rushed in and out each day, powering a gristmill and roiling the garbage and sewage deposited freely on the barren flats. By the 1850s, it was plain that Boston's growing population demanded a better use for the Back Bay, which the board of health had already described as a "nuisance, offensive and injurious to the large and increasing population" living nearby.

Boston was indeed feeling the pressures of rapid expansion, much of it through immigration. The 1840 population of some 93,000 had grown by 1850 to nearly 137,000; in the single year of 1847 better than 37,000 immigrants had stepped ashore at the Boston wharves. By 1875, Boston's population would hit the 342,000 mark, nearly six times the number of just a half century before. In his boyhood, Henry Lee Higginson recalled later, "there were only enough foreigners to exercise benevolence on, not to intrude." By the time Higginson was ready to set up a home of his own, the newcomers had made heavy intrusions into the old residential areas of the city, driving the well-to-do merchants, manufacturers, and financiers to new parts of town. The growing demands of Boston's thriving commerce had also encroached on older residential areas. Charles Bulfinch's graceful Tontine Crescent, along with many surrounding blocks of homes, had come down in the 1850s to make room for stone stores and warehouses. And as business buildings moved into other areas as well, Pemberton Square, once home to the likes of Amos Adams Lawrence and Nathaniel Goddard, was leveled in the 1880s to accommodate a new courthouse. As they had in the early part of the century when Beacon Hill began coming into its own, Boston's wealthy were looking for new places to live.

For a time, it seemed that the new South End, land filled out along the narrow neck that had been the old Shawmut peninsula's sole natural link with the interior, might fill the bill. Beginning in the 1840s, a number of large houses were raised in this section, and for decades afterwards real estate developers built graceful town houses, many of them reminiscent of earlier Beacon Hill mansions, in the area. For a variety of reasons—it was a bit far from the State Street financial district, not to mention its separation from Beacon Hill—the South End never caught on among the really wealthy men of Boston, and by the time Charles Francis Adams was ready to build his in-town house, the Back Bay had taken over as the favored spot for Boston's moneyed elite who couldn't find places or chose not to live on Beacon Hill. The South End, meanwhile, had drifted into a region of rooming houses.

The filling of the Back Bay lands got under way in 1858 after much wrangling among the state, the city, and private property owners. (There had also been those who objected to the project on grounds that it would deprive citizens of salubrious whiffs of salt air at high tide, but such claims had been easily belied by the unmistakable odor of sewage seeping from the flats.) With gravel and earth brought from Needham by train—there were no more hills left in Boston to provide fill—large sections of new land were soon created, and by the early 1860s brownstone houses were rising on freshly laid out streets which, in contrast to the crooked, narrow ways of the old city, were wide and arrow-straight. It was not long before the Back Bay was peppered with the homes of Boston's commercial and financial leaders, and the region quickly came to rival Beacon Hill as a fashionable and proper place to live. The profits of trade and textile manufacturing had made Beacon Hill; profits from railroads, copper mines, and other domestic investments had helped make the Back Bay.

Charles Francis Adams, for one, did more than merely move to the newly made region. With his brother John Quincy Adams, II, who had also moved to the Back Bay, he organized the Riverbank Improvement Company in the 1880s to fill and create even more acreage on the western reaches of the Back

Bay. Adams may have had most of his real estate ventures in the West, but he didn't neglect his own backyard, either. The Adams brothers' Bay State Road was soon the site of numerous palatial houses, but its greater distance from the center of town kept it from ever competing with the Back Bay as a desirable place to live. Today, it is flanked primarily by Boston University.

The business district was also undergoing change in the post–Civil War years—though not by design. The city had seen many devastating fires during its long history, but nothing that could match the disastrous blaze of November 9, 1872, which in less than twelve hours ravaged about sixty acres, destroying $75 million in property.

Henry Lee Higginson, living at the time in a Back Bay hotel, was entertaining his father-in-law, Professor Louis Agassiz, at dinner on that Saturday night. At about eight o'clock, some forty-five minutes after the fire had broken out in a basement furnace room, Higginson spotted a great glow on the eastern horizon, beyond the Common. He rushed immediately to the State Street offices of Lee, Higginson & Company, and did not return home until the next afternoon. "I had had nothing to eat or drink in all that time," he said later, "but was in duty bound to look after the Union Safety Deposit Vaults."

These vaults, though not an official part of Lee, Higginson, were located beneath the firm's property on State Street, and were the principal repository of stocks and bonds held by Boston investors. They had been built four years before by Higginson's uncle, Henry C. Lee, who tested the strength of their protective roof by letting a heavy safe fall on it from a height of four or five floors. The roof had withstood this trial, but fire was something else again. When Higginson arrived on the scene, hordes of investors were clamoring to get in and rescue their securities from the rapidly advancing flames. With the help of his father, who in the meantime managed to hustle Lee, Higginson's record books to the safety of his house, Henry managed to keep the crowd at bay. Later, his cousin Thomas Wentworth Higginson—who had had problems of his own with a mob during the attempt to free a fugitive slave from the Court House—suggested that the elder Higginson should have his portrait painted, outlined against the glowing fire, his back to the wall of the vaults, holding off the "anxious mob of respectable capitalists."

As it happened, the fire did not reach the Lee, Higginson offices or the safe-deposit vaults below, and another fitting subject for a painting might have been Henry Higginson's daring stunt to help contain the fire. To make a gap in the ranks of buildings in the path of the flames and prevent further spreading, it had been proposed to blow up a number of buildings, and powder from the harbor forts had been sent to the end of Long Wharf. There was no one willing or able to bring the explosives to the scene of the fire, Higginson recalled, so "I found a covered wagon open at the sides, got it to the end of Long Wharf, and loaded some thirty kegs of powder on it and drove up State Street, which was full of engines pumping, and sparks were flying in every direction."

Blowing up buildings turned out to be of scant use in fighting the fire, and though operations were considerably hindered by the effects of an epizootic ailment that had felled most of the horses used for pulling fire apparatus, the flames were eventually quenched. But not before they had leveled many of the residential and commercial landmarks of earlier days. Out of the ashes a new Boston was to rise, a Boston whose spirit was flickering but not yet burned out.

FOUR. "ONE OF THE WONDERFUL COMPANIES OF THE WORLD"

Charles Francis Adams had moved to the Back Bay primarily to have a convenient spot to entertain business associates. This scion of America's most distinguished family cared little about a fashionable address, and cared even less about the first-family social whirl of Beacon Hill and the Back Bay. Indeed, Adams despised Boston's "society" life, found it provincial and pretentious; not long after his Union Pacific debacle, in fact, he bought a place in the exurban town of Lincoln and sold his Back Bay mansion. With two presidents in his family tree, with considerable achievements of his own behind him, Adams did not need proximity to others in the so-called Brahmin class to ratify his position in the world. He could well afford to say, as he did toward the end of his life, that "I have tried Boston socially on all sides: I have summered it and wintered it, tried it drunk and tried it sober; and, drunk or sober, there's nothing in it—save Boston!"

For somewhat different reasons, Adams's friend John Murray Forbes shared similar misgivings about Boston society. Perhaps remembering how the sons of James and Thomas Handasyd Perkins had been corrupted by the life of ease and sure social position made possible by their fathers' enterprise, Forbes took care that his own children should be relatively untouched by the temptations of unearned riches. Even at the height of his involvement in the western railroads, he declined to live in the city, preferring to remain in the more bucolic precincts of suburban Milton and instructing potential guardians of his children that he wanted the young Forbeses to continue living there in the event of his death. Not only would it be healthier for them, he said, but "with their rich circle of acquaintance in Boston, and with their probable wealth, they would, if in the city, be liable to get injurious ideas of their own consequence. . . ."

William Hathaway Forbes, for one, never suffered from inflated notions of his own worth. Always in the shadow of his successful and autocratic father, seldom allowed to make major business decisions on his own, William Forbes was plagued with doubts about his abilities, frequently fearing that he might not live up to the example of his father. Years later, in fact, his friend and frequent business associate Henry Lee Higginson would say of the younger Forbes that he "thought very little of himself." The cavalry officer who had stood in his stirrups and defied John Singleton Mosby's whooping rangers with a flashing saber had come home to find it hard to stand up to his own father.

Alexander Graham Bell, inventor of the telephone, had a

higher opinion of William Forbes than Forbes had of himself. Writing to his wife from Forbes's Milton home in January, 1879, Bell said that "I have come here tonight as the guest of Mr. Forbes, one of the new Directors, a wealthy man of great influence and who has a reputation for thorough integrity." Comparing him with other officials of the newly formed National Bell Telephone Company, Bell added that "the only man who impresses me as possessing marked ability is this Mr. Forbes." In the months and years to come, Forbes would surely need marked abilities, for he was soon to face off with Jay Gould and William Vanderbilt, those buccaneering bugbears of Boston's capitalists.

Forbes seemed ill-prepared for such combat. In an earlier time, he might have broken into the business world as a super-cargo on distant voyages, then been seasoned in Canton or some other Asiatic outpost. But when William Forbes came of age, John Murray Forbes had not even offered his son a chance to prove his mettle with one of the Forbes-backed railroads in the American West. After his expulsion from Harvard—and his father's stern warnings of early failure—Forbes had clerked for a time at the Boston office of the Chicago, Burlington & Quincy before serving with honor and valor in the Civil War. Back home, he married a daughter of Ralph Waldo Emerson and settled in as a junior partner at J. M. Forbes & Company, where his father kept a close eye on him as he handled correspondence with agents in China and evaluated domestic securities for possible addition to the firm's own portfolio and for trust accounts of relatives and friends. Quite early, he showed a strong conservative streak, and when a cousin asked about buying some Calumet & Hecla shares for one of these trusts, Forbes balked, explaining that "I know it is likely that the purchase of Calumet & Hecla stock at present prices may be a good business operation, but if I should buy into it and it should go wrong I should be directly responsible, because no one can claim that copper stocks are safe and judicious investments for trustees."

Forbes did a bit better by his father-in-law, and when he saw that the sage of Concord was getting only niggardly returns on valuable downtown Boston property inherited by his wife, he investigated and found that the Emersons had for years been cheated out of their fair share by a smooth-talking agent. Eventually, Forbes talked an unbelieving Mrs. Emerson into selling the property, and invested the proceeds in railroad stocks—but not in Calumet & Hecla—that paid twenty times the income doled out by the dishonest agent, who was later sentenced to ten years in prison for his malefactions. Forbes also discovered that Emerson's publisher had been holding back on the author's royalty payments, and from then on acted as his father-in-law's literary agent.

With his own money, Forbes could be more venturesome than with funds entrusted to him by others. Unfortunately, when he strayed from fields familiar to the family firm, his investments were not always wise ones. In the early 1870s, for example, he followed in the unsure footsteps of Henry Lee Higginson, and with six associates organized the Florida Plantation Fund to raise cotton. It was Higginson's ill-fated Cottonham in spades; the crop failed for three years running, and the partners finally bailed out with considerable losses.

Even when Forbes was onto something promising, his father—who kept the firm's healthy railroad investments to himself and turned what he called the invalids over to his son—sometimes squelched him. Not long after the Florida cotton venture, Forbes wanted to move the firm into some promising railroads in Florida and Georgia. His cousin Charles E. Perkins, then manager of the Chicago, Burlington & Quincy, was also enthusiastic about the lines, which Forbes said would give them "a hold on the whole Florida trade. . . ." Like his father in an earlier day, William Forbes was looking for an outlet for his constructive drives.

He was not to find it in the industry pioneered by John Murray Forbes. In the spring of 1877, he wrote to Perkins of the southern railway scheme that "Father is blue on account of the general rather depressed look of things . . . and doesn't want to. So he is at the moment down on new projects. The fact is," Forbes added petulantly, "that if we could put many of the old invalids on the footing of cost of this Florida project, they would be good paying investments today." As he had so many times before, Forbes had deferred to his father's judgment and gone back to tending the machinery of wealth set in motion by others. But he would soon break away and become a pioneer in his own right, if not with his father's complete blessing, then at least without his interference.

In 1868, a teacher of elocution and linguistics from Edinburgh, Scotland, had visited Boston to deliver a series of Lowell Institute lectures. Two years later, with two of his sons dead from tuberculosis and the third showing early signs of the disease, Alexander Melville Bell moved with his family from Scotland to the healthier climate of Brantford, Ontario. By 1872, his twenty-five-year-old surviving son, Alexander Graham Bell, had set himself up in Boston to teach speech at a school for the deaf.

The young Bell was something of a tinkerer, too, and it wasn't long before one of his ideas had attracted the attention of Gardiner Greene Hubbard and Thomas Sanders, the fathers of two of his students. In 1874, as William Forbes was analyzing railroad securities and watching his Florida cotton venture trickle down the drain, Hubbard and Sanders were staking Bell to his experiments in sending multiple telegraph messages over a single wire at the same time, informally agreeing to a three-way split of any profits that might come from the invention.

Bell's interest in phonetics soon gave him the notion that speech as well as telegraphic dots and dashes could be carried by wire, and though Sanders and Hubbard considered this a somewhat visionary scheme, they continued to fund Bell's research. With the help of mechanic Thomas A. Watson, Bell made rapid progress, and on March 7, 1876, he was granted a patent for the basic telephonic process. Three days later he placed his epoch-making phone call to Watson in the next room of his Boston laboratory. That same summer, Bell demonstrated the telephone at the Centennial Exposition in Philadelphia; the British physicist Sir William Thompson declared that it was the most amazing thing he had seen on his visit to America.

The three partners knew that they had a tiger by the tail, but they weren't quite certain what to do with it. Their first impulse was to sell their rights to the telephone for what they considered the princely sum of $100,000, but when they made the offer to the Vanderbilt-controlled Western Union they were turned down. Bell, on a wedding trip to England in the summer of 1877—he had married a former speech student, the deaf daughter of backer Gardiner Hubbard—had tried to line up British capital, but found no takers. In early 1878 Hubbard and Sanders organized the New England Telephone Company to lay out and run a system in New England, and several months later they formed the Bell Telephone Company to handle rights in the rest of the country. At about the same time, Hubbard hired Theodore N. Vail, the talented superintendent of the federal Railway Mail Service, as Bell Telephone's general manager.

Western Union, meanwhile, after spurning the chance to buy Bell's patents, was still bidding for a chunk of the telephone business. Through its subsidiary, American Speaking Telephone Company, Western Union had acquired other telephone patents—including one granted to Thomas A. Edison—and was not only seeking to set up a competitive telephone system, but had also challenged Bell's claim to be the inventor of the telephone. Lacking sufficient capital, the Bell Telephone Company seemed doomed to play the role of paper tiger, crushed by a stronger competitor.

By the end of 1878 the desperate search for funds had led to William Forbes, who quickly saw the company's potential. He must have seen, too, his chance—perhaps his last and only chance—to break away from a domineering father and strike out on his own on what promised to be a great national enterprise, something that might in time rival his father's achievements as a railroad builder. John Murray Forbes declined to put any of his own money into the venture, but gave William free rein. If the company prospered, he felt, his son would gain the glory and the profit; if it failed, William would bear both the blame and the loss.

Forbes acted quickly, first to consolidate control of the company, then to fend off the threatened competition. In early 1879, with the help of Boston friends who had also invested in the company, a new National Bell Telephone Company was formed, with Forbes as president. With control of the companies consolidated, Forbes now moved single-mindedly against the corporate marauders from New York. Earlier, in a letter to Ralph Waldo Emerson, Forbes had referred to the Emersons' deceiving agent as "the enemy"—now, his enemy was far bigger game indeed.

While the Vanderbilts' Western Union was gunning for the Bell company's business, suing for patent infringement and setting up rival systems, the equally rapacious Jay Gould was stalking the Vanderbilts. Trying to knock William Vanderbilt out of his catbird seat at Western Union, Gould set up the American Union Telegraph Company soon after Forbes was named head of National Bell. At the same time, Gould began buying up local Bell system companies as a foil to Western Union's telephonic ambitions. No matter who won out in this contest of giants, the smaller National Bell stood to be a loser.

To counter the pressures from Western Union, Forbes beefed up management in cities where the Vanderbilt interests had set up rival exchanges. He also encouraged National Bell's counsel, James Jackson Storrow, Sr., to vigorously defend the company in pending patent suits and to rebut any claims that the Bell equipment was inferior. "It looks now as if the big gun in reserve which the enemy is supposed to have is the testimony of their experts that instruments made after Bell's patent of them will not work," Forbes wrote to one of his directors, adding by way of reassurance that "As made by our people exactly by specification they talk perfectly well."

Luckily for Forbes, Vanderbilt soon caved in to Gould's attacks, and it turned out that Gould had been acquiring pieces of the Bell system merely to use as a club against Vanderbilt rather than because of any real interest in the telephone business. Fearing that Bell telephones might start horning in on his telegraph interests, Vanderbilt, in November, 1879, agreed to sell all his telephone properties to National Bell in exchange for a 20 percent share of Bell's future licensing fees and an agreement that Bell would stay out of the telegraph business. With Western Union out of the telephone picture, and with all Bell licensees barred from handling telegrams, Jay Gould's interest in buying up National Bell evaporated, and he went after Vanderbilt through the more direct telegraph route. Little more than two years later, Gould had displaced Vanderbilt at Western Union.

With Vanderbilt and Gould off his back, Forbes and his Boston associates had the nation's telephone industry virtually to themselves. They had established primacy of the Bell patents, which were not to expire until 1893 and 1894, and had more than a decade to entrench their company in an impregnable position. "With a thorough occupation of the principal cities and towns by our licensees, [and] the ownership of the broad patents covering the use of the speaking telephone," Forbes wrote in a report to stockholders in early 1880, "the danger of competition with our business from newcomers seems small." At about the same time, Forbes applied for and received a state charter for the more generously capitalized American Bell Telephone Company to proceed with National Bell's mission. In urging quick action on the application, Forbes wrote to the governor that "We believe it is for the interests of the state to keep such corporations here, and hope that some little pride will be taken in keeping the headquarters in this state of a business growing out of a Massachusetts invention."

The American Bell Telephone Company now had an effective monopoly of its field, and was a thoroughly Boston concern. Officers, directors, and their relatives, nearly all of them from Boston, owned more than 50 percent of the some 73,000 shares outstanding. Forbes alone held 4,961 shares; his brother Malcolm owned 3,325. Lee, Higginson & Company had 3,367 shares, while partner Henry Lee Higginson held 3,510 shares in his own name. Considerable blocks were also owned by Forbes's friends and fellow company officials Alexander Cochrane, George L. Bradley, and Charles P. Bowditch. Later, reminiscing about past failures and triumphs, Higginson would remember these pioneers as "Some idiots" who "risked our money on the Telephone in a dream. . . ."

Forbes was acutely aware of his company's monopoly situation and sometimes had chilling fears that this exclusive position might work against the Bell system. Writing in 1884 to attorney James Storrow about some "night cogitations" regarding one of the incessant patent suits that plagued the company in its early days, Forbes noted that "Perhaps our most serious danger is in the possibility that the Judge may look upon us, as so many do, as a monopoly really hostile to the true interests of the public, using our rights to make excessive charges. . . ." Indeed, though Forbes and his fellow investors made much of the public service aspects of the telephone, and of the social and communications revolutions that would be ushered in by its widespread use, they actually seemed more interested in large and steady dividends than in rapid expansion and improvement of telephone service. Forbes, like his general manager, Theodore Vail, foresaw the nationwide communications network that would grow out of Bell's invention, but cautious trustee that he was at heart, he opted for high rates and the certainty of current profit over the lure of spending and building for the distant future. For the Boston investors, it was a richly rewarding policy, and during the years of absolute monopoly the company paid out dividends that ran as high as $18 a share. Between 1880 and 1894 the total payout to stockholders was a hefty $25 million, and over the same period the price of stock jumped from about $75 to more than $200. The telephone was not yet another Calumet & Hecla, but it would do till something better came along.

Unfortunately, much of the profits doled out in dividends would probably have been put to better use expanding and refining the growing telephone system, whose most visible sign was the network of overhead wires lacing through the streets of every city and town served by telephone. Partly because of technical difficulties, but largely because of the expense involved, Forbes resisted mounting pressures to put these unsightly bundles of wire underground, and it would be years before the Bell system would live down its reputation as an uglifier of the urban landscape.

High rates—$150 per 1,000 connections during the 1880s—

permitted high dividends, but the stiff tolls also inhibited rapid growth of service and left Bell wide open to competition when its exclusive franchise ran out in 1894. By the end of the century, this competition would set in motion a train of events that would see control of the Bell system wrested from its original Boston backers and put in the hands of Wall Street. Forbes, meanwhile, had been forced into a move that made such a power play almost inevitable. In 1885, seeing that long-distance as well as local service would have to be provided by any communications system worthy of the name, he sought to raise funds to finance intercity connections. With a sizable slice of profits earmarked for dividends, internal financing was out, so Forbes chose to issue new stock. But the Massachusetts legislature, perhaps troubled by visions of more wires snaking through the air from pole to pole, turned down the company's request to issue additional shares. The directors then proceeded to organize, in the more expansive atmosphere of New York, a subsidiary company to develop long-distance telephone lines. Theodore Vail, general manager of the parent American Bell, was named president of the New York operation, which was called the American Telephone & Telegraph Company— A.T.&T., for short.

Forbes, worn down by the pressures of his position, resigned the presidency of American Bell in 1887, and was replaced by the proper Boston banker Howard Stockton, who had married a granddaughter of textile magnate Amos Lawrence. The able and ambitious Vail, miffed at being passed over for the job as president of the senior corporation, quit his post at A.T.&T. But the Bell system had not heard the last of its old general manager; in the early years of the new century, Vail was to return to the company as the chosen instrument of the New York financiers who took it away from the old Bostonians.

If Vail had felt bridled by some of his Boston associates' conservative financial policies, these policies were generally applauded by the staider Bostonians who had let their yen for dividends supplant the old passion for building. Besides, Forbes had steered the fledgling Bell system through some stormy weather, and it may well be that his steady hand and counsel were just what the company needed in the early stages of its development. When Forbes came on the scene, the Bell company seemed set to be drawn into the maw of a much larger and more powerful competitor; when he left, the company was firmly positioned as the leader presumptive in the telephone field. Years later, Henry Lee Higginson would write to William Forbes's son Cameron that "Your father 'set agoin' one of the wonderful companies of the world; and he gave it a tone that it has never lost."

John Murray Forbes, the old China trader and railroad builder, was pleased—and perhaps a little bit surprised, too—by his son's performance as head of the telephone company. It all showed that William had real ability, the elder Forbes said, and that he "was not spoiled by his too easy surroundings."

FIVE. "DISTINGUISHED AND SUBSTANTIAL BACKING"

The telephone company was not alone among the great enterprises grounded in the Boston of the nineteenth century's closing decades. And at least one of the ventures was born of the same maritime spirit that had fired the city's earliest traders.

Captain Lorenzo D. Baker, a Cape Codder whose mother had had the unlikely maiden name of Thankful Rich, was always on the lookout for promising cargoes. Returning in 1870 from Venezuela, where he'd taken a party of gold miners up the Orinoco River, he stopped off in Jamaica and took on a load of return goods that included about 160 bunches of bananas. The exotic yellow fruit was a definite luxury item at the time, and Baker was more than a little impressed when he put in at Jersey City and sold the bananas—which had cost him about fourteen cents a bunch—at a comfortable profit of two dollars per bunch. Back in Boston, young Andrew Preston was impressed, too, when Baker told him of the sale, and for the next few years Baker brought bananas as spare cargo from Jamaica and turned them over to Preston to sell on commission. The future looked good for the banana trade, and by 1877 Baker—now involved with the Standard Steam Navigation Company—moved to Jamaica to handle tropical affairs and assure a steady stream of bananas to Boston. In 1885, Baker, Preston, and a group of nine minor merchants and capitalists set up their own selling agency, calling it the Boston Fruit Company. Their capital was a minuscule $15,000, and they cautiously agreed that the company would not be expected to pay dividends for five years.

Boston Fruit was lucky. It had no monopoly on the banana trade, but while other firms were plagued with crop failures and rotted cargoes, the sun seemed always to shine on the company's plantations, and its shipments arrived on the market in succulent good order. In just five years the puny $15,000 nest egg had swelled to $531,000, and Boston Fruit had begun to expand its operations into other cities. It was well known as one of the top new enterprises in Boston, but it was still venturing into a field fraught with risk and danger. One bad crop or one delayed shipment could spoil the most careful plans, and chancing money on tropical fruits held little appeal for Boston's old-rich capitalists. Years later, Henry Lee Higginson would regret that he and his Brahmin colleagues had not cashed in on the banana bonanza earlier.

Meanwhile, Brooklyn-born Minor Keith was also getting big in bananas, primarily to supply freight for the railroads he was building in Central America. He didn't really compete with Boston Fruit—his main port of entry was New Orleans, far from the Boston company's outlets in the Northeast—and when his operations fell on hard times from fire, flood, and other disasters, some sort of combination seemed in order. It came in 1899 with merger of the Keith interests and Boston Fruit, to form the United Fruit Company. Bananas were a solid, respectable investment by now, and one of the men instrumental in the merger was Thomas Jefferson Coolidge, Jr., who, with his father's backing, had established the old-school Old Colony Trust Company in 1890. It was the beginning of a sometimes difficult marriage between staid Boston capital and exotic tropical enterprise, a marriage that would, in another generation,

be threatened almost to breaking by a tough-talking Bessarabian immigrant from New Orleans.

Yet another merger took place in Boston in 1899, one between rival companies in the shoe machinery business. Lynn, to
the north of Boston, had been a shoemaking center since early
colonial times, when the first handcraftsmen set up shop there
in so-called ten-footers—tiny shops, often with living quarters
overhead. Until the Civil War, shoemaking had remained a
laborious hand operation, but the vast amount of footwear required by the Union army had spurred the use of machinery to
stitch soles to uppers. Not until the late 1880s, however, did a
real mechanical breakthrough come. Jan Matzeliger, a black
native of Dutch Guiana working at a Lynn shoe plant, accom-
plished what most shoe men had insisted couldn't be done: he
invented a machine to perform the lasting operation, the pulling and stretching of leather to the shape of the foot. The
Consolidated Hand Lasting Machine Company was formed to
exploit the invention, which, working in tandem with stitching
equipment, quickly turned shoemaking into a big business. At
the same time, shoe machinery became a big business, too, and
within a decade it occurred to the major machinery builders
that instead of fighting over slices of the market, they should get
together and feast on the whole pie. The resulting combination,
put together largely by future Supreme Court Justice Louis W.
Brandeis, was called the United Shoe Machinery Corporation.

A salient feature of the company—borrowed from one of the
component companies—was a strict policy that none of its machinery would be sold outright. Instead, United Shoe leased
equipment to shoe manufacturers and collected a royalty on
every pair of shoes that went through its machines. In time, this
restrictive practice would bring the company considerable and
lengthy legal grief at the hands of federal trustbusters; while it
lasted, though, the lease-only practice, coupled with United
Shoe's control of patents, would give the company a royalty on
nearly all the shoes manufactured in the United States, plus a
good share of the overseas market. And it would enable the
company to thrive even as the shoe industry, lured by lower
taxes and a more congenial labor climate, abandoned the Boston area for other parts of the country.

Both United Fruit and United Shoe were based on established patterns of enterprise or existing industries. But another Boston-backed venture was rooted, like the telephone, in a new and unproved field—though its prime mover came from the shoe industry.

Maine-born Charles A. Coffin was one of several shoe manufacturers in Lynn, Massachusetts, approached in 1882 about joining a syndicate set up to buy the Connecticut-based American Electric Company. Formed just two years before by Professors Edwin J. Houston and Elihu Thomson, the company was in sore need of funds to carry on its business of manufacturing dynamos, and the two inventive professors were happy to be rescued by an infusion of cash from Massachusetts. They were more interested, anyway, in puttering around their laboratories than in making a commercial success of their equipment. With Coffin in charge, the company was reorganized, renamed the Thomson-Houston Electric Company, and moved to Lynn in 1883.

The use of electricity was just catching on at the time, and there was some disagreement over which course the industry should take—whether it should sell generating plants to individual companies and householders, or whether it should build central generating facilities to produce electricity for distant customers. Coffin wisely opted for the central-station route, and the business grew rapidly, so rapidly, in fact, that Thomson-Houston found itself in need of more funds than it could come up with on its own. Coffin turned naturally enough to Boston for help and was able to sell his company's stock to such influential investors as Henry Lee Higginson, Thomas Jefferson Coolidge, and George P. Gardner.

Meanwhile, on the banks of the Mohawk River at Schenectady, New York, the Edison General Electric Company was prospering, too, and officials of both Edison and Thomson-Houston were beginning to see the value of a merger that would put an end to patent fights and form a giant in the field. The union came in 1892, when the two companies combined to form the General Electric Company, with Coffin as president and guiding light. Among the Boston directors were Higginson, Coolidge, and F. Lothrup Ames; the New York board members included the omnipresent J. P. Morgan. Years later, General Electric Chairman Owen D. Young would say of his company's first directorate that it was a reflection of "distinguished and substantial backing." Indeed, in terms of financial power, it was probably the strongest assemblage of men yet gathered together in behalf of an industrial corporation. The balance of this power, however, was tipped decidedly toward New York, and the Bostonians who sat on the board were there not as builders or promoters but as investors and fiduciaries, keeping watchful eyes on the portfolios placed in their care.

In August, 1898, as he had done for decades, John Murray Forbes attended the directors meeting of the Chicago, Burlington & Quincy Railroad. He was eighty-five now, and feeble, his mind frequently wandering back to wooden sailing ships and the distant days of the China trade. The friends of his youth and prime manhood were mostly dead. His brother, Black Ben, called Commodore in his old age, had been buried out of King's Chapel nearly nine years before, his coffin topped with a sheaf of ripe wheat on a wreath of ivy. Even William, his son, weakened by tuberculosis, had died the previous October, and the flags on the family island of Naushon had flown at half-mast in mourning.

It was a real effort for Forbes to drag himself to the directors' meeting, to sit and hear younger men making plans for days he knew he wouldn't see. Indeed, as his faculties had failed, Forbes didn't even want to read newspapers; he didn't want to know about current events. He couldn't help hearing about the quickly fought Spanish-American War, though, of the sinking of the *Maine* and of Dewey at Manila Bay. And through the fog of age the old China trader saw trouble ahead with the islands—Puerto Rico and Guam, the Philippines—signed over to the United States by Spain. "I would give Spain the amount of our war debt five times over," Forbes said, "to take those islands back again."

John Murray Forbes died at his Milton home on October 12, 1898, a year and a day after the death of his son. Alexander Agassiz and Henry Lee Higginson were among the few nonfamily members who attended the private and simple Unitarian service two days later; the casket was banked with many flowers as the assembled mourners joined to sing the "Battle Hymn of the Republic." Years before, his good friend Ralph Waldo Emerson had composed a fitting epitaph for Forbes when he wrote, "How little this man suspects, with his sympathy for men and his respect for lettered and scientific people, that he is not likely, in any company, to meet a man superior to himself. And I think this is a good country that can bear such a creature as he is."

Boston would not see his like again.

Chapter Eight

DECLINE AND
DISINTEGRATION

It was as if the argosies of Venice had been realized and the proceeds
placed with Shylock at four per cent.
                                        —Frederic J. Stimson, 1931

In 1900, stock in the Calumet & Hecla copper mines of Michigan was selling at a high of $840; the previous year, each of the 100,000 shares—most still owned by Bostonians—paid $100 in dividends. It was a heady record for a stock that just thirty years before had sold for as little as $60 per share, and it was continuing testimony to the enterprise and vision of nineteenth-century Boston. But with the coming of the new century, this enterprise was blunted, the vision dimmed. At Calumet & Hecla and other Michigan properties, mining had become a more costly deep-hole operation to reach less valuable ore, and copper men with big ideas for the long-term future were now looking to the richer lodes of the West and Southwest. In the early days of Calumet & Hecla, Alexander Agassiz had planned for the future by buying equipment much larger than required by the mine's production at the time; now, he was content with current income, and showed little interest in making plans for the coming decades. Approached in 1894 by officials of the Anaconda Company with a joint venture proposal for a promising western property, Agassiz declined, replying that "Mr. Shaw was getting old and hard to move to anything new and that I was always away and could not run anything new." The brothers-in-law who had so energetically exploited Michigan's greatest copper lode for the enrichment of their Boston friends and kin had now grown tired. "We have ground enough for this generation and one or two more," a Calumet & Hecla official wrote in 1892 to an English correspondent, "and we therefore are not looking for further fields for our energies."

By the 1920s Calumet & Hecla was known scornfully in copper-mining circles as "the white-haired Grand Uncle from Michigan ... jealously guarding the last of his treasure...." The same might have been said for all of Boston, for more than mortal remains had been entombed with John Murray Forbes on that bright fall day in the old century's penultimate year. Something of the old spirit was buried with him, too, something of the confident energy that had spurred his charmed generation across the seas in search of fortune, that had raised the textile cities of Lowell and Lawrence, that had pushed iron rails over unsettled plains and through the Rocky Mountains.

In the 1880s and 1890s, Bostonians had owned and run the Bell Telephone Company, had been financial powers behind General Electric, had controlled thousands of miles of western railroads; the counsels of State Street, Beacon Hill, and the Back Bay were sought and valued throughout the nation, and Boston still warmed the seat of enterprise occupied ever since its daring merchants had put out in frail ships to bring home to America the riches of the world. Before two generations had passed, in 1928, Elmer Davis stood on the banks of the Charles River, looked up at the vista of Beacon Hill, and wrote that "It is flawless, complete, finished, static, dead; it lies before you in an autumnal sunset splendor, like Rome under the Ostrogoths." Just five years later, *Fortune* magazine, that great celebrator of the industrial capitalism that got its start in Boston more than a century before, would observe that "there can be no doubt but that the Bostonian has suffered a decay and disintegration of tragic proportions ... the Bostonian of today has withdrawn from productive enterprise. He has lost the active management of his industries." The Boston of the Faneuils and the Hancocks, of Thomas Handasyd Perkins and Francis Cabot Lowell, of Amos and Abbott Lawrence and John and Bennet Forbes, had become a listless shadow, a pale reflection of former days. Boston's Back Bay and Beacon Hill mansions, and the great houses of Brookline and Milton, were redolent now of wealth but not of enterprise.

TWO. "DEALING IN REAL ESTATE IN KANZAS CITY"

The coming of this decline had been augured even in Boston's great days of commercial and industrial supremacy. In 1846, at the same time the Lowell and Lawrence mills seemed unshakable in their power, at the same time that John Murray Forbes was taking his first plunge into the railroads of the West and hailing Boston as the nation's foremost source of capital, a gossipy catalogue of the city's rich appeared in Boston bookshops. Titled *Our First Men*, the book noted that the "best society" comprises wealthy men who, if they did not inherit their money, had some social standing before they made it, or at least are able to behave like gentlemen. The authors further observed that "As a general rule ... wealth does not long remain in the same families, but frequently in the second, very frequently in the third, and almost always by the fourth generation, vanishes and disappears—a process which the equal distribution of property among all the children greatly facilitates." By the logic of *Our First Men*, the scions of Boston's early nineteenth-century moneyed aristocracy had seemed fated to fade away, their place in "best society" filled by freshly rich newcomers of gentlemanly bearing.

Fortunately for coming generations of Boston's merchant and manufacturing families, this somewhat facile logic was considerably less than relentless, and the same *Fortune* article of 1933 which so pityingly described the industrial impotence of the Bostonian noted at the same time that "No great Boston family of the first rank has lost either means or position." And this at a time when the brutal stock market crash of just four years before had wiped out many fortunes, both large and small.

What the authors of *Our First Men* had not reckoned with was the Boston Brahmin's ingenuity at preserving and protecting his wealth for his progeny and the ability of upper-class Bostonians to become an effectively closed society from which outsiders and newcomers were barred. This husbanding of wealth, combined with the hardening of Boston's social arteries in the mid-nineteenth century, assured the hereditary Brahmin's position in Boston; it could not, however, preserve Boston's position as a center of national economic and entrepreneurial enterprise.

In another city, an upper class based on past achievement and inherited means might have been only a minor curiosity, a fossilized survival of olden times having little to do with the present and nothing with the future. The swashbuckling New York robber barons were scarcely inhibited by the presence in their midst of a social aristocracy; almost by definition, the newer cities of the West were havens for new men unfettered by the usages of the past. But Boston was different. With an older and larger store of common traditions behind them, Boston's Brahmins had been granted generations to construct a code of "proper" social behavior; having made their money earlier than the rich of other cities, the Bostonians had had ample time to build a wall of fashionable churches, clubs, and other institutions as a barrier against invaders. And the city's long period of stable and homogeneous population had enabled the Brahmins to stamp Boston with a tone that would linger on even in the face of pounding waves of Irish immigrants and eventual Irish political domination.

If Boston's prickly social barriers repelled ambitious outsiders in favor of more open and hospitable cities, the comforts of Boston society also dampened the commercial and industrial ambitions of succeeding generations of insiders. The city was indeed a pleasant place for its wealthy upper class, whose younger members seldom felt a compelling need to seek new fortunes in fresh fields. Even Peter Faneuil and John Hancock, richly topping the Boston society of their days, had lacked the merchant drives of their benefactor uncles; the sons of neither James nor Thomas Handasyd Perkins had been merchant successes. Thomas Gold Appleton, son of the Nathan Appleton who had come to Boston from a New Hampsire farm at the age of fifteen and grown to be a towering figure in the textile industry, lived out his own life as a peripatetic gentleman aesthete, supported by his father's fortune.

It was a tempting course for a young Bostonian to take, and it is no wonder that John Murray Forbes had tried to insulate his own children from the long-standing blandishments described by Dr. Oliver Wendell Holmes in 1886: "What better provision can be made for mortal man than such as our own Boston can offer its wealthy children? A palace on Commonwealth Avenue or on Beacon Street; a country-place at Framingham or Lenox; a seaside residence at Nahant, Beverly Farms, Newport, or Bar Harbor; a pew at Trinity or King's Chapel; a tomb at Mount Auburn or Forest Hills; with the prospect of a memorial stained-window after his lamented demise,—is not that a pretty programme to offer a candidate for human existence?"

Indeed it was, but it was not calculated to encourage continuation of the sort of enterprise that had made it all possible in the first place. J. R. Sturgis, recalling that his father's generation had gone such great distances—even to the other side of the earth—to seek out fortunes, lamented that by the 1890s "only a very few [young Bostonians], not driven by necessity, can be induced to leave the delights of Boston to seek, even at a few days' distance of railroad, the better chances of the West...." In newer generations, he feared, "the spirit of manly adventure is yielding to the mere appetite of comfort."

British lecturer James Anthony Froude, on a visit to Boston in 1872, had spotted even more ominous signs. Writing of the men he met there—among other things, he had dinner with the membership of the Massachusetts Historical Society—Froude observed that "Their physical frames seem hung together rather than organically grown.... They are generous with their money, have much tenderness and quiet good feeling; but the old Anglo-Saxon power is running to seed, and I don't think will revive." Froude was surely stretching his point, and according to Professor Charles Eliot Norton, the Britisher's own physiognomy left something to be desired—"His face," wrote Norton, "exhibits the corporeal insincerity of his disposition." But it was a telling observation, marking the steady erosion of the old spirit. And as more and more Bostonians stepped aside from the path of enterprise and opted for Holmes's "pretty programme," other men in other cities were becoming movers and shakers in the economic life of the nation.

Additional influences, too, had sapped Boston's position as a stronghold of creative American enterprise. The city's out-of-the-way location in relation to national markets had put the port of Boston at a disadvantage that was made up for in earlier times only by the competitive energy of its merchant mariners. The Erie Canal sealed Boston off even more from the western hinterland and assured eventual maritime supremacy to New York. When Samuel Cunard chose Boston as his American port of entry in 1839, Bostonians took it as their due, but in the main they stuck to their own wooden sailing ships and allowed Cunard's steamers to pluck the choicest passenger and freight trade. New Yorkers, not bound so tightly to a seafaring past, were more willing to adapt to steam, and by the time the panic of 1857 and the Civil War dealt their heavy blows to foreign trade, Boston had long since been surpassed by the port of New York. By 1868, Cunard had abandoned Boston for the more thriving piers of New York—in Boston, the British steamers had been hard pressed to put together full cargoes for the return voyages to Liverpool. Boston service was restored two years later, but the city's maritime doom had already been sealed.

By itself, the decline of Boston as a center for foreign trade need not have been an unalloyed disaster. The merchant trio of Francis Cabot Lowell, Nathan Appleton, and Patrick Tracy Jackson had made a smooth transition from trade to textiles, and it was Boston's merchant money and management that had done so much to build up the western railroads. Bostonians of the past had found ways to adapt to changing economic conditions and to squeeze advantage out of seeming adversity. But as

Boston dwindled in importance as a seaport, the city's role in other areas diminished as well. With New York's growth as a commercial center, the great Boston textile-selling houses opened branches there, and soon the branches were doing more business than the home offices. As New York became the coastal center of market distribution, it became, too, the city where the financial and commercial action was, the city that beckoned in the dreams of ambitious young men on the make. And while New Yorkers had been carving out this position for themselves, digging canals and making their port the Atlantic terminus of the western railroads, Boston sat back, wrote Charles Francis Adams as early as 1867, "with a lack of perception, a want of foresight, an absence of enterprise, and a superabundance of timidity, in sad contrast with the great promise of an earlier and brighter day." Even Chicago—much of which John Murray Forbes could have bought in the 1840s for $1.25 an acre—came to overshadow Boston, said Adams, noting that Chicago was not only larger than Boston, but performed "far greater functions in the economy of the continent."

Bostonians had only themselves to blame for being upstaged by other cities, wrote Adams, claiming that Boston investors who put their money and talents into projects far from home did so at the expense of their own city's development. Strange sentiments indeed for a man who just twenty years later, as president of the Union Pacific, would write with some exaggeration that "all the money I have made has been in dealing in real estate in Kanzas [sic] City."

Boston was also penalized for its early start and outstanding performance in the money-making game. As the center of American foreign trade for more than a century, as the cradle of industrial revolution and capitalism, Boston was the first U.S. city to offer a considerable number of its citizens the opportunity to grow rich. Inevitably, Boston became, too, the first city to spawn a really wealthy urban upper class, an aristocracy based, not on merit or achievement, but on inherited wealth and position. As early as the 1830s and 1840s, while the founders of many a durable New York fortune were retailing pots and pans, pants and sundries, the heirs of Boston fortunes were graduating from Harvard, or, in the case of Thomas Gold Appleton, dabbling in the arts and wintering in the capitals of Europe. Men like Amos Adams Lawrence or William Hathaway Forbes might follow in their fathers' footsteps—if on tiptoe, and wearing smaller shoes—but neither genes nor exhortation could vest succeeding generations with the old entrepreneurial spirit or repress the natural instinct to steadfastly preserve a fortune already made. As the first city to make large amounts of money, Boston became also the first city to grow preoccupied with conserving it.

THREE. "HOW MEN OF PRUDENCE MANAGE THEIR OWN AFFAIRS"

Just as Bostonians had pioneered in finding new ways of making money, they had broken fresh ground in developing corporate means for its management and care. As early as 1784, a group of prominent citizens that included Judge John Lowell and the merchants Thomas Russell and Stephen Higginson, had joined together to found the Massachusetts Bank, second only to Philadelphia's Bank of North America among banks chartered in the new nation. The fledgling Boston bankers had indeed struck out into virgin territory, and when they wrote to the Bank of North America's president for guidance, he advised that "The world is apt to Suppose a greater Mystery in this sort of Business, than there really is," adding wistfully that "Perhaps it is right they should do so, & wonder on. ..." Other banks followed, perhaps most notably the Suffolk, which in 1824 introduced the so-called Suffolk System, requiring country banks—which had been flooding the state with unbacked paper currency—to redeem their banknotes in specie on demand.

Chartered in 1818 as Boston's seventh bank, the Suffolk numbered Patrick Tracy Jackson and William Lawrence among its initial directors, and the slate of later directors would continue to read like a who's who of Boston's merchant and manufacturing establishment. Kirk Boott, John Amory Lowell, Nathan Appleton, William Appleton, Amos Adams Lawrence—all would serve on the bank's board and leave their imprints behind them.

The ponderously named Provident Institution for Savings in the Town of Boston—the first incorporated savings bank in the United States—was another financial institution established by the traders and textile men, though its original intent was to encourage frugal habits among the town's "industrious mechanics . . . seamen, laborers, and all men of small capital." When it opened for business in 1816, the Provident was backed by the likes of John Lowell—son of the Old Judge and brother of Francis Cabot Lowell—and the merchants Russell Sturgis and Joseph Coolidge. In years to come, men like Nathan Appleton, Peter Chardon Brooks, Patrick Tracy Jackson, Amos Lawrence, and Amos Adams Lawrence would serve as trustees, and there would not be a time when the Provident's board was without a Lowell.

Important as they were in institutionalizing the commanding financial station of Boston's early aristocracy—by 1850 about 40 percent of Boston's banking resources were controlled by that tight circle of friends and kin—the banks were overshadowed by another institution, one that would have deep and lasting influence on the course of Boston's economic fortunes.

Despite strong financial support from the leading citizens of Boston, the Massachusetts General Hospital had been hard pressed to raise sufficient funds. After toying with the idea of going into the annuity business to generate the needed cash, the hospital's trustees put together the Massachusetts Hospital Life Insurance Company in 1818, with the proviso that a third of the company's profits would go to the hospital. Not much came of the idea until five years later, when the trustees assured prospective investors that the hospital's share of the profits would be doled out only after stockholders had been paid 6 percent dividends. Bostonians were always willing to do their part for charity, but they were even more willing if they could rake off some profits in return. Among the early investors were

Peter Chardon Brooks, David Sears, George Cabot, Amos Lawrence, William Sturgis, Patrick Tracy Jackson, Nathan Appleton, Joseph Coolidge, and the ubiquitous Thomas Handasyd Perkins.

As actuary—or chief executive—of the new company, the trustees chose Nathaniel Bowditch, the noted mathematician whose *New American Practical Navigator*, published in 1802, was for years a bible for Boston's ship captains, guiding them across the seas to distant markets and safely home with rich cargoes from all the world. This navigational aid had done much to make possible the maritime prosperity that launched Boston's early burst of enterprise and underpinned the city's great fortunes; at the helm now of Massachusetts Hospital Life, Bowditch would begin to steer those fortunes to a safe haven—out of harm's way, but beyond the reach of new opportunity.

Even before he accepted the post of actuary, Bowditch determined that there wouldn't be enough life insurance business in Boston to support a company of the size envisioned by the Hospital Life's backers. As an alternative, he suggested that the company accept money in trust and pay depositers an attractive yield while keeping the principal amount intact. Later, this would become common enough in the financial world, but in Bowditch's time it was a unique proposal. Individuals frequently put the care of their money in the hands of others, but this was generally done on a relatively informal basis. A successful merchant might manage investments for far-ranging traders and sea captains or for less enterprising relatives and friends; a wealthy man might, in his will, direct that his estate be tended to by a trusted friend on behalf of his beneficiaries. Bowditch himself was trustee for the estate of a deceased Salem merchant. But for an institution to perform these services was something altogether different and new. It was, according to Bowditch, "a Species of Savings Bank for the rich and middle class of Society."

For the rich in particular, this was an inviting prospect. The ½ of 1 percent fee on income was less than generally charged by private trustees, and turning funds over to an institution rather than to an individual provided the kind of long-term

continuity desired by men planning for the welfare of generations yet unborn. Appletons, Lowells, Lawrences, Perkinses,
Cabots, and Lees were among families that were soon putting a
part of their fortunes in the care of Massachusetts Hospital
Life, which was quick to become a social as well as financial
institution.

The company offered two forms of trusts that were especially
attractive to rich and successful fathers who doubted the
abilities of their sons or who feared that their financially well-
endowed daughters might be plucked by unscrupulous fortune
hunters. Under terms of these trust arrangements, known as
the "strict male" and "strict female" forms, a specified sum was
put on deposit for the life of the beneficiary, who was paid an
income but could not under any circumstances or at any time
withdraw any of the principal amount. To protect women from
grasping husbands, the "strict female" trust could come with
the provision that her income was "for her separate use, free
from the debts, control, or interference by any husband she
now has, or may hereafter have. . . ." Having thus provided for
a beloved daughter, a wealthy father could rest easily, freed
from what Francis Grund in 1839 termed wealthy Boston's
"great dread of poor bachelors." By tying up a son's inheritance
in a "strict male" trust, a rich Bostonian could be assured that
his bequest would not be risked on some hazardous or visionary
scheme. The purpose of a trust, after all, was to provide a
safe and steady income for its beneficiary, while carefully preserving, never dipping into the principal amount. And Massachusetts Hospital Life's directors had made it plain in their
original proposals that their aim was to be safe and steady,
keeping "always in view the safety of the Capital, rather than
the greatness of the income."

To arrive at this target, the company invested its funds
primarily in carefully chosen, well-secured mortgages, all close
to home in Massachusetts—land is an abiding treasure, a solid,
safe investment. Later, the company became heavily involved in
the textile industry, many of whose leaders were also directors
of Massachusetts Hospital Life. In 1826 the pioneering Boston
Manufacturing Company in Waltham took a $20,000 loan, se-

cured by five shares of stock in the Suffolk Bank and the signatures of Patrick Tracy Jackson and Nathan Appleton. In 1827 and 1828 the Dover Manufacturing Company, backed by William Appleton and David Sears, took four loans totaling $200,000, and in the coming years nearly all the great textile mills would call on the resources of Massachusetts Hospital Life from time to time, generally putting up their stock as collateral. The fortunes of the financial institution and the textile industry became closely intertwined; by 1856, the company held more than 10 percent of the stock in five of the largest Lowell and Lawrence mills. At about the same time, textile magnate John Amory Lowell began establishing trusts in Massachusetts Hospital Life at the birth of each grandchild, so that they might "never suffer want." Lowell's trusts provided for payment of a lump sum when the beneficiaries came of age, but the "strict male" and "strict female" varieties were growing in popularity; in 1858, such trusts accounted for more than a third of the total amount held in trust by Massachusetts Hospital Life.

From the start, the company determined to be a regional institution, encouraging depositers primarily from the Boston area and investing mainly in Massachusetts property—whether it was real estate or securities. Its influence was felt far beyond this purposely narrow sphere, however. As the nation's first corporate trust operation, it soon inspired counterparts in other cities, most notably the New York Life Insurance & Trust Company, the Ohio Life Insurance & Trust Company, and the Girard Life Insurance, Annuity & Trust Company. In time, it would breed competitive companies at home, too, but its most immediate impact on Boston was to set standards by which both clients and practitioners measured the conduct of private trusteeship. Because it was owned, managed, and patronized by Boston's wealthiest families, the mercantile and manufacturing elite who had laid up America's first great fortunes, its policy of scrupulous preservation and protection of wealth rubbed off on Boston's private trustees—many of whom, in any case, served as officers and directors of Massachusetts Hospital Life. The ever popular "strict" trusts caught on, too, and were refined into that peculiarly Boston fiduciary instrument, the "spendthrift" trust. This device put the principal out of reach of both the beneficiary and his creditors—indeed, said *Fortune* in 1933, it could tie up an estate "beyond the reach of any power but the Communist International"—and permitted the trustee to dole out income as he saw fit. Given Boston's prudent trustees, a spendthrift trust was—and still is—hardly the type of inheritance calculated to encourage high living or venturesome investments.

Trustees did not operate in a vacuum, of course, and if they seemed tightfisted or unimaginative it was only because they were carrying out the bidding of wealthy men who wanted their fortunes handed safely down the family tree to as many generations as possible. Such men were not about to let something so bothersome as a feckless son or flighty daughter break the chain—a prospect frequently seen as a distinct possibility to be forestalled by the strictest measures. It was for the good of the family, born and unborn, in a Boston where sense of family had reached almost Oriental proportions. And if provident ancestors were to be venerated, then the young had to pay a price in the esteem of their elders. Writing in 1936, the quintessential Boston trustee E. Sohier Welch observed of the salad days of trust formation that "Confidence in the ability of the younger generation was even less common then than now. . . ." and noted that a rich man's goal was to insure the wealth and happiness of his distant descendants "in spite of the frailty of his children. . . ." It is a custom honored today in the common Boston dogma that it isn't how much money a person has that counts—what matters is how long the money has been in the family.

As conservation became the byword of the Boston trustee, increasing amounts of Boston's wealth were squirreled away and removed from productive enterprise. By definition, trusteed wealth must not be put at hazard, must not be risked on chancy ventures, and the proper place for money held in trust was in solid real estate, in the steady cotton mills, in tried-and-true railroad securities. Fortunes made by taking risks must not be risked again.

For all that, Boston trustees had more leeway in their operations than did their fellow fiduciaries in other parts of the country. Unless directed otherwise, trustees had been bound by tradition, if not by law, to make riskless investments that did not jeopardize principal for the sake of income. So it was that Harvard College sought to recover its full share of the $50,000 that merchant John McLean had left in 1823 to provide income for his widow, with the stipulation that the sum should be divided equally between Harvard and Massachusetts General Hospital after Mrs. McLean's death. Meanwhile, Jonathan and Francis Amory, the trustees, had invested the $50,000 in comi on stocks which at the time of Mrs. McLean's death were worth a good deal less than the original fund. Justice Samuel Putnam found in favor of the trustees. "All that can be required of a private trustee," he declared, "is, that he shall conduct himself faithfully and exercise a sound discretion. He is to observe how men of prudence manage their own affairs, not in regard to speculation, but in regard to the permanent disposition of their funds, considering the probable income, as well as the probable safety of the capital to be invested."

This landmark ruling, laying out what came to be known as the Prudent Man Rule, gave Boston trustees a flexible edge over their counterparts elsewhere, but did not break the fetters clamped upon them by the growing Boston preoccupation with preserving old fortunes for the benefit of new generations. The Boston trustee could buy common stocks in likely industries, but as conservator of other people's money he was rightfully careful to choose solid and seasoned companies, preferring a proven past to a promising but problematic future. He was nothing if not prudent. As a private investor, a William H. Forbes might take a flier in Florida cotton and bet on the telephone; as a steward of others' funds, he shied away from Calumet & Hecla because copper stocks were not "safe and judicious investments for trustees," and balked at the future blue-chip Pullman Company, explaining that "I do not consider that the property rests on as sure and permanent basis as many others that will pay good interest, though probably not as good. . . ."

In 1868 a young Charles Francis Adams had faulted Boston capitalists for neglecting their home state's economic interests in favor of the "chance of fifty per cent in Colorado" that seemed more enticing than "the certainty of six per cent at home." Little more than a generation later, certainty had far outpaced chance in the eyes of most Boston investors, and it was sometimes said that there were Bostonians who declined to put money into anything that they couldn't keep an eye on from their office windows. By then, the tide of national growth and innovation had receded far from the old Shawmut peninsula, leaving Boston alone with its rich memories of past achievement. Their energies directed now toward preservation and slow, steady magnification of previous fortunes, Bostonians assumed a vested interest in olden times, a seeming disinterest in things to come. As Charles Francis Adams had observed as America entered the great period of post-Civil War industrialism, "The new era found [Boston] wedded to the old, and her eyes, dimmed with experiences of the past, could not credit the brilliant visions of the future."

FOUR. "A MONEY GETTER WITH STRUGGLES FOR BETTER THINGS"

His eyes dimmed with tears, Henry Lee Higginson stood in the ballroom of the two-year-old Copley Plaza Hotel on the night of November 18, 1914. From the head table, he nodded stiffly to the three hundred leading Bostonians who stood to applaud their city's undisputed first citizen on his eightieth birthday. Senator Henry Cabot Lodge had presided over the dinner, reading letters of congratulation from the likes of Justice Oliver Wendell Holmes, Charles Francis Adams, and Harvard President Abbott Lawrence Lowell. Among the speakers who had praised Higginson for a life of achievement was Episcopal Bishop William Lawrence, son of textile magnate Amos Adams Lawrence. It was a gathering of the clans, an assembly of all that Boston was and all that it had been, come to bear tribute to its most faithful paladin.

Major Higginson—he would always bear his old military title, just as he would always be badged with the saber scar that slashed across his cheek and disappeared into his now-white hair—waited for the applause to die down, then fumbled at the response that he had so carefully prepared. All he could manage were a few grateful sentences and a reaffirmation of what he called "the keynote of my faith"—"From my boyhood," he said in a voice that broke with emotion, "I have had a deep and passionate wish that we should live according to our highest ideals."

Higginson had been true to Boston and its traditions of upright and honorable conduct. Striding from his home on Commonwealth Avenue to his State Street office in his old age—he never quite came to terms with the automobile, though he once bought two cars on impulse—wearing a nondescript suit and one of his famous straw hats, Higginson seemed the very personification of all that commercial Boston stood for. Doubts about the value of his calling assailed him throughout life, but he came to terms with them, learned to resist the temptation to sit on the doorstep at Lee, Higginson and cry for unfulfilled dreams. He became, in fact, an archetypal proper Bostonian, stern, austere—he slept in a simple iron bunk bed in a plain room with only a table and few chairs for furniture— and a bit priggish at times. Once, praised by a prominent citizen for his myriad accomplishments and good works, Higginson complained bitterly to Harvard President Charles William Eliot. "What right has he to do that?" asked the onetime Bully Hig. "He and I never played together when we were boys."

For all that, Higginson had a bizarre sense of humor, and liked to tell of the time he saw a crowd gather around an overturned automobile. A woman newly arrived at the scene called out, "Anybody hurt? Anybody hurt?" and was taken aback when Higginson bowed and replied, "I hope so, madam." Thinking that the elderly Higginson must have been hard of hearing, the woman repeated her question, only to hear him say, "Yes, madam, I heard the first time. I said, I hope so; think how disappointed all the people would be if nobody were hurt."

Muttering under her breath about the wretched, wicked old

man, the woman started to walk away, then turned back and looked closely at Boston's leading citizen. "Aren't you Mr. Higginson?" she asked. "No, madam," said Higginson. "You look very much like him," the woman said. "I have been told so," Higginson replied with a tip of his hat. The point of this tale, Higginson once explained to a younger associate, was that while truth-telling is essential in business dealing, a little lying can be a great social diversion. Another story that Higginson liked to tell was of the day a colleague, upset over some business misunderstanding with Higginson's father, stalked into the offices at Lee, Higginson and said "Mr. Higginson, I always supposed you were an honest man." "No, you did not," the elder Higginson snapped, "you *knew* it."

This was the faith of his father and his friends. Higginson and his generation had kept and nurtured that faith and its attendant dogmas of probity and rectitude, but in his own lifetime, Higginson had seen the coming of infidels in the land, robber barons unchecked by Boston's long traditions. And John Murray Forbes had been right; Bostonians were no match for the Goulds and Morgans and Vanderbilts of the world. In his own lifetime, too, Higginson had seen Boston's attitudes toward the time-honored pursuit of wealth—no matter how creditably conducted—change from approbation to scorn.

In the old Boston, the high status and motives of the merchants and capitalists had been unquestioned. The great manufacturer Nathan Appleton could say in 1828 that he knew "of no purer morality in any department of life than that of the counting room," and be bolstered by the historian William Hickling Prescott's reference to "the noble post of head of a cotton factory." Through much of the nineteenth century, Boston's commercial and intellectual communities lived together in easy harmony. Indeed, they composed a single community whose bonds were often knit by marriage; a daughter of Nathan Appleton married Henry Wadsworth Longfellow, and William Hathaway Forbes married a daughter of Ralph Waldo Emerson. Boston entrepreneurs and financiers were willing patrons of the arts, and cultivated friendship with scholars and writers. The life of the mind was generally honored in the countinghouse, and merchants and industrialists were in turn honored by Boston's intellectuals—whose contemplative lives were, in any case, frequently made possible by kinship or friendship with the city's capitalist class.

William Appleton noted in his diary in 1858 that at the age of seventy-one he marveled at his continuing interest in business, and chalked his enthusiasm up to "the pleasure of doing what others cannot do, & to get applause for so doing." It may not have been a high motive, the self-made millionaire said, but it was "better than a sordid one." At the time, Appleton could be assured of the applause of both his colleagues of the counting room and the intellectual community; it would not be long, however, before the ovation would begin to fade. Boston's romance between mind and Mammon was not to last, and doubts would soon be raised about the motives behind the money-making urge. Coming at a time when Boston's long-standing commercial, financial, and industrial supremacy was being challenged from many sides, these homegrown qualms would accelerate the city's decline in national economic importance. Happily for the Bostonians' peace of mind, they would also help to rationalize this loss of position, making it seem the result, not of Boston's shortcomings, but of its transcendent virtues.

The early merchants and manufacturers had had little time or inclination to examine the fundamental value of what they were doing. Indeed, to the extent that they believed riches to be the just reward of diligence and virtue, the laying up of wealth was by definition a worthy enterprise. Some, like Amos Lawrence or the profit-ridden Augustus Hemenway, would agree that they were throwing themselves a little too energetically into the race for riches, but none questioned the ultimate merit of their goal. Later, as the pace of industrialism quickened, and as Boston's wealthy families—their fortunes secure in the hands of prudent trustees—bound themselves together as an exclusive urban upper class, there was a pronounced shift in attitudes toward the entrepreneurial zeal that had fired the old traders and textile men. The ideal citizen was no longer the self-made man, but the man with inherited means and position.

Oliver Wendell Holmes, Boston's great breakfast table autocrat, sounded the keynote when he wrote that "Other things being equal, in most relations of life I prefer a man of family," which in Holmes's lexicon meant a man who could claim as forebears "Four or five generations of gentlemen and gentlewomen," and whose portrait gallery included a "great merchant-uncle ... with a globe by him, to show the range of his commercial transactions." There would also be some honored ancestor whose "smile is good for twenty thousand dollars to the Hospital, besides ample bequests to all relatives and dependents."

In a community grounded on such sentiments—the humbler origins of those already enrolled in the dominant upper class were conveniently overlooked—the rise of newly rich capitalists was a clear threat to the established order. In response, eloquent spokesmen for Boston Brahminism came to scorn not only money-makers but money-making itself—careful always, of course, to exempt their own ancestors and those friends and kinsmen still toiling in the counting room. According to this new Boston litany, the growing American drive for wealth was vulgar and corrupt, totally destructive of the old cultural values and traditions so prized in the Back Bay and on Beacon Hill. To Brooks and Henry Adams, brothers of Charles Francis Adams, the archvillains were gold-hungry Jewish bankers bent on destroying Western civilization; James Russell Lowell spotted the enemy as "the increasing power of wealth and its combinations." But it was only new wealth that Lowell feared. Boston wealth, the wealth passed from generation to generation, was a benign treasure, "the security of refinement, the feeder of all those arts that ennoble and beautify life."

Writers and intellectuals were not alone in the chorus of contempt for the newly rich. Charles Francis Adams, following his own career as a national railroad leader, surely did not include his Boston financial peers among the rich and famous men whose company he did not care to share again either in heaven or on earth. And Henry Lee Higginson, fearful of being tarred with the same dripping brush that was swiping at the robber barons, minced no words when it came to fingering the nation's true malefactors of great wealth. ". . . 'The predatory rich!' as T. R. says," Higginson snorted. "Who are they? Sons of farmers, mechanics, day-laborers, etc., who fought hard for their first $100, and so believe that they can do as they like with their millions. They never had any good traditions, never had any high fine talk and should not be expected to act well. . . ."

Higginson had high hopes that the heirs of these coarse nouveaux riches, exposed to the benefits of wealthy surroundings and traditions more elevated than those of mechanics and day laborers, might prove themselves socially acceptable and worthy of a Bostonian's respect. Meanwhile, he had little use for their fathers, for the rich and ambitious men, risen from doubtful antecedents, who were beginning to make their place in the complex and growing world of American business. Higginson was perfectly in tune with his brother and fellow financier Francis Lee Higginson, who wrote of a mutual associate that "He is a self made man without the backing of a family to keep him straight. I have never met one such yet in my business life who has not sooner or later lied to me, or at least tried to cheat me."

The proper and established Bostonian's deepening distrust of outsiders, his suspicion of those cut from cloth of a different color than Boston's own somber hues, worked in tandem with other factors, slowly and surely isolating Boston from the mainstream of productive American enterprise. The selectivity of the drawing room and private club was extended almost intact to the business office, with such smothering pomposity that Harvard Professor Barrett Wendell, commissioned in 1918 to write an authorized history of Lee, Higginson & Company, could say of former partner Charles Fairchild: "He joined the firm in 1880, and left it in 1894. Of western origin, he had been a good soldier; later he had shown ability in the conduct of considerable manufacturing affairs; he had a bluff heartiness of address which all who knew him must always pleasantly remember; his social propensities, however, were perhaps less fashionable than Bohemian—he was a great friend of Robert

Louis Stevenson." Allowed to color business judgment, such priggish snobbery deprived Boston of the lasting infusion of new blood and spirit that might have helped keep the city in the vanguard of economic life.

For all that, Boston probably felt little need to man the front lines of American commerce and industry. As the nation moved into a period of mammoth corporations and industrial trusts, the men who managed Boston's great capital resources lacked the overweening imperial ambitions of the robber barons. With their comfort assured, with a time-honored stock of traditions to draw upon, Bostonians of means had no compulsion to control and manipulate far-flung commercial dominions. John Murray Forbes, with all the great energy and resources at his command, might well have become overlord of a coast-to-coast railway system, but did not feel that the prize was worth the effort. One of the most visionary men of his generation, he had wider interests, and as early as 1848 could write that "I am determined to get my affairs into a very narrow compass within the next six months, so as to have more time for farming, shooting, and other gentlemanlike occupations. I suppose my property has shrunk 20% or 25% within the past year but with habits of economy this is of no consequence."

Even as a Harvard senior, Amos Adams Lawrence had circumscribed the scope of his ambitions, vowing to be a litterateur and farmer while at the same time administering the textile empire carved out by his father and uncle. Lawrence's literary hopes bore no fruit, but he did manage to be a gentleman farmer of sorts, always practicing the kind of frugal economy so characteristic of Boston. Lawrence was a great believer in kindness to animals—he frequently bought worn out horses and shot them to put them out of their misery—and one day he told his gardener to dig a deep, wide trench the whole length of the grape arbor at his Longwood estate. He then rode to the nearby Brighton cattle market and returned leading a string of nine old nags that he'd bought for $2.50 to $10.00 each. Lining the horses up at the edge of the trench, Lawrence shot them all between the eyes and then had the gardener cover them over. Combining good works with self-interest, he had released the horses from their suffering and enriched the soil of his grape arbor in the bargain.

With honored intellectuals sniping at the values of market-place and factory, with their own ardor for unstinting business pursuits on the wane, it is no wonder that Boston's leading capitalists were afflicted with nagging misgivings about the worthiness of their occupations. Charles Francis Adams branded the urge for riches a "low instinct." Henry Lee Higginson perceived material success as a corrupter of his generation, and in 1878, at the near peak of his business career, he lamented to his literary cousin Thomas Wentworth Higginson that "I wanted to do something decent, to leave a little relic behind me, or at least to lead a life full of something to satisfy one's soul—a little—I tried, but failed—partly by accident, chiefly however, from want of brains—and so with the really bright interlude of the war I have become and am a money-getter with struggles for better things." But for all his talk of failure, Higginson had not given up, and his struggles would soon take a turn for the better.

FIVE. "WEALTH AND THE KNOWLEDGE OF HOW TO USE IT"

As the centennial year of 1876 drew near, the state of Massachusetts dispatched a commission to observe and report on the Vienna Exposition in hopes of turning up some pointers to aid in preparing for the upcoming national celebration in Philadelphia. Henry Lee Higginson was named an honorary commissioner, and among his traveling companions when he sailed for Europe in 1873 were Charles Francis Adams, chairman of the commission, and Greely Curtis, a childhood friend and comrade from that bright and brave interlude of battle. In some ways, the trip was a reprise of Higginson's youthful wanderings on the Continent, though he was mindful now, as a prosperous American financier, not to appear on the streets in the shabby and peculiar clothes that had so distressed his father just thirteen years before. He did, however, look up a number of his old friends from the world of music, many of whom had risen high in their professions. One, he noted, was "the piano professor at the Conservatorium, and *the* pianist of Vienna." It was the kind of life that Higginson had once wanted for himself, and being exposed to it again rekindled old musical dreams.

Happily for his business affairs, Higginson had also found the time to visit with several British investors, and money raised from them went a long way toward helping Lee, Higginson & Company weather the stormy half decade following the panic of 1873. John Murray Forbes's western railroads and the Calumet & Hecla copper mines, in which the firm had major interests, continued to prosper, and so did Henry Higginson.

Back in Europe once more in 1878, Higginson again renewed old musical acquaintances, was again fired with the vision which he would later say had first struck him as long ago as 1857, the same year that he wrote from Vienna to his father back on State Street that "Trade [is] not satisfying to the inner man as a life-occupation." What was satisfying to Higginson was music—"I enjoy in the depths of my soul music as nothing else," he had once told his father—and he was determined now that Boston should share in this satisfaction. In the spring of 1881, following several years of notable financial successes, Higginson announced the formation of a sixty-man symphony orchestra, directed by the German-born Georg Henschel. "The intention is," Higginson wrote, "that this orchestra shall be made permanent here, and shall be called 'The Boston Symphony Orchestra.'" To insure its permanence, Higginson agreed to make up the difference between receipts and expenses, moving a breathless San Francisco newspaper editorialist to cry, "Oh! for a few such men in our midst."

Some Bostonians were a bit cool to Higginson's symphony scheme—they feared its impact on long-established amateur musical groups, and resented its foreign conductor—but the symphony soon became a Boston institution, even a national institution. And it did not come cheap to its founder, who had purposely pegged ticket prices relatively low. Against the advice of friends who urged him from time to time to drop his support, Higginson during his lifetime made up a deficit that came to considerably more than one million dollars. "The Boston Symphony Orchestra," wrote Richard Aldrich in *Century Magazine*, "is Mr. Henry L. Higginson's yacht, his racing stable, his library, and his art gallery, or it takes the place of what these things are to other men of wealth with other tastes."

Higginson's virtual gift of a great symphony orchestra was totally in keeping with nineteenth-century Boston's attitudes toward the arts and education. Bostonians did not go in for such things as yachts and racing stables, at least not on the conspicuous scale that these pleasures were pursued by the sporting rich of New York and other cities unendowed with Boston's peculiar traditions. (Sadly for Henry Higginson, his own son Alexander was a rule-proving exception. At an estate in Lincoln, Alexander Higginson kept an expensive string of horses and so indulged his appetites for high living that his hardworking father frequently reminded him that his elevated standard of living was possible only because of parental generosity that was fast wearing thin. In desperation, Higginson finally composed a standard letter to fire off to irate creditors, informing them that he was paying his son's bill for the last time and that in the future they would be well advised not to sell him or his wife anything on credit.)

Long noted for the willingness of its wealthy to support the cause of culture, the city was, said Edwin L. Godkin in 1871, "the one place in America where wealth and the knowledge of how to use it are apt to coincide." For Godkin, this happy coincidence had brought in money from John Murray Forbes and other Boston capitalists when the Irish-born intellectual launched the *Nation* in New York just after the Civil War. Closer to home, it had meant generous support of such institutions as the Boston Athenaeum, the Boston Public Library, and the Museum of Fine Arts—which was, indeed, an outgrowth of the Athenaeum's own art collection. And it had, of course, led John Lowell, Jr., feverish on the banks of the Nile, to remember his native city with the magnificent Lowell Institute. Not for nothing was Boston frequently called the Athens of America.

But it was Harvard, fair Harvard, that had taken the greatest share of Boston's mercantile and capitalist wealth, which had become the quintessential Boston appendage on which to lavish a share of the rewards of enterprise or inheritance. Since its founding in 1636, it had been more than merely Harvard College; it was The College, the place where the wealthy sent their sons to learn and mingle with other young men who would soon be holding positions of leadership in the tight little world of Boston. Much later, as Harvard grew to become a national and even international institution, the school remained for Boston what the great state universities so frequently were in other parts of the country—the place, the *only* place, for the education of the man who planned to make his way in his home community. And just as loyal legions of nonalumni respect Old State U. and cheer for the triumph of its athletic squads, Bostonians who in their youth had not so much as set foot in the Harvard Yard were dedicated to its goals and traditions. They were not Harvard men, but they were Harvard's men, and they gave Harvard their sons as well as their steadfast support.

For the college did supply an occasional intellectual prop to merchant values, and if a master's degree candidate in 1725 could argue in favor of government price regulations, a postgraduate in the next generation would maintain the thesis that "the cultivation of commerce [is] of more benefit to the state than that of science." And in 1765, Harvard student Elbridge Gerry, whose name would become a part of the coming new republic's political argot, would take the affirmative side on the question: "Can the new prohibitory duties, which make it useless for the people to engage in commerce, be evaded by them as faithful subjects?" Little more than a decade later, Gerry would join his fellow Harvard man—and frequent duty-evader—John Hancock in signing the declaration that made such questions purely academic.

John Hancock's uncle, benefactor, and adoptive father, Thomas Hancock, had not attended Harvard. Indentured at fourteen to a Boston bookseller, he'd had little time for formal education, though he appreciated its value. His clergyman father was a graduate of the college, as were many of his merchant associates. So the self-made merchant Thomas had left in his will a bequest for a chair of Oriental languages (Hebrew, in the parlance of the time) at Harvard, and it is likely that John Hancock might have made a similar provision—if he had ever taken the time to compose a will. Other Bostonians preferred to do their duty for Harvard while they still lived, as Abbott Lawrence did with his 1847 gift of $50,000 to establish the Lawrence Scientific School, a donation augmented at his death eight years later with another $50,000, which was in turn matched in 1865 by an additional $50,000 from his son James.

Like Thomas Hancock, Abbott Lawrence had signed on in a counting room at too young an age to leave time for Harvard, but he surely agreed with his older brother, Amos, who wrote of the college when he heard of Abbott's benefaction that "Instead of our sons going to France and other foreign lands for instruction, here will be a place, second to no other on earth, for such teaching as our country now stands in absolute need of." It would hardly be the last of the great textile family's gifts to Harvard, and the Lawrences would later join with the Lowells to produce one of the most towering presidents in Harvard's long history, Abbott Lawrence Lowell. Grandson of the manufacturing magnates Abbott Lawrence and John Amory Lowell—and brother of the poet Amy and the astronomer Percival, who discovered the planet Pluto—A. Lawrence Lowell presided over Harvard during its period of greatest expansion in the first third of the twentieth century. Largely through his efforts, Harvard did indeed become, as Amos Lawrence had hoped it would, a university "second to no other on earth."

Not everyone shared in wealthy Boston's love affair with Harvard. Through much of the nineteenth century, in fact, it was regarded by some educators as little more than a glorified high school whose appeal was based on social éclat rather than on academics; until shortly before the Revolution, students had been ranked on Harvard's rolls on the basis of social position, and long after the end of this practice the rich and wellborn set the prevailing tone of the school. William Hathaway Forbes, responding in 1868 to a request for contributions, groused about this when he wrote of Harvard that "I do not believe that it owes its popularity to its value as a good and well conducted school but to the good company which it affords and to the fact of its being convenient and fashionable." Forbes complained further that Harvard's professors would do well to spend more time inspiring and teaching their students and less time writing books; and adding injury to his verbal insults, the wealthy young Forbes put himself down for a pledge of just $25 a year for the following ten years. For his children's sake, he bowed nonetheless to convenience and fashion and sent all five of his sons to Harvard.

Charles Francis Adams shared some of Forbes's misgivings about the value of a Harvard education, and in 1883—just a year before taking the reins of the Union Pacific—he created a stir at Harvard and throughout the entire academic world when he delivered a Phi Beta Kappa address lambasting Harvard's insistence on requiring a knowledge of ancient Greek as a ticket for admission. This was, said Adams, useless and ridiculous—as was Harvard's partiality for the classics—and had nothing whatever to do with preparing students for the real world. Still, Adams's fondness for Harvard remained undimmed, and at his fiftieth class reunion in 1906 he said that he wished he could have put together "one of those vast fortunes of the present day rising into the tens and scores of millions—what is vulgarly known as 'money to burn'"—not for himself or for his family, but to give to Harvard.

Making enough money to burn was never a part of the Boston style, but generosity to educational institutions certainly was. And Harvard was not alone among schools with a claim on wealthy Boston's affection and largesse.

SIX. "A POLYTECHNIC SCHOOL IN BOSTON"

Fresh from its great voyage of merchant adventure, the ship *Columbia* had been hailed by a cannonade of thirteen guns when it sailed home to Boston Harbor in 1790 to the cheers of citizens come to greet the tea-laden vessel at dockside. Plowing through the same waters on a June morning in 1916, the passenger steamer *Bunker Hill* was welcomed by a twenty-one-gun salute as it eased toward India Wharf—halved now by an interloping waterfront roadway that had severed but not quite destroyed Charles Bulfinch's graceful temple of Boston's old mercantile supremacy. Along the wharf, a crowd of alumni and students from the Massachusetts Institute of Technology stood to cheer the arrival of five hundred alumni and guests who had taken ship from New York the night before to participate in ceremonies marking the opening of M.I.T.'s sprawling new campus on the banks of the Charles River in Cambridge.

Later, in a pageant of mystic and medieval splendor—made more awesome by the lights of modern science—the celebrants saw a snow white vessel, modeled after the Venetian Republic's barge of state, moving slowly across the river from the Boston shore. Fitfully lighted by soaring rockets that punctuated the icy beams of searchlights slashing through the darkening sky, the craft was bearing the charter and seal of the institute to their new home. Architect Ralph Adams Cram, the M.I.T. professor who had engineered the spectacle, spared nothing when it came to allegory—the barge was captained by an alumnus clad as Christopher Columbus; on its prow sat a figure of Mother Technology, holding high a flickering Torch of Progress. As the charter and seal were placed reverently on an altar in the new M.I.T.'s great courtyard, the lights were suddenly doused, playing now only on Cram himself, garbed as Merlin as he struck the ground with his staff. It was the signal for a whirling, kaleidoscopic celebration of man's long and tortuous climb from ignorance and superstition to rational science. At the end, a lone searchlight on the newly consecrated cathedral of technology knifed across the sky until it touched the one bright beam still lofting from the brick Victorian pile that had housed M.I.T. for nearly half a century. Briefly, the two lights stood locked in the night; then the beam from the old Back Bay building faded and disappeared, leaving the newer light pointing to the stars, a pale herald of days to come.

As such matters are often reckoned in Boston, M.I.T was
something of a brash newcomer, having opened its doors to the
first fifteen students only in 1865. But the civic jubilee attending the dedication of its new quarters was brilliant testimony to
the school's relatively rapid rise to nearly the same state of social
and cultural grace as Harvard in the Boston scheme of things.
From the very start, M.I.T. had been closely twined with Harvard and Harvard's wealthy stalwarts. It could trace its roots
back to 1842, when the brothers William Barton Rogers and
Henry Darwin Rogers presented to a Boston meeting of the
Association of American Geologists and Naturalists their ponderously titled paper "On the Structure of the Appalachian
Chain as Exemplifying the Laws which have Regulated the Ele-
vation of Great Mountain Chains Generally." Their work was
well received in Boston—the textile magnate Nathan Appleton,
an amateur geologist of some repute, backed the publication of
the meeting's proceedings—and the brothers Rogers were impressed with the intellectual and industrial ferment that they
found in the city. They had long thought that America needed
a first-rate technical and engineering school, and Boston
seemed an ideal location for such an undertaking. Henry was so
taken with the town that he resigned his professorship at the
University of Pennsylvania and moved to Boston to become an
independent lecturer and geological consultant; among other
things, he surveyed the shores of Lake Superior for a group of
would-be copper investors, and delivered a series of Lowell
Institute lectures.

In 1846 Henry Rogers approached John Amory Lowell, textile man and trustee of the Lowell Institute, to sound him out
about prospects for the institute's financing a technical school.
Lowell was interested in the idea, but the terms of the bequest
barred him from putting Lowell Institute money into such an
enterprise. For a time, the plan lay dormant, but not even Abbott Lawrence's gift to establish the Lawrence Scientific School
at Harvard could dampen the Rogers brothers' enthusiasm for
what they called "A Plan for a Polytechnic School in Boston."
By 1861, spurred by calls for parts of the newly filled Back Bay
to be used for "public educational improvements," the state

legislature chartered the school, known from the start as the Massachusetts Institute of Technology, but sometimes called Boston Tech.

The Civil War interfered with the institute's building plans, and the first class met in makeshift quarters at the Mercantile Library. It was no Harvard, but M.I.T. was no coarse parvenu, either; in its minuscule maiden class were a Forbes and a Cabot, and its first professor of analytical chemistry and metallurgy was the well-connected Charles W. Eliot, who would soon become president of Harvard.

During Eliot's long presidency, several attempts were made to merge the young M.I.T. with the venerable Harvard. It seemed like a reasonable enough idea; Harvard could use M.I.T. to shore up the never-robust Lawrence Scientific School, and M.I.T. could use Harvard's reputation and stability. But M.I.T. partisans would have nothing to do with such a plan, fearing that the institute's practical approach to education would not mix well with Harvard's classic liberal arts tradition. Instead, they pressed for an independence that became more readily maintained as the school's endowment and reputation continued to grow. The institute had its closest call with union with Harvard shortly after the turn of the century, when merger seemed so imminent that Henry Lee Higginson and Andrew Carnegie bought a parcel of land along the Charles River adjacent to Soldiers Field—a Higginson gift to Harvard— as a site for the school. Later, the tract became the home of the Harvard Graduate School of Business Administration.

From the start, M.I.T. had been generously supported by Boston's merchant and capitalist grandees, who saw the value of hard-nosed technical education in a rapidly changing world. John Amory Lowell and his son Augustus were both active backers, and while they could not commit Lowell Institute funds directly to M.I.T., the two institutes worked closely together in several areas. John Murray Forbes and his son William each served on the institute's governing body, and Edward Austin, Henry Lee Higginson's old merchant mentor, gave $400,000 to establish an M.I.T. scholarship fund. Later, as the old Boston Tech became a national institution, support poured in from many quarters. T. Coleman du Pont, of the class of 1884, made a gift of $500,000 in 1911, enabling the expanding institute to buy land in Cambridge for its new and larger campus. George Eastman, impressed with the M.I.T. graduates who had come to work for him at Kodak Park, supported the school in 1912 to the tune of $2.5 million for its new building program. Wary of publicity, the photographic pioneer insisted on anonymity, and for years the donor of his gift was known only as Mr. Smith. Eventually, Eastman's total gifts to M.I.T. came to some $20 million.

For the nation, for the world, and for Boston, this support for technology would yield a fruitful harvest in years to come. When Boston's decades of maritime and industrial prosperity had receded into dim memory, M.I.T. would become a catalyst for revival of the city's ailing economic fortunes.

While much of Boston slept, its spirit of earlier days was sustained in the classrooms and laboratories of the Massachusetts Institute of Technology, ready to rise again in an hour of need.

SEVEN. "SLICK AS SNOT ON A DOORKNOB"

On the day of M.I.T.'s pyrotechnic celebration of triumphant technology, better than five thousand alumni and other well-wishers had gathered to the south of Boston at Nantasket Beach for a round of merrymaking that included a burlesque preview of Ralph Adams Cram's carefully orchestrated pageantry. Suddenly, the festivities were jarred by the insistent roar of an aircraft engine—a rare enough sound in 1916—and the appearance from the north of a ponderous, biwinged seaplane. Circling over the grandstand, the plane skittered through the air in a figure-eight maneuver followed by a straight line—forming the numerals of the class of '81—and then banked to fly off in the direction of Boston.

At the controls in the open cockpit, face framed by his leather flying helmet, grizzled mustache bristling beneath large goggles, was Godfrey Lowell Cabot, a living Boston anachronism, a virtual throwback to Boston's earlier times of commercial and manufacturing adventure come back in a torpid time.

By biological inheritance, if nothing else, Cabot was well suited for a career of old-school business zealotry—leavened with incredible luck—that would make him not only the richest man in Boston but one of the richest men in America, at a time when Boston's fortunes had been far eclipsed by the greater riches piled up by less inhibited capitalist corsairs. Descended from privateer Samuel Cabot—the same Samuel Cabot accused by John Singleton Copley of euchring him out of a fair profit on the sale of his Beacon Hill lands—Godfrey Cabot was a grandson of textile magnate Patrick Tracy Jackson and a great-grandson of merchant prince Thomas Handasyd Perkins. In others of his generation, this heritage may have gone to seed, but Cabot proved to be a hardier sprout: born six days before the first inauguration of Abraham Lincoln, he lived to see the presidency of John Fitzgerald Kennedy. Along the way, he soared far above the prevailing Boston obsession with mere preservation of wealth already made.

Despite his aerial stunt over Nantasket Beach, Cabot was not a graduate of M.I.T., but a Harvard man, *magna cum laude* in chemistry. He had, however, attended the institute for a year before enrolling in the college, and had a lifetime attachment to both schools. At M.I.T., Cabot had taken only a couple of drawing courses, leaving him plenty of time to hang around the small factory where his older brother Samuel turned out roofing oil and lampblack. It hardly seemed the sort of thing to hang a fortune on, but lampblack, or carbon black—soot, as Cabot always called it—would make Cabot far wealthier than his forebears had ever become from privateering, trade, and textiles combined.

After his Harvard graduation, Cabot went to work for his brother as a chemist, trying to figure out better ways to make carbon black, which is nothing more than the soot left behind by burning petroleum, kerosene, or gas. Used primarily in ink, it also found its way into shoe polish, stove polish, paints, and other products requiring black pigmentation. Seeking a cheap way of turning out a blacker black, Samuel Cabot had inspected the booming oil fields of Pennsylvania, where it was common for drillers to burn off huge quantities of surplus natural gas released during the search for oil. The gas was cheap and seemingly endless in supply, and in 1883 Godfrey Cabot was dispatched to Pennsylvania to study the possibility of setting up carbon-black production facilities there. It looked promising, but Godfrey was in no hurry to get too involved in business affairs. Back from the oil fields, he took a long and leisurely tour of Europe—where his priggish Boston-Puritan nature was scandalized by much of what he saw—before settling down and setting himself up as a chemical consultant. In his first four months he made only $120, but he was hardly in need of money; his father died in 1885, leaving Godfrey a comfortable $80,000, unencumbered by any such nuisance as a spendthrift trust. Together with a legacy from his grandmother, this gave him $102,000 to spend or invest. He decided to use this small unearned fortune to earn an even bigger fortune on his own.

Cabot had brushed aside his brother's previous offers of a partnership, but when Samuel asked him to join in making and selling a new gas regulator in Pennsylvania, he agreed, and was soon spending considerable time peddling the device and setting up his collecting plates and burners for production of carbon black. In the fall of 1886 he bought Samuel out of the partnership. He was on his own now, and at a time when so many of his friends and contemporaries back home in Boston were going into banking and brokerage, minding the stocks and bonds of enterprises not their own, Cabot hurled himself into his business with a gusto that would have done credit to the Bostonians of a much earlier time. Roaming through the Pennsylvania and West Virginia countryside, covering much of his ground on foot, he bought up cheap gasland, drilled wells, and built rambling carbon-black plants. Then he'd start selling his gas to householders and industries and move on to a fresh field for his carbon-black factories. By 1890, he was the nation's fourth largest carbon-black maker; approached by competitors about the possibility of entering into a trust arrangement,

Cabot declined—he didn't want to "milk the public," he said, nor did he want to give up any of his independence.

He may not have wanted to milk the public, but Cabot had nothing against driving hard bargains that were to his decided advantage. In the true tradition of his class and time, he was a scrupulously honest man—he once wrote to his brother that "I do not wish, ever, for my own or any one else's pecuniary advantage, to utter a single word calculated to convey other than the exact fact..."—and he neither engaged in chicanery nor suffered gladly those whose ethics he deemed less lofty than his own. But when buying up cheap gaslands in the rural counties whose trapped gas would inflate his fortune, Cabot quibbled to the last nickel, and never felt bound to inform owners of their property's true value. Later, as his company grew huge in an industry where payoffs and kickbacks were pandemic, Cabot barred his operatives from such tainted business, warning that instant dismissal was the penalty for tendering bribes or extraordinary favors. Cabot's executives honored their employer's moral stand by carefully concealing from him any shady transactions that they judged necessary.

Ironically, Cabot did not take to the motor car, the twentieth century's great contribution to the mobility and independence that he so highly prized throughout his long and active life. Like Henry Higginson, he distrusted the automobile, and though he became an avid pilot and promoter of aviation, he never in his long life learned to drive. Yet it was the automobile, mass production of which was a high point of the industrial revolution introduced to America by the early Boston cotton manufacturers, that was to become the largest factor in the success of Cabot's carbon-black business. When he began, printer's ink took the largest share of his output. Later, as Henry Ford set out to put a car in every garage, huge amounts of black were consumed by makers of automobile tires; as much as six pounds went into each tire as a reinforcing agent. Ranging the hills and hollows of West Virginia in his early days as a soot-maker and gasman, Cabot had no inkling of this coming bonanza that would gobble up black as quickly as he could ship it out, or of the ballooning demand for natural gas that would turn his cheaply bought reserves into virtual gold mines. Like his ancestors, Cabot was lucky; unlike his Boston contemporaries, he had an enterprising spirit that put him in the right place when his lucky ship came in. In 1902, his income was a respectable $30,000 a year, but by the 1920s he was pulling in as much as $500,000.

Like Cabot, James Jackson Storrow, Jr., seemed to be an energetic, hard-driving remnant of earlier times. It would become Storrow's lot to spearhead a salvage operation that put a faltering General Motors Corporation back on its feet and set it running again in the race with the pioneering Henry Ford.

Storrow was ideally suited for the sort of enterprise which most of his contemporaries were content to leave to men from other cities. Building was in his blood, and while his domineering but unattentive father had bred in the son an almost painful reserve, his constructive spirit had not been bent. Storrow's grandfather, the talented engineer Charles Storer Storrow, had been tapped by the textile Lawrences to design and build the Merrimack River mill city that bears their name, and young James, born in 1864, was frequently regaled with grandfatherly tales of city building, of the construction of the Boston & Lowell Railroad, of raising the great water-harnessing dam across the river at Lawrence. His father, too, had set a good example, though in so doing he worked so hard that he had little time to spend with his family. An acknowledged genius at patent law, the senior James Storrow had captained American Bell Telephone's battles against the host of patent infringement suits that harried the company in its early days, winning not only his court cases but the undying gratitude of William Hathaway Forbes. Sticking ever to his last, the elder Storrow collapsed and died one day in 1897 while toiling over a legal brief at the Library of Congress.

James Storrow, Jr., had followed doggedly in his father's footsteps, graduating from the Harvard Law School and working for a year in an old-line law office before forming a firm of his own. He may have had some things in common with Godfrey Cabot, but the two were perhaps as different as they were alike. While Cabot, wearing as always his lumpish suits and heavy shoes, was slogging through the backwoods bargaining for rock-bottom land, the impeccable Storrow was at home in Boston, practicing the Byzantine intricacies of corporate law, doing legal work, and serving as a director of United Fruit and United Shoe. Much more than Cabot, he was in tune with Boston's new times.

But he was not content to leave things as he found them, as the old firm of Lee, Higginson & Company was about to find out. At the death of his kinsman James Jackson in 1900, Storrow was named to take Jackson's place as a partner in Lee, Higginson. All things being equal, Boston business seemed still to be a family affair, even in the age of industrial capitalism. And by standards of either talent or blood, Storrow was a prime prospect for such a partnership; besides being talented, he was also related in one way or another to Higginsons, Jacksons, Lees, and Cabots. By Boston reckoning, he was far more equal than most.

The Lee, Higginson that Storrow joined was symbolic of the torpor that had begun to settle like some smothering fog over the once-bright bastions of Boston enterprise. Still ensconced in its unassuming three-story granite building hard by the old State House, the firm did a full 95 percent of its business in safe, solid, unimaginative railroad bonds, held mainly by a small group of wealthy friends and relatives of equally wealthy partners. It seemed more a club than a bustling brokerage house, a condition ratified by the nearly constant presence of Henry Lee Higginson's cigar-smoking cousin, the railroader and yachtsman Charles Jackson Paine, who habitually settled into a comfortable leather armchair and dispensed data about stocks and bonds. In the absence of computers and even a systematic filing system, Paine's voluminous memory was the next best thing. Henry Higginson, meanwhile, though seen by the world at large as "Mr. Lee, Higginson" himself, was more and more occupied with the affairs of his symphony orchestra and his beloved Harvard, giving little more than token attention to the enterprise that made his benefactions possible.

Perhaps most telling of all, the firm had only two salesmen; with its inbred clientele there was little need to go out and drum up business from customers with slimmer purses and unknown antecedents.

But times had changed, and Storrow intended to see that time did not pass Lee, Higginson completely by. The job of a Lee, Higginson now was not to raise huge sums to back new ventures but to peddle established securities to large numbers of relatively small investors. To that end, Storrow began hiring platoons of salesmen to carry the banners of people's capitalism, and with senior partner Henry Higginson's blessings opened up branch offices in other cities. A Chicago branch opened for business in 1905, and the following year saw offices in New York and London. By 1913, the firm had moved so far from its old standby railroad bonds that some 75 percent of its volume was in public service and industrial securities. It was still a solid operation, though, and the conservative Storrow wrote to a younger partner to caution him that the firm's aim was to provide clients with "safe securities, and this involves sticking closely to the things which we are trained to analyze and know how to weigh in the balance."

Little analysis had been required in 1910 to see that the two-year-old Buick Motor Car Company of Flint, Michigan, was in deep trouble, trouble that was showing up on the books of the company's creditors. To make matters worse, Buick's parent company, General Motors, was in equally bad shape, and there was open talk that the whole GM operation was tooling not so merrily toward bankruptcy. Alarmed at the prospect of having to write off their considerable loans to the floundering automaker, a group of creditors—among them the First National Bank of Boston—undertook to reorganize the management and operation of the company, in hopes of staving off disaster. As chairman of a five-man committee of trustees charged with administering General Motors' affairs for a five-year period, the creditors named Storrow, who quickly threw himself into the salvage operation. It was no easy job, and for the next two years Storrow would take an almost weekly trip to Detroit.

His first order of business was to raise $15 million from skeptical bankers to keep the sinking company afloat, and it took all of the reticent Bostonian's powers of persuasion to convince the doubters that they were not throwing good money after bad. He had an even harder time of it a short time later when he had to go back for $9 million more. But his money-raising skills and his eye for detail began to pay off. Manufacturing costs were cut considerably after Storrow ordered workers to strip down a fully assembled Buick and spread the component parts out on the floor; it was the first time that anyone had thought to catalogue all the pieces that went into making the product, and it allowed for combining some parts and eliminating others. Storrow was also a good judge of men: he hired Walter P. Chrysler, manager of Pittsburgh's American Locomotive Company plant, as general manager of Buick, and was later instrumental in choosing Charles W. Nash as president of General Motors. Still later, he helped Nash form the Nash Motors Company, and served as chairman of the board.

Storrow's herculean labors on behalf of the ailing auto operation paid off handsomely—during the last year of his trusteeship, General Motors stock paid a first-ever $50 dividend—but they proved no bonanza for Lee, Higginson. Throughout, Storrow had insisted that the firm should have no self-interest in General Motors, and it did not buy great blocks of stock in the company.

Their active devotion to big business affairs and money-making may have cut against the prevailing Boston grain, but neither James Storrow nor Godfrey Cabot suffered in the eyes of their peers for such nonconformity. Cabot, far and away the most aggressive and hard-driving of the two (a competitor once described him as "slick as snot on a doorknob"), occupied so unassailable a position in the Brahmin firmament that he was beyond the criticism of his class for any offense save the unlikely one of moral turpitude; Storrow, no piker, either, when it came to family credentials, leavened his tireless business pursuits with an equally untiring attention to civic matters. (For that matter, so did Cabot, though his quixotic run for mayor of Cambridge as a Republican reformer was a fool's errand at

best, and his prudish crusades on behalf of the book-banning
Watch & Ward Society made Boston the laughingstock of the
country.) Even at the height of his expansion of Lee, Higginson
and the midwifery of a robust General Motors, Storrow found
time to devote to the common weal. During the early years of
the century he served on the Boston School Committee, leading
the fight for reform of that politics-ridden body, and was one of
the foremost proponents of recreational development along
the Boston bank of the Charles River—ironically, the six-lane
roadway that slashed through the graceful Charles River
Esplanade years later was named Storrow Drive in his honor.
Storrow also spearheaded the organization of a workable
Boston Chamber of Commerce and served as its first president.

His most visible—and most disappointing—entry into the
public lists was his 1910 campaign for mayor. Boston had long
since come under the political control of its large Irish population, and it seemed the height of folly for a patrician like Storrow to try to dislodge the city's firmly entrenched politicos. But
he fought a good fight in what turned out to be a hot and close
contest and won the support of the city's major newspapers;
some said the papers took his side because of his lavish spending on advertising space. When the votes were tallied, Storrow
had failed by a narrow margin to capture City Hall, though a
financial postmortem disclosed that his defeat had cost considerably more than his opponent's victory. Storrow, the loser, had
pumped $103,250 into the campaign; the winner, John F.
"Honey Fitz" Fitzgerald, had spent just $48,140.

EIGHT. "THAT WORST OF ALL
ECONOMIC PARASITES"

Four years after whipping James Storrow at the polls, John
Fitzgerald suffered what he deemed at the time a loss of his
own—his sparkling daughter Rose, reigning princess of the
city's Irish society, married a young Harvard graduate named
Joseph P. Kennedy. Kennedy seemed solid enough—at
twenty-six, he was said to be the nation's youngest bank
president—but the doting Honey Fitz had wished better things

for his favorite girl, though he would live to see her presented to the king and queen of England as the wife of the United States ambassador to the Court of St. James's.

The grandson of an Irish cooper who had fled his potato-starved native country in 1848, Kennedy had worked hard from an early age, but not by necessity. His father had done well by himself as a saloon keeper turned politician and banker, and encouraged his son in the ways of money-making. While his Brahmin contemporaries were being groomed as lawyers or fiduciaries, the Catholic Kennedy was being fired with the hard-driving Protestant work ethic that had galvanized Bostonians of an earlier time. Even at Harvard—his parents wanted their boy to have the best that Boston offered—Kennedy had a penchant for big profits, and operated a sightseeing-bus business that netted him a substantial $5,000 over three summers. He also had a craving for social acceptance, which would not be satisfied at Harvard or in Boston either. He would spend a good part of his life trying in sundry ways to prove that he was not just as good as, but better than, the Boston aristocrats who could not bring themselves to accept the brash grandson of an immigrant Irish barrelmaker. In return, proper Boston would regard Kennedy as a less-than-upright wheeler-dealer, a coarsely vulgar parvenu—which in many ways he was.

Fresh from Harvard and intent on becoming rich, Kennedy worked briefly at the Columbia Trust Company, an East Boston bank founded by his father and some friends in 1895, before being named assistant bank examiner for Massachusetts. Eighteen months later, with funds borrowed primarily from contacts he'd made as a bank examiner, he bought control of Columbia Trust and installed himself as president. He was clearly a young man on the way up, and he avidly courted the attention and favor of those already at the top, a suit that was rewarded in 1917 with his election as a trustee of the powerful Massachusetts Electric Company, where he sat with some of the kingpins of Boston's social and financial establishment.

Godfrey Lowell Cabot, who never quite came to terms with the fact that he had been born too late to fight in the Civil War, rushed uncalled to the colors during World War I. Buying his own seaplane to patrol coastal waters searching for German U-boats, he badgered the Navy Department to commission him, at the age of fifty-four, a lieutenant in the Naval Reserve Flying Corps. The much younger Joseph Kennedy chose a safer course, serving out the war years as assistant general manager of Bethlehem Steel's shipyard at Quincy, Massachusetts, turning his bank presidency over to his father. While there, he dealt occasionally with Franklin D. Roosevelt, the assistant secretary of the navy who had signed Godfrey Cabot's naval commission. Following the war, Kennedy was offered a job as head of Hayden, Stone & Company's Boston brokerage office—the firm's Galen Stone was a fellow trustee of Massachusetts Electric and had been impressed with Kennedy's style. The pay wasn't much, but the post gave the ambitious young financier-to-be a chance to learn the mysteries of stock trading and manipulation, at which he soon became a master. At the same time, he and some friends bought a string of New England movie theaters, marking his first tentative move into the growing motion picture industry. By the late 1920s Kennedy was a bona fide movie mogul, a self-assured Irish Catholic from Boston who sneeringly called his predominantly Jewish competitors a gang of "pants pressers." Uninfluenced by traditional Boston's uplifting cultural ideals, his studios cranked out reel after reel of low-grade pictures, and when an interviewer once complimented Kennedy for producing some good films, a dumfounded movie magnate had to ask which ones they were.

More fields awaited the Kennedy Midas touch—real estate, liquor, and always, high-stakes stock market speculation—but his millions would not be "Boston money," would not trace itself in fact or in spirit to the prevailing winds of Boston commerce and industry. Indeed, just as he was fairly started on his whirlwind financial career, and sorely stung by a turndown from a Boston-area country club, Joseph Kennedy pulled up stakes and moved with his growing family to the more hospitable atmosphere of New York. As the whole world knows, he would send his sons to Harvard and maintain a base in Massachusetts, but he would always remain an outsider in old-line Boston. And not solely because of his Irish background, but because of his wheeler-dealer ways, because in Boston's eyes he was, as the *New Republic* described him when damning his appointment as chairman of the newly formed Securities and Exchange Commission, "that worst of all economic parasites, a Wall Street operator." President Roosevelt, it is said, named Kennedy to the SEC post in the only half-facetious belief that it takes a thief to catch a thief. This assessment came as no surprise in Boston, where Kennedy's career was seen as solid evidence that earlier Brahmin alarmists had been right in their warnings of the mischief that is worked by the untrammeled drive for profit on the part of the newly rich.

Joseph P. Kennedy was not, of course, a thief in the strictly legal sense—though he once remarked to a colleague that the time was ripe to cop fortunes from stock manipulations "before they pass a law against it." But other actors on the Boston financial stage were not even that scrupulous, and their singular, if brief, success was perhaps a measure of Boston's own decline.

NINE. "A 100 PER CENT ON THE LEVEL WIZARD"

From the front door of the Washington Street office building where he conducted his thriving soot-and-gas business out of two cluttered, sparsely furnished rooms, Godfrey Lowell Cabot could look toward City Hall in the summer of 1920 and see a roiling mob of men and women trying to get into the offices of the adjacent Securities Exchange Company. Cabot had little in common with the horde of "investors"—they were mainly Irish and Italian, little people who saw nothing suspicious about a man who promised them 400 percent a year on their investment—and was in even less harmony with Charles Ponzi, the short, glib charlatan who was fleecing large numbers of New Englanders like so many innocent lambs. Ponzi had come to staid, conservative Boston to make a killing, and before his short-lived scam was over he would give his name to an age-old con game that had previously been known simply as borrowing (or stealing) from Peter to pay Paul.

Charles Ponzi had looked like a million dollars when he first stepped ashore in Boston on a drizzly November Sunday in 1903, fresh from his native Italy. He was dressed in the latest fashion even down to mouse gray spats, accompanied by several pieces of matched baggage. Unfortunately for Ponzi, it was all an illusion, and by his own account he was merely "one of those immigrants; one of the motley crowd oozing out of the ship's side." He had just $2.50 in his pocket, having frittered away the rest of his $200 nest egg in shipboard drinking and card games. Seven years later, after beating around the United States and Canada working at a variety of menial jobs, he was little better off; released from a Montreal prison after doing twenty months on a forgery conviction, he had $5 in cash, but he was wearing a baggy suit. Ponzi was soon behind bars again—this time for helping Italian workmen to sneak into the U.S. from Canada—and when he'd finished doing his time in Atlanta he bounced around the South for awhile longer, then headed for Boston and a lowly clerkship in an import-export firm. He was not exactly a young immigrant made good.

But Ponzi was ambitious, and if he was untouched by Protestant ethics, he was filled with the greedy independent streak that frequently underlies them. He quit his job in 1919 and set up in his own office, renting out desk space to cover his rent. The problem was that he couldn't figure out what kind of work to do. He dabbled for a time in importing and exporting, then turned briefly to publishing a trade directory for foreign firms seeking to do business in the U.S. His *Trader's Guide* died aborning—he couldn't raise the cash to get it under way—and Ponzi was racking his brain for another big idea when he was struck by a perverse inspiration.

Ponzi had sent out letters to prospective users of his directory, and while idly going through a stack of mail one day he came across a Spanish firm's request for a copy. Pinned neatly to the letter was an International Reply Coupon, issued by the International Postal Union and redeemable in U.S. postage for the return mailing to Spain. It was the birth of the Ponzi scheme, and the making of a momentary millionaire.

Ponzi's plan was beautiful—too beautiful—in its exquisite logic and simplicity. By sending American dollars abroad for conversion into generally depreciated foreign currencies, he could buy reply coupons exchangeable in the U.S. for stamps worth considerably more than their purchase price in foreign money. Mailing one dollar each to friends and relatives in France, Italy, and Spain, Ponzi tested his theory and found that it worked just as he dreamed it would. The Securities Exchange Company was in business, and before a year was out a wondering writer for the *Washington Evening Star* would observe of Ponzi that "It must be said of him that whatever his game, he has certainly played it well."

By definition, trading in stamps was a nickel-and-dime operation, and Ponzi himself sometimes wondered at the gullibility of people who failed to realize that there could not be enough reply coupons—or stamps and money, for that matter—in the whole world to allow him to deliver as promised. What counted was that it was theoretically possible to rake in huge profits buying and trading the coupons. Building on that demonstrable base, the fast-talking Ponzi was off and running. Conning one of his creditors into lending him still more money, Ponzi printed up stationery and notes pledging to pay investors 50 percent on their money in just forty-five days—this at a time when bank interest was running to about 5 percent a year. Word of Ponzi's generous wizardry soon spread—he used no advertising, only word of mouth, primarily in the large Italian community of Boston—and when the handful of initial investors were indeed given the promised 50 percent after forty-five days, an avalanche of customers began pouring into Ponzi's offices overlooking City Hall. He soon had branches pulling in funds from all over New England.

The grandiose scale of Ponzi's operation quickly overtook the underlying concept. There was no trade in reply coupons, but who knew, who cared? Ponzi was, after all, paying as promised to those who wanted their interest, though most investors chose to leave both their interest and principal in Ponzi's hands for reinvestment. And the money continued to pour in. Ponzi bought control of a small bank, downtown real estate, and a suburban home. He even bought a macaroni company. But his bubble couldn't last. Postal officials and other authorities had been suspicious of him from the start, but he'd managed to bluff his way through. The press was a different story, and when the Boston papers began spotlighting his affairs in July, 1920, little more than six months after the start of his operation, Ponzi sensed the beginning of the end.

His offices were mobbed, partly by previous investors wanting to withdraw their funds, but largely by fresh faces seeking to get in on the bonanza while there was still time. Ponzi cheerfully accommodated both, taking in new money and using it to pay off old notes. At times, it took a dozen mounted policemen to control the crowds, and by Ponzi's account he once raked in a million dollars in a single three-hour period. "Madness, money madness, the worst kind of madness, was reflected in everybody's eyes," he wrote later of the eager throngs that stormed the offices of his Securities Exchange Company. For his own part, he added, money meant little to him. He just wanted to test its power.

Its power was not sufficient to fend off disaster for Ponzi. Forced to agree to an audit of his haphazard books, he was confronted with figures showing he owed millions that he just didn't have and had no way of raising. "Gee," said the dapper Ponzi, flashing the broad grin that had seen him through so many a close call in the past, "then I guess I'm not solvent." Indeed he wasn't, and he was soon behind bars, though he maintained that he was being railroaded by bankers fearful of his competition for the public's funds, and must certainly have concurred with the wording of a handbill distributed on the streets of Boston by one of his clerks, James Francis Morelli. Ponzi, Morelli said, was "a 100 per cent on the level wizard."

A federal judge disagreed, finding that while Ponzi may have been a wizard of sorts, he was by no means on the level. The penalty: five years in prison. Ironically, Ponzi's defense counsel, Daniel H. Coakley, also wound up in a cell not long afterward, though his imprisonment stemmed not from dealings with his notorious swindler client but from a set-to with the redoubtable Godfrey Lowell Cabot. Cabot, whose indignant self-righteousness when it came to sin frequently led him into unlikely combat, had become incensed when the district attorney for

Boston, Joseph C. Pelletier, had merely chuckled when Cabot informed him that a Beacon Street physician was administering to nervous female patients a dose of what in a later generation would be called sex therapy. Never one to shirk his duty, Cabot determined to remove Pelletier from office, no mean feat in a city where political power had long since been snatched from the hands of Cabot's class. In the course of his crusade, Cabot discovered that Pelletier not only snickered at vice in the examining room, but was also conspiring with lawyer Coakley and the district attorney of a neighboring jurisdiction to uncover substantial citizens in staged sexual situations. For a sizable fee, the conspirators would agree to drop all charges and forget what they knew. It took him several years—during the course of which he was tried and acquitted for the larceny of materials from Coakley's office—but Cabot at last succeeded: Coakley and the two offending district attorneys were disbarred, and Coakley was jailed. Later, this episode would inspire John P. Marquand to have his fictional George Apley involved in a somewhat similar adventure, though with quite different results.

TEN. "FIRMS SUCH AS LEE, HIGGINSON SIGNED THEIR NAMES"

One day in 1922, as Charles Ponzi was languishing in his cell, two New York partners of Lee, Higginson & Company were having lunch with one of Europe's most brilliant industrialists. Donald Durant and Frederic W. Allen sat enthralled as the soft-spoken Ivar Kreuger described how he had started out with two modest family match companies, then built them into one of the largest industrial trusts in the world. He seemed to be a genius, all right, and what was possibly even more important to the representatives of an old-line Boston banking house, he was every inch a gentleman. His suit was a conservative pin stripe; his tie, if not old school by Boston standards, was in impeccably good taste. Here was no olive-skinned Italian sharpie sauntering about in flashy clothes and waving a gold-headed walking stick; here was a dignified Swede who could match patrician bearing with any man, just the kind of solid businessman who was deserving of the aid and backing of one of the nation's most respected banking and brokerage houses.

This was precisely the impression that Kreuger had set out to make on his American luncheon companions. He knew that Lee, Higginson, while small by New York standards, was so rightly famed for integrity and rectitude—those twin trademarks of Boston finance—that the firm's sponsorship would stamp his far-flung enterprises with instant good repute. Henry Lee Higginson had died three years before, but his spirit lived on in the echoes of words spoken to a group of bond-salesman trainees just months before his death: "The house has always tried to do its work well and to have and keep a high character..." Higginson had said, adding that "Character is the foundation stone of such a business, and once lost, is not easily regained...." The public believed in Lee, Higginson, and knew that the firm would not put its upright character at hazard on behalf of ventures that it had not weighed carefully in the balance and deemed sound. And if anything, the fine old firm of Lee, Higginson had become more prudent and trustworthy with the passage of time. "As the house grows older," wrote Higginson to the New York-bred Frederic Allen in 1915, "I think it grows more careful."

Ivar Kreuger, peering intently across the table at the two Lee, Higginson men, mesmerizing them with his dream of worldwide control of the match market, was careful not to press his case too hard, skillfully casting himself, not as a suitor, but as one whose financial favors were worthy of ardent courtship even by prudent men. He did not let on that he needed Lee, Higginson and its reputation far more than the firm needed him, for he was a master of his art, a con man of the first water; the tens of millions of dollars' worth of securities that he would soon be selling through the agency of Lee, Higginson would in the end be worth little more than Charles Ponzi's fabulous 50 percent notes. And when he was finally brought down, he would fall far harder than the swaggering wizard of international postage stamps. Ponzi paid for his peculations with a mere prison sentence; Kreuger would pay with his life, taken by his own hand, and Lee, Higginson, promoter of railroads and copper mines, of American Telephone, General Electric, and General Motors, would forfeit its character, its reputation, and its very name.

When he first met with Durant and Allen, Kreuger was in fact master of a considerable fortune and head of a complex network of companies that controlled match production in several European countries. He had considerably overextended himself, however, and was in sore need of the sort of capital which in the uncertain postwar years could be had only in America. His two primary companies, Kreuger & Toll, Incorporated, and the Swedish Match Company, had sopped up nearly all the funds available to them in Europe, and Kreuger's imperial designs seemed made for the recruitment of American investors. What he had in mind was nothing short of a global monopoly on matches, complete control of every single one of the tens of millions of matches struck each day. A mundane product, perhaps, but still a universal one that promised stupendous profits to a monopolist.

The promise seemed bright to Lee, Higginson, which felt honored that Kreuger seemed to have singled out that firm from among all the others that were unashamedly scrambling for his business. Kreuger was pleased, if not honored, by Lee, Higginson's ardor, but he moved slowly. Leaving Durant and Allen to wait hopefully in their Wall Street offices, the match mogul steamed off to London and arranged with the Boston firm's English affiliate, Higginson & Company, to handle a major stock issue for Swedish Match. To keep things honest, Kreuger invited the London partners to visit Stockholm and look over his properties there. They were impressed with what they saw, but they were perhaps even more impressed with the discount that he gave them on the stock.

Before long, Kreuger was ready to start giving American investors a shot at the match game, and by the end of 1923 he and Lee, Higginson had joined to set up the imposingly titled International Match Corporation. Though real power in the company was securely vested in Kreuger and his Swedish cronies, the board of directors was graced with numerous prestigious Americans, among them Durant and his fellow Lee, Higginson director, Percy A. Rockefeller, a nephew of John D. With names like that behind it, International Match stock was gobbled up in short order by eager American investors who were soon crying for more. Kreuger readily obliged, and by 1932 Lee, Higginson had unloaded nearly $150 million worth of the company's stock.

Oddly enough for a firm that had always prided itself on pushing only those stocks whose value it had carefully determined, Lee, Higginson had only the vaguest notion of where the proceeds were going. When asked, Kreuger gave blithe and convincing explanations—the near-$22 million net from one big offering, he said, was earmarked for "transactions in Greece, Portugal, Algiers, Norway and Manila"—but there was seldom any proof, any documentary evidence to point to. What seemed to matter was that Kreuger was a gentleman, and a gentleman's word was proof enough. ("Never make a gentleman's agreement," Godfrey Lowell Cabot always warned his sons, "or you will find you are the only gentleman party to it.")

In fact, though he did indeed manufacture and market a lot of matches, Kreuger was pulling a magnificent financial caper that made Charles Ponzi look like a small-town pool hustler. And his victims were not, as Ponzi's had been, merely the greedily naive—"children in finance," one writer had called them—but the canniest investors in the country.

The key element of Kreuger's grand deception was government-granted monopolies which supposedly gave his companies the sole right to manufacture and market matches in a given country. Such monopolies were costly, of course, and required considerable payments and loans to governments and to government officials. And because of delicate matters of international relations and internal politics, it was often necessary to keep the payments under wraps. Or so the suave Kreuger told anyone who inquired about what he was doing with all those millions put into his hands. In Poland, he actually did shell out a $6 million loan in exchange for a match monopoly, but an additional $17 million, raised largely from American investors under the pretense that it would be used for expanding the Polish operation, simply disappeared in the complex maze of real and bogus corporations that Kreuger had set up to conduct his ever more complicated affairs. As for Italy, Kreuger merely printed up and forged government bonds and notes totaling $142 million, which he flourished before the eyes of doubters and carried as assets in his tangled books.

Without the intervention of global economic collapse, Kreuger's fragile empire might have wheezed along for a considerable time, buoyed by profits from the legitimate side of his operation and paying out dividends with funds raised from fresh stock issues. For the world had faith in Kreuger, so much so that his visits at the White House with President Herbert Hoover were regarded as major steps in sorting out what was wrong with the general financial situation. But Kreuger was in worse shape than the world economy. As money supplies began drying up, he was caught increasingly short when it came time to pay off his obligations. Prices of Kreuger company securities plummeted on every stock exchange in the world despite the efforts of Lee, Higginson and other houses to shore up the shares on the bellwether New York Stock Exchange.

Trying desperately to wheel and deal himself out of fiscal quicksand, Kreuger could finally no longer stall a full and close accounting of his affairs. Two Lee, Higginson partners, calling on the match king at his New York apartment in early 1932, found him babbling patent nonsense; the doctor summoned by the worried pair informed them that their golden Swede was on the verge of total insanity that could be prevented only by the avoidance of bothersome pressure. Now Lee, Higginson, its reputation riding on the outcome, was drawn into the maze of Kreuger's real and phantom enterprises, and tried to get a solid purchase on elusive assets whose nature and whereabouts seemed known only to the master himself. Rallying, Kreuger managed once more to brazen his way through a crisis, to regain the all-important confidence of Lee, Higginson.

But he could not hold back the day of reckoning or dodge the inevitable end. When he sailed back to Europe in early March,

1932, he was accompanied by Donald Durant and his fellow Lee, Higginson partner N. Penrose Hallowell, who, if they had kept their faith in Kreuger, were nursing nagging doubts about his bookkeeping practices. They planned to be at his side when he sorted through his ledgers in search of salvation. It was a leisurely crossing, a welcome respite—for the beleaguered Kreuger, at least—from the pressing reality of the match king's swaying house of cards. In Paris, where the party had determined to hold a preliminary accounting before moving on to the other outposts of the Kreuger empire, Kreuger spent a somewhat nervous first afternoon parrying queries from close associates in preparation for the next morning's full-dress session—which only Kreuger knew would not take place quite as planned.

At about ten o'clock the next morning, New York time, a cablegram was delivered to the Wall Street office of Lee, Higginson. George Murnane, the senior partner in the office that Saturday, read the message with stunned disbelief. Dispatched by Donald Durant in Paris, it was short and pointed: Kreuger had "died very suddenly" that very day. The cable did not describe how Durant and the others had waited nervously for Kreuger to appear at the appointed meeting; how finally they had dispatched one of their number to call at the match magnate's plush apartment; and how Kreuger, immaculate in silk shirt, muted tie, and pin-stripe suit—coat and vest carefully moved aside—had been found in bed, shot neatly in the heart. Nor did it tell of the wild fears, the shock of realization that had struck the men waiting vainly for Kreuger to explain himself. It didn't have to. For Murnane, without knowing the grim details, knew enough. He knew, as he said later, that "we had all been idiots."

And so did all the world. Kreuger's ashes had hardly cooled—despite the family's request that contributions be made to charity in lieu of flowers, Lee, Higginson, along with many others, sent a huge floral wreath to the fallen financier's funeral—before the cynics' worst suspicions began to be confirmed. A preliminary announcement from a hastily convened investigating commission observed laconically that the flagship

Kreuger & Toll's assets were in all likelihood insufficient to cover its liabilities, to which the esteemed Lee, Higginson could only reply that true or not, this state of affairs was at considerable variance from the information provided by the late Ivar Kreuger. So much for high character, so much for James Jackson Storrow's old injunction that the firm should stick "closely to the things which we are trained to analyze and know how to weigh in the balance."

And there were no answers for those who asked why, who wondered how it happened—no answers, at least, that would have suited founding partners John Lee and George Higginson. For Kreuger's part, that enigmatic deceiver had been driven by his own twisted demons to seek financial power, no matter what the cost in gold or honor. If he ended badly, he had lived well, or at least comfortably, though probably no more luxuriously than if he'd chosen to be an honest man. Lee, Higginson, on the other hand, had simply fallen to the credulous, speculative craze of the time, been caught up in the fevered pace of the 1920s. As the firm had grown and branched out, it had moved from State Street to Wall Street.

Called to testify at a bankruptcy hearing held to unravel International Match's intricately knotted affairs, Lee, Higginson officials were forced to concede that no, they had never examined or even asked many questions about Kreuger's alleged worldwide assets, and that yes, they had such implicit confidence in the monumental swindler's integrity that they believed nearly everything he ever told them. Said partner Frederic Allen: "up to the time he committed suicide I personally had no doubt of the integrity of the man." In fairness, so too did nearly everyone else, save those who made their more critical judgments with the considerable advantage of hindsight. Indeed, Kreuger had so bedazzled Lee, Higginson with his apparent honesty, virtue, and all-around worthiness that the firm had lent him a full $15 million, secured only by his reputation.

In the swirling haze of Kreuger's smoking pistol, Lee, Higginson died, too, its once-bright legacy riddled almost beyond recall by all but the charitable. Most of the proceeds from the some $150 million in Kreuger securities marketed by the firm to U.S. investors had simply vanished, swallowed without trace or residue by the inscrutable match magnate's labyrinthine corporate sham. Investors who had taken Lee, Higginson's word on the value of Kreuger's bogus issues were badly stung, as were the partners and their friends and families, who saw some $9 million of their own run down the drain. Abbott Lawrence Lowell—whose young relative, Ralph Lowell, was a Lee, Higginson partner in Boston—alone lost nearly $195,000. The shock and the shame, not to mention the acute financial embarrassment, were too much to bear, and just three months after Kreuger left his shambles behind him, the old and honorable banking and investment firm announced curtly that it was going into liquidation. Sixteen branch offices were shuttered, and though the reorganized firm continued to do brokerage business in Boston, Chicago, and New York as Lee Higginson Corp., it was, like Boston itself, a pale and blurred copy of what it once had been. Disgraced by fortune and in men's eyes, the firm's most dolorous epitaph was written, not by a Bostonian, but by a Swede, the economist Gustav Cassel. In the *Svenska Dagbladet*—which, ironically, had once been controlled by Ivar Kreuger—Cassel spoke for many when he observed that "If firms such as Lee, Higginson & Co. signed their names to Kreuger's issues, it was natural that we in Sweden—and even more people all over the rest of the world—should suppose that they had thoroughly investigated the position of the firm and were exercising a comprehensive supervision over its management. We were mistaken. . . . They gave Kreuger & Toll their moral support for many years without taking any steps to make themselves acquainted with the firm's real position."

It was a fair and fitting summation of the Lee, Higginson–Ivar Kreuger romance and a stinging slap across the face of Boston's time-tested traditions of honorable and upright conduct in business affairs.

ELEVEN. "THE MAINTENANCE AND PERFECTION OF WHAT ALREADY EXISTS"

Godfrey Lowell Cabot, James Jackson Storrow, Lee, Higginson's ambitious but ill-considered fling with Ivar Kreuger—all were a part of Boston's first few twentieth-century decades; happily and unhappily, they were atypical, variants from the steady, plodding theme that would mark the Boston business spirit until the post–World War II years. As the nation's center of capital and enterprise had shifted relentlessly to New York, Boston had been eased into the role of financial spear carrier, upstaged by the bigger guns of Gotham. In the words of novelist and diplomat Frederic J. Stimson, himself a product of Boston, Bostonians had to be "content with the crumbs from J. P. Morgan's table."

Ownership of the great Boston-backed railroads had been diluted or grabbed by others—the Chicago, Burlington & Quincy, once the pride of John Murray Forbes, shuttered its general office in Boston before World War I—and Boston's pivotal role in developing the nation's railway system was a receding memory. Early in the century, American Telephone had slipped away. "We used to sell all the Telephone bonds," wrote Henry Higginson in 1910, "but now the company has outgrown us and passed into other hands." The "other hands" were mainly those of J. P. Morgan, who had easily outmaneuvered and outbid the Bostonians at every turn; ironically, he was assisted in this enterprise by the Boston investment banker T. Jefferson Coolidge, Jr. General Electric, too, had fallen to Morgan and his minions, though Bostonians continued to sit on the board of directors—as they did on the boards of other companies that they had founded and once controlled. But these were mainly "Boston seats," honoring the large stockholdings controlled by the city's fiduciaries. They carried with them little power or influence; Bostonians were no longer lords of industry, but virtual vassals of more puissant men. Responding in 1913 to General Electric President Charles A. Coffin's query about the possibility of Lee, Higginson's underwriting a debenture issue, Henry Higginson replied meekly that "we can not without disrespect to Messrs. Morgan, make any definite propositions to you until after you have talked with those gentlemen,—and those gentlemen means Jack Morgan." On yet another occasion, Higginson wrote that "our relations with Messrs. Morgan & Company are entirely friendly, and we wish to do as they wish."

United Fruit's mighty fleet, its vast tropical landholdings, railroads and radio-telephone system had made the company an all-but-sovereign power in Latin America, but this great banana empire had been easily plucked away by Samuel Zemurray, whose rival Cuyamel Fruit Company was merged with United Fruit in 1929. Under terms of the purchase, Zemurray "retired" as United Fruit's largest shareholder, but when the fortunes of the company and of Zemurray's sizable block of stock began to decline, the tough-talking Bessarabian immigrant came to Boston from his home in New Orleans to save his investment. Hardly inhibited by Boston's rules of decorum, Zemurray strolled into the company's board room on lower State Street, hurled a sheaf of empowering stocks and proxies on the table in front of the startled directors, and snarled: "You've been fucking up this business long enough. I'm going to straighten it out."

United Shoe Machinery—"The Shoe," as it was known familiarly around town—remained a Boston company in both ownership and control, but its very success only underscored the city's overall decline in power and initiative. The company's key founders and top executives, Sidney W. Winslow and George W. Brown, were "new" Bostonians from out of town, operating outside the sluggish main currents of what now passed in Boston for enterprise. The First National Bank, too, though it could (and proudly did) trace its corporate ancestry back to the first John Lowell, owed its success to outlanders—which may explain why it was far and away the largest bank in Boston. Known for years as the "Winslow bank" because of the strong influence of United Shoe and Sidney Winslow, the First had risen from virtual obscurity through a series of mergers that put Daniel G. Wing in the president's chair. Wing, who proceeded to lead the bank to a commanding position that it would never lose, had had the temerity to be born in Iowa, and began his banking career at the age of fourteen as a lowly messenger boy in the State National Bank of Lincoln, Nebraska. At a time when the Brahmin-run Massachusetts Hospital Life Insurance Company was mindlessly putting its money into mortgages in the deteriorating downtown area—which could be seen from the office window—the First National Bank was investing in Texas real estate and Hollywood and opening up a net of offices overseas.

United Shoe and the First, strong as they were, were merely exceptions to Boston's ruling disintegration, fruited islands in a stagnant sea. Even the Gillette Safety Razor Company, built around the inspired invention of a Boston-based but Wisconsin-born and Chicago-educated bottle-top salesman, did not attract any great attention from old-line Boston until the disposable blade's wide use by World War I doughboys made it obvious to all but the dullest minds that the safety razor was here to stay. Meanwhile, bankrolled primarily by a collection of bottle- and cap-manufacturers and a prosperous Irish immigrant, the company had become an international concern.

Boston itself seemed a reflection of washed-out glory, of blunted enterprise, and nowhere was this apparent more than on the wharves, raised as testaments to a thriving commerce but standing now as galling monuments of vanished and better days. Despite the steady decline of the New England textile industry as low-cost labor made southern mills more economical and productive, Boston remained the world's largest wool center; the still-thriving footwear industry made the city the center for export of boots and shoes and imports of leather. But such workaday commerce was a far cry from the days when sailing ships had put out to sea with mixed cargoes and come proudly home with holds bearing the riches of China and the Indies. By the eve of World War II, nearly half of the ships docking at Boston came filled to the hatches with coal, leaving vast stretches of waterfront clouded in perpetual fogs of black and choking dust.

Only Long Wharf, once the pride of Boston, bore any likeness to the old times of maritime prosperity and romance, and then only on days when ships of United Fruit's great white fleet were docked alongside to unload lush stems of tropical bananas. Other storied wharves had not fared so well. Lincoln Wharf had become a powerhouse for the Boston Elevated Railway Company, whose girdered tracks slashed along the

waterfront and destroyed the city's vista of the harbor. Constitution and Battery wharves were warehouses for soap and
groceries; day-excursion boats were the only vessels setting out
from Foster's Wharf, where Black Ben Forbes had watched
with childish fascination as sailors beat the ice from the sails and
rigging of the ship that took him on his first ocean voyage.

The sagging, rotting, disused, misused wharves were not the
only battered remnants of days long past. There were also
ships, or what was left of them after the ravages of time and
scavengers. Like dead and foundered sea creatures nipped by
marauding sharks, a fleet of derelict hulls littered the harbor,
bleached by the sun at low tide. Even at that, their day was not
yet done: in the grim and needy winters of the early 1930s,
some 120 of these skeletal vessels were dragged ashore, broken
to bits, and picked over for firewood by the poor.

Downtown Boston, now a citadel of prudence and trusteeship, had fared only a little better than the old waterfront.
Largely rebuilt following the great fire of 1872, it had remained
virtually static ever since, a shabbily genteel image of its
fiduciary role. The soaring hopes of the 1920s had spurred
building booms in the more dynamic cities of the nation, but
not in Boston. Save for the United Shoe Machinery Company's
twenty-four-story headquarters building—hailed as a marvel
when it opened its doors in 1930—and a handful of other ran-
dom structures, the Boston skyline was all but unchanged since
the Doric Custom House was defaced in 1914 with an incon-
gruent office tower that would overshadow other downtown
buildings for fully two generations. In stark contrast to earlier
days, Boston had little need for building. And the men who
held the purse strings, who tended the insurance companies
and investment trusts and great family nest eggs, had mostly
moved from the city, to Wellesley or Westwood or Milton or
Manchester-by-the-Sea. They were commuters now, daytime
transients in a city that was no longer their home.

Few Bostonians slumped on the mourners' bench lamenting
what time had done to their city and to themselves. If the
wharves were falling, so be it. There was no good use for them
anyway, and to fix them up would be to throw good money

after bad. As for the down-at-the-heels business district, what did it matter? Fast operators in New York or Chicago might need fancy new offices in towering buildings, but the slower, more prudent men of Boston could get along just fine in more modest and traditional quarters behind frosted glass doors on Milk Street. Godfrey Lowell Cabot made do with a couple of unpretentious rooms, and his far-flung business activities had made him one of the richest men in Boston. There must have been a broader meaning behind the story that Cabot steadfastly refused to buy overshoes on grounds that Boston winters, severe though they might be, did not last long enough to make such a frivolous investment worthwhile.

Indeed, Boston drew such generous dividends from past achievement that it seemed almost a duty to pay homage to history at every opportunity. The banker Allan Forbes, grandson of Robert Bennet Forbes, began writing and publishing in 1906 a series of booklets glorifying the deeds and men of Boston's venturesome past. When it came time to move his State Street Trust to a new headquarters building in 1925, Forbes made sure that the new granite structure would have been in harmony with Boston business buildings of the early nineteenth century, and he had the main banking floor done up in such a way that it looked as appropriate a place for checking on the arrival of a ship from Canton as for cashing a check. For his own corner office on the first floor, Forbes designed a replica of an eighteenth-century counting room, its walls lined with pictures and mementos of long-ago times. The small window behind his desk looked out across the site of the Boston Massacre to the Old State House, a scene that had remained little changed with the passage of generations. But this was not enough for Forbes: the modern pavement intruded, and so did the modern pedestrians and the coughing, horn-blowing automobiles jockeying for position at the intersection. When all this became too overbearing, Forbes could almost wipe it away by pulling down his shade, on which was drawn the same scene as it had appeared in the days when his grandfather had strode through Boston with such sure and certain purpose.

Boston lived easily with the past, perhaps more easily than

with the present or with prospects for the future. As long ago as 1912 the writer Isaac Marcosson had noted the city's reputation as a "clannish repository of old family wealth," a place where the achievements of ancestors were favored topics of conversation, and it seemed that the passage of time had only hardened this backward disposition. To be sure, the conservative trustees and other money managers, those prudent custodians of well-ripened wealth, had brought themselves and their clients relatively safely through the great stock market crash of 1929, and were rightfully proud of that feat. Too proud, some thought, and there was a waggish story going around that the Boston Safe Deposit & Trust Company was so conservative that it didn't even know there was a depression.

As the world inched toward the watershed global war with Germany and Japan, Boston was far from a city of builders and promoters, of innovators and visionaries. Like an elderly gentleman of means snoozing in a well-worn leather chair and scanning from time to time the morning's stock quotations, the city had settled easily into its fiduciary role. Its power and initiative gone, it seemed content as an investor's city, living on dividends gleaned from the imagination and enterprise of others. Noting without apparent irony that Bostonians had from the beginning shown "their ability to adapt themselves to changing conditions," the private trustee and investment manager Donald Holbrook went on to write smugly in 1937 that in Boston "one finds little evidence of frenzied pursuit of expansion and grandiose development. There is far more concentration upon the maintenance and perfection of what already exists. . . . Boston has an attending degree of stability more in keeping with its maturity, and gladly turns over the exuberance of pioneering to other sections of the country. . . ." So much for voyages of adventure.

In a way, such widespread thinking was indeed an adaptation, a face-saving acceptance of Boston's loss of national influence. But it was far from the way Francis Cabot Lowell and his friends had turned boldly from a withering commerce to found a thriving new industry; it was hardly of a piece with John Murray Forbes's move from the China trade to railroad building; it was a sodden echo of the pathfinding days of copper lodes and telephones. It was, indeed, nothing less than rationalization for a monumental surrender of power and will, a prim damnation of what Bostonians of an earlier and more ambitious day had called enterprise. It was a virtual celebration of the decrepitude gripping a once-dynamic city.

Chapter Nine

AWAKENING

We cannot float along indefinitely on the enterprise and vision of preceding generations.

—Ralph E. Flanders, 1946

Amid fanfare and well-wishing, Lee, Higginson & Company had occupied in late 1925 a spacious building of its own on Federal Street. James Jackson Storrow, Jr., drained by the cancer that would claim his life within three months, came in from his Lincoln estate for the occasion, to mark the proud firm's move from the long-familiar State Street address into quarters that it fully expected to maintain for at least as long as it had the old. By the war years, a humbled and shrunken Lee, Higginson had moved to more modest offices just doors away. The letters of the firm's name had been unceremoniously pulled off—leaving telltale scars on the granite walls—and its nearly abandoned building was being used as headquarters for United War Fund drives, whose chairman's desk sat in the same chandeliered oval room where Ivar Kreuger had once lectured young stock- and bond-salesmen on "How to Succeed."

Not all of Boston had been brought so low, and the real home-front war was being waged not in the shells of an old Boston, but in the incubators of the new, in the classrooms and laboratories of Harvard and the Massachusetts Institute of Technology.

For even at its most moribund, Boston had pulsed with an

occasional vital sign, a harbinger of renewal and better days ahead—and not only in its academic world. In 1924 a trio of young Boston investment men organized a fund to enable investors to pool their resources and put them in the care of prudent Boston money managers. This allowed the small investor to buy a piece of a well-handled securities portfolio far more diversified than he could ever hold on his own; as an added bonus, shares in the fund—dubbed the Massachusetts Investors Trust—were redeemable on demand at the current proportionate value of the fund's assets. It was a novel concept, so novel that at the time it didn't even have a name. When it spawned the inevitable imitators, they were all called Boston funds. Later, they were known as mutual funds.

At about the same time, a small Cambridge concern known as the American Appliance Company, established a few years before to make refrigerators, acquired the rights to a new kind of radio tube that would permit radios to run on household current rather than on bulky batteries. One of the company's key advisers was M.I.T. Professor Vannevar Bush; the investors included J. P. Morgan, Jr., along with a handful of Bostonians, among them Thomas Jefferson Coolidge, III. Then in 1925, the fledgling company got an unexpected jolt: there already was an American Appliance Company, out in Indiana, that had no intention of letting an upstart steal its good name. At a special meeting of the board, the company was hastily rechristened the Raytheon Manufacturing Company in honor of the futuristic name that had been picked for the revolutionary radio tube. By the 1930s, annual sales were running to several million dollars. And in August, 1938, a young Boston stockbroker named Charles Francis Adams, Jr., son of Boston's first citizen, joined Raytheon's board of directors. In a way, it was a family matter—Adams's sister was married to a Morgan son, and the new director's main task was to keep close tabs on the Morgan investment in the company—but Adams would later see in Raytheon a chance to build a new industry, to help reverse his home state's steady decline.

Just a year before Adams slipped into his director's chair at Raytheon another young man was forming his own small company not far from Raytheon's Cambridge plant. His aim was to capitalize on an idea he'd been tinkering with for more than a decade, ever since the night in 1926 when, as a seventeen-year-old Harvard freshman from Bridgeport, Connecticut, he'd been walking along New York's Broadway squinting into the blinding glare of oncoming automobile headlights. He was a clever young man with a consuming interest in physics, and it occurred to him on the spot that the glare could be erased with special polarizing filters. Driven by a vision of these filters installed on the headlights and windshields of every automobile, Edwin H. Land took a leave of absence from Harvard and spent the next two years boning up on the problem by day in the New York Public Library and experimenting by night in a rented room and a Columbia University physics laboratory that he entered through an unlocked window. His idea virtually perfected, Land returned to Harvard in 1929 and was provided lab space to continue his research. He never did get around to graduating, and in 1932 took a permanent leave of academic absence and set up a small research and production company with a Harvard physics instructor. Five years later Land was ready to go it alone. Through a New York lawyer friend he'd made some substantial contacts on Wall Street with men who had both wherewithal and forward vision, a combination not notably present in Boston at the time. His original investors and directors included the likes of James P. Warburg, W. Averell Harriman, and Lewis Strauss, and these financial titans had such faith in Land's genius and the prospect of mounting his product on millions upon millions of automobiles that they struck a most unusual bargain. They invested $375,000 in the new company—which Land dubbed the Polaroid Corporation—and agreed to give Land voting control and the complete direction of the company for a ten-year period. There would be some rough times ahead, and a sharp departure from the company's original goal, but at the end of that decade no one would regret the trust placed in the brilliant and broodingly handsome Edwin Land.

Land chose a Boston-Cambridge location for his enterprise because the area's endemic intellectual ferment suited his scholarly temperament—despite his lack of a diploma, he would later lecture at both Harvard and M.I.T. (and cherish his honorific title of "Doctor"). He got his financing in New York because he had contacts there and because that's where the big money seemed to be for the sort of venturesome undertaking he had in mind. But there was money to be had in Boston, too, if not on so grand a scale. As in times past, there were men willing to bet on something new, to back promising people and ideas. One of them was William A. Coolidge, a lawyer and investment banker—and grandson of the coin-tossing rail-roader, textile man, and financier Thomas Jefferson Coolidge —who had seen the need for investments that went beyond the standard portfolio of blue-chip stocks and bonds. With some like-minded Bostonians, Coolidge had formed a loose group called Enterprise Associates, which soon crossed paths with Richard S. Morse, a young man with a somewhat novel idea. A 1933 graduate of M.I.T.—like Land, he majored in physics—Morse had done graduate work in Germany, then taken a research job at Eastman Kodak and later another Rochester, New York, company. It seemed to Morse that much of the industrial research activities he observed were not par-ticularly productive, that too many processes and products were found, filed, and soon forgotten. What was needed, he thought, was a research organization that would not only be a consultant, but would also put things into production. Scouting around for guidance, Morse met the French-born Georges F. Doriot, gifted and popular Harvard Business School professor who always found time for extracurricular activities; one of them was acting as an adviser to Coolidge's Enterprise As-sociates. Morse's idea sounded good to Coolidge and his friends, and at a Somerset Club dinner one night in the spring of 1940, Morse learned that out of hundreds of projects con-sidered by Enterprise Associates, his would be the first to obtain financial backing, to the tune of $50,000.

Morse grandly called his company the National Research Corporation, and he wasted little time in getting it under way. Coincidentally enough, his first move was to get a license from M.I.T. to use a vacuum technique for coating glass to prevent glare, and lenses treated with the process were widely used in bombsights and periscopes during the war. National Research also developed a process to speed and cheapen the production of penicillin, and its work with concentrated orange juice led to the formation in 1945 of the Minute Maid Company. By that time, the company was moving along at such a rapid clip that it had been able to make a public stock offering the year before. There would be many more such companies to come, companies conceived in war but ready to respond to the needs of peace.

More than any previous conflict had been or could have been, World War II was a battle of technology; in the final accounting, victory fell to the side that had the best scientists as well as the most battalions. And there were probably no better scientific brains on earth than those toiling along the Harvard—M.I.T. axis. In solid campus buildings, in quickly rented space, in hastily built wooden structures thrown up for the duration, the Boston area's great technological resources were mobilized to thwart and destroy the war machines of Germany and Japan. At M.I.T.'s Radiation Laboratory, essential radar and other detection and navigational systems were developed and honed to fine reliability. Harvard did critical work on problems of submarine warfare, among other things; other Boston-area universities did their share as well. But it was M.I.T., old Boston Tech with its long dedication to purely practical matters, that carried the heavier burden, that contributed possibly more than any other research and development organization to the overall war effort. Out of its laboratories and work rooms came a bewildering array of methods, systems, and devices relating to fire control, missile guidance and navigation, metallurgy, optics, photography, and, above all, the burgeoning new world of electronics. Marching to war, M.I.T. and its myriad scientists and technicians helped bring closer the inevitable peace and became a catalyst for the renaissance of a Boston that had already begun to stir, to shake off more than a generation of fitful sleep.

TWO. "NEARLY EVERYONE THOUGHT WE WOULD FAIL"

Technology: it had saved the world from Hitler and the ravenous rising sun; now it had a more mundane—but hardly unimportant—mission. Properly exploited, it could save Boston from the great slough that the city had fallen into, restore the constructive spirit of old. Boston faced many of the same problems that had plagued it from its very beginnings on the barren Shawmut peninsula three centuries before. It had no easy access to natural resources; it was remote—even more remote now—from population centers; fuel costs were high. But it was not without counterbalancing assets. And as they had in the past, the elements of success seemed happily conjoined. All that Boston had been and done for generations seemed to come together in a pattern of prospective achievement. The city was the center of the largest congregation of scientists and technicians ever assembled: in 1950, M.I.T. president James R. Killian, Jr., would observe that the so-called Research Row, embracing Harvard, his own school, and the many nearby industrial laboratories, could boast "probably the greatest concentration of scientific, engineering, and research talent in the world." The lovingly nurtured educational and cultural climate of the city combined to make the Boston area attractive to intellectuals and scientists poised at the cutting edge of advancing technology. Equally important, Boston contained great amounts of capital which, if not lying idle, was not being used quite to full capacity, and was looking for more venturesome outlets. Most promising of all, there was an almost pioneering spirit abroad in Boston, an inclination to find new ways to blend finance, technology, and brainpower into a productive recipe.

Perhaps nowhere was this spirit made more manifest than in a tiny room on Congress Street, in the heart of Boston's financial district, where the fledgling American Research & Development Corporation first opened for business in mid-1946. ARD, as the company soon was known, was a unique organization, a publicly owned investment company formed to supply venture capital to new research-based enterprises bent on peaceful exploitation of the technology that had only recently been turned to the destruction of men and cities. Cold war had not yet come, and it was time to beat swords into plowshares for the benefit of a nation saved from economic depression only by the intervention of a long and costly conflict. But money, funds to set new ventures rolling, was a distinct problem. There were a few wealthy individuals and private groups sniffing around for likely investments in the highly speculative technical field, but it seemed that most of the nation's wealth—and certainly most of Boston's—was in the grip of fiduciaries such as insurance companies and investment trusts which by their very nature were not given to risk-taking. A man with a new and untested idea had to look long and far to scare up the capital to set his venture going.

Few saw the dangers of this financial bottleneck more clearly than Ralph E. Flanders, a Vermont machine tool company executive who started his business career as an apprentice machinist and rose to be president of the Federal Reserve Bank of Boston and later United States senator from his home state. It was in 1946, the last year of his two-year stint at the Federal Reserve, that Flanders decided to take steps to crack open the bottle. "I became increasingly concerned," he wrote at the time, "with the increasing degree to which the liquid wealth of the nation is tending to concentrate in fiduciary hands. This in itself is a natural process, but it does make it more and more difficult as time goes on to finance new undertakings." As Flanders saw it, there were two large repositories of wealth with a stake in putting some of their funds into enterprises other than the well-aged blue chips so favored by fiduciaries. These were insurance companies and investment trusts, with which Boston, a long and honorable record of prudent money management behind it, abounded. To help channel some of this money into new fields, said Flanders, there was a need for "a development corporation financed in a large measure by these two groups of institutions, under the directorship and management of the most capable men available in the fields of business and technology." It was an imaginative prescription— there was nothing like it in the country—and it was one that Boston, with its great stores of intellectual and financial capital, was ideally suited to fill.

To insure institutional participation in ARD, Flanders and his fellow founders specified that their company would start rolling only when half of its 120,000 initial shares, valued at $3 million, had been purchased by institutions. Among those that anted up: the John Hancock Mutual Life Insurance Company; the Massachusetts Institute of Technology; and that pioneering and prestigious mutual fund, the Massachusetts Investors Trust—"the other M.I.T.," it was sometimes called—whose crusty chairman, Merrill Griswold, was one of the key founders of ARD.

Flanders did not serve long in the twin offices of president and treasurer which he held at the birth of American Research & Development. Elected to the U.S. Senate in the same year that the company opened its doors, he stayed on as a director but resigned his executive posts. But with or without Flanders, ARD was in capable hands. Elected president in his stead was the Harvard Business School's Georges Doriot—Brigadier General Doriot now, following World War II service in a high army research and development post in Washington. The treasurer's job was taken on by Horace S. Ford, who was also treasurer of the Massachusetts Institute of Technology. And serving with Doriot and Ford as chairman of the three-man executive committee was Merrill Griswold of "the other M.I.T." Together, the three represented that great triple-threat combination that helped provide the strength for Boston to pull itself out of its long sleep: the Harvard Business School, M.I.T., and the financial community.

ARD's first investment was not particularly auspicious: a new line of degreasing equipment for automobile engines and parts that flopped when a nationwide chlorine shortage cut off supplies of needed solvent. Subsequent ventures proved more fruitful and more in keeping with Boston's new technological times; the degreasing equipment maker had been located in Cleveland, Ohio.

At about the time that groundwork was being laid for ARD, John G. Trump was mulling over the possibility of starting a company to build and market a scaled-down version of the famous particle accelerator, or "atom smasher," developed in the 1930s by Robert Van de Graaff. Trump, an associate professor of electrical engineering at M.I.T., had come up with a way to reduce the size of the machine even before the war, and when he returned to academia after serving as director of the Radiation Laboratory's British branch, he got several inquiries from hospitals seeking to use the machines in cancer therapy. There was an obvious demand for such equipment, and Trump hoped to capitalize on it. When he told M.I.T. President Karl Compton of his plan, Compton immediately saw it as a hot prospect for help from ARD—he had been a prime mover behind the firm, and was on its board of technical advisers— and pushed strongly for its financial support. Georges Doriot, though not a technical man, agreed with Compton's assessment, even though the giant General Electric Company had already entered the market. Drawing on the talent available from M.I.T., Doriot reasoned, the prospective company could match or excel whatever brainpower GE could muster, and besides, the Trump-designed machine could sell for considerably less than the GE model. On the last day of 1946, ARD put $200,000 behind the newly formed High Voltage Engineering Company, headed full time by Denis Robinson, who had led a British technical mission to the Radiation Lab. It was not long before industry observers were marveling at the run this upstart Cambridge company was giving GE for its money.

The founders of High Voltage Engineering had had a firm idea of what business they were getting into, but the men behind ARD's next investment had not been nearly so certain. "We didn't have the slightest idea what we wanted to do," one of them said later, recalling how he and three other Radiation Lab alumni had pooled their meager resources right after the war, rented a small room in Cambridge, and called themselves the Industrial Electronics Laboratory. (They were, perhaps, living examples of what would become a byword at ARD and among other investors in new technology: "The longer I stay in this business," said Merrill Griswold in the early 1950s, "the more convinced I am that it is better to back a smart person with a fair invention than a fool with a good one.") The four found few takers for their offers to do just about anything from repair radios to tinker with shipboard radar, and then one day one of them, Ray Ghelardi, was talking over his problems with an M.I.T. physics professor, a friend from wartime Radiation Lab days. Why not, the friend suggested, get into providing electronic gear and radiochemical services to the hospitals, universities, and industries that were interested in peacetime uses of radioactive isotopes in a variety of testing and tracing operations? It sounded like a good idea, better than fooling around with radio repairs, and when Ghelardi and his partners drew in William E. Barbour, Jr., another M.I.T. friend, things began falling into place. Barbour had worked at Raytheon before the war, had pulled a coup in the company's stock, and was willing to put some cash into the new venture. With what seemed like the munificent sum of $26,000 from Barbour and about $1,500 apiece from the original Industrial Electronics Laboratory crew, a new company, Tracerlab, Incorporated, was formed in March, 1946, just three months before the incorporation of American Research & Development.

In rundown quarters near Boston's financial district, the company went into swift operation, and was ready to sell its first products by December. But an unexpected problem had cropped up along the way—with no money coming in, the original nest egg had all but disappeared by October. Barbour, who had become Tracerlab's money man, turned to New Enterprises, Incorporated—the postwar guise of William Coolidge's Enterprise Associates—but was turned down when a dip in the stock market made new and untried enterprises look singularly uninviting. Next he tried some New York venture capitalists who would gladly come through with $100,000 or so, but they wanted control of the company in exchange, something that Tracerlab management did not care to give up. Then Barbour heard of ARD. Tracerlab—the first company to really commercialize a by-product of the atomic bomb—seemed promising, and ARD invested $150,000 on terms that left the founders in full charge.

And so it went. With quickening speed and growing momentum, new companies—cranking out either products or research and development projects, and sometimes both—

began dotting the landscape in and around Boston. Pent-up demand for consumer goods, things like television and home deep freezers, kept war-born electronics alive; by the mid-1950s or so, things seemed to reach a critical mass, a period of self-sustained and almost unstoppable growth. The Russians had helped push the process along when they touched off their first nuclear bomb in 1949—long before the world had guessed they could. There was a rush to develop advanced air defense systems to guard against attack, and as it had in the hot war that had ended in the mushroom clouds of Hiroshima and Nagasaki, the U.S. military again enlisted the help of the nation's universities, among them M.I.T., for extended duty in a new kind of cold war. At the joint request of the army, navy, and air force, M.I.T. established the Lincoln Laboratory to work on long-range radar, distant radio communications, and high-speed digital data processors to digest and interpret masses of information. Later, when the Russians surprised the world once more by orbiting the first man-made earth satellite, M.I.T.'s Instrumentation Laboratory, which had long done yeoman work in developing sophisticated aircraft and missile navigational equipment, was given the task of devising guidance systems that would in time lead American astronauts safely to the moon and back.

It was a time of bubbly ferment and expansion, of high purpose and promise. Seeing the success of some of the earliest technology-based enterprises—Tracerlab, for one, was posting annual sales of more than $10 million within five years of its founding—engineers with an entrepreneurial spirit broke away from their laboratories or companies to form new businesses of their own. They were called spin-offs, these newly spawned companies, and their number was legion. By the early 1960s, it was estimated that Raytheon alone—whose huge defense contracts had made it the state's largest industrial employer—had spun off nearly 150 enterprises; M.I.T., with its yeasty classrooms and laboratories, could account for 100 or so such enterprises—including, in what now seemed the dim past, Raytheon itself. Like some biblical patriarch, M.I.T. begat companies that begat companies in a chain reaction that seemed to have no ending.

Boston had once measured capital in dollars; now the equation was fleshed out with brainpower and technology. And there was no dearth of men eager to prove their new ideas worthy of financial commitment, men seeking to meld their intellectual capital with whatever financial capital could be found, whether it was in Boston or elsewhere.

David Bakalar, with a doctorate in physical metallurgy from M.I.T. and a temporary job at Bell Laboratories, had no trouble getting the needed cash from his older brother, Leo, when he decided in 1952 to go into the new field of transistors. Indeed, Leo Bakalar had pushed and shoved his more scholarly brother into the business world, and gladly put about $1 million—made from scratch in liquidating unwanted goods and then in plastics—into the pioneering Transitron Electronics Corporation. Within seven years, these two sons of a Lithuanian immigrant were sole owners of a company valued at some $150 million.

When a cadre of researchers from Boston University spun off in 1957 and formed the Itek Corporation, they got their start-up money from the Rockefellers; Kenneth H. Olsen and Harlan E. Anderson, when they spun out of M.I.T.'s Lincoln Lab in the same year to set up their own small company, turned to Georges Doriot's American Research & Development for both funds and an organizational assist. They had intended to make electronic modules for designing and testing computers, but their Digital Equipment Corporation quickly outgrew its youthful bounds and introduced a computer of its own in 1960. Soon the company was the hands-down leader in the small computer field, an industry that it had created almost single-handedly. Along the way, it proved fabulously profitable to ARD, whose initial $70,000 investment soared in value to better than $300 million in the years after Digital Equipment went public in 1966.

It was sweet success, savored with particular relish by Georges Doriot, who remembered the skepticism that had greeted the first announcement of ARD's venture-capital plans. "People said that it couldn't be done," he recalled later, "and that we'd lose all our money. They said it was too dangerous, and nearly everyone thought we would fail."

But it had not been long before even the most confirmed nay-sayers saw sure and certain signs that the new technology was more than mere curiosity, and that it was sinking strong roots in the near hinterland of Boston.

THREE. "THE PROXIMITY OF M.I.T."

When the textile men of old got cramped for space and needed room to expand their ranks of looms and spindles, they moved out boldly to create whole new riverside cities. Their spiritual heirs in the twentieth century's technology-based industries had no such luxury as they multiplied and strained at the available quarters in Boston, Cambridge, and nearby towns. Some, like Transitron and Digital Equipment, made do with what was at hand. Transitron achieved a crowning position in its industry while operating out of an old knit-underwear mill and a converted bakery; Digital is still going strong with headquarters and considerable manufacturing facilities in a rambling brick mill that once wove woolen blankets for Civil War soldiers. Others—many others—chose a sprawling counterpart of Lowell and Lawrence, located not on a riverway but along a divided highway that scribed an asphalt arc around Boston.

It had been there in embryo for years, a narrow country road snaking through the woods and rolling fields, broken here and there by truck farms, piggeries, and poultry farms, running lazily from Peabody on the north through Wakefield to Woburn and storied Lexington, then south to Waltham and through the Newtons. Its main reason for being was to carry traffic from the north and south around Boston, bypassing the city's narrow and congested streets. Something like a superhighway for the route—dubbed Route 128—had been discussed in the 1920s, and a four-lane segment got started on the northern leg in the late 1930s. But the war put an end to such civil projects, and it wasn't until 1948 that things got going in earnest. By 1951, the road was all but finished, curving gracefully through open land from ten to fifteen miles out from the heart of Boston. It was an ideal route for an unhurried Sunday country ramble, and some cynics wondered what an expensive superhighway was doing in such relative wilderness. It would not be wilderness for long, however, and Route 128 would soon become a generic name for research-based companies. It bore the official designation of Boston Circumferential Highway, or Yankee Division Highway, after the Massachusetts National Guard. But it was to be better and more widely known by such nicknames as the Golden Belt, the Electronic Highway, the Miracle Highway, and the Golden Semicircle.

No one really planned it that way, but the completion of Route 128 and the rapid ballooning of the Boston area's research-based industries coincided with such artful symmetry that the Miracle Highway seemed almost foreordained. And few saw this more clearly, or did more to bring it to full and fruitful flower, than the real estate development firm of Cabot, Cabot & Forbes Company.

There was little in the company's history to indicate that it would be in the vanguard of a faltering Boston's rebirth through technology. It had begun in 1892 when George E. Cabot, a cousin and contemporary of Godfrey Lowell Cabot of carbon-black fame, went into the real estate business after trying his hand at managing a telephone exchange and running a couple of small electric companies. George's younger brother Norman came into the office right after his graduation from Harvard in 1898 and was made a partner five years later. Taken on as a third partner at the same time was Francis Murray Forbes, who had spent his childhood in China when his father—a New York cousin of the Boston Forbeses—was serving there as a partner in Russell & Company, the old China trade concern that had failed at last in 1891. The Cabot firm was incorporated in 1904 and went on with its business of managing Boston properties owned by some of the city's first families. Cabot, Cabot & Forbes did a fair amount of construction on State Street and along Boylston Street, the Back Bay's main business drag, and then served as trustee for the buildings' owners. It was a solid, respectable company whose slogan—"The Care and Management of Property"—neatly summed up the scope of its activities. But it was ready to change with the times, to listen to new ideas and give them a chance. It just needed a little prodding.

The prodding came from Gerald W. Blakeley, Jr., a young Bowdoin College graduate—his father was a professor at M.I.T.—who optimistically started up his own real estate development company when he got out of the navy in 1947. It was Blakeley's idea to build garden-type industrial parks, neatly landscaped bunches of manufacturing and research facilities in an almost campuslike setting, just the kind of place for all those academic types spinning out of classrooms and laboratories to try their hands at building companies of their own. It wasn't long before Blakeley crossed paths with F. Murray Forbes, by then the head of Cabot, Cabot & Forbes, and it wasn't long, either, before Forbes was taken with the younger man's enthusiasm and vision. He was in his seventies now and not ready to go off on new and untried paths himself, but he was willing to make the paths easier for those who wanted to give them a try.

It was a fine idea, Forbes told Blakeley, a fine idea indeed. But there was one slight problem: no one in Boston knew who Blakeley was, which wouldn't make it any easier for him to sell his industrial park idea. Why not, asked Forbes, join forces with Cabot, Cabot & Forbes? It was probably fair to say that the prestige of the company could save the young upstart about twenty years of groundwork, which would certainly make the association worth his while. Blakeley agreed that this might be something to think about, but Forbes didn't give him much time for reflection. "He said that in this business you have to make decisions quickly," Blakeley recalled later. "It was four o'clock in the afternoon, and he said he wanted to know by noon the next day whether I'd join the company." The following afternoon, Blakeley was head of the newly established industrial division of Cabot, Cabot & Forbes. And the cagey Forbes had been right. Even with the old names of Cabot and Forbes behind his ventures, Blakeley ran into skeptics. An old-line banker, for one, taken to see the site of an early Cabot, Cabot & Forbes industrial park, turned to Blakeley and advised him that he was much too bright to get himself involved in such an enterprise. Such foolishness might go over in Texas or California, he said, but never in New England.

He was wrong, of course. Nearly as soon as Route 128 was opened to traffic, technical companies were attracted to its bordering expanses of open land, so near to the university research facilities and their pools of brainpower and new ideas—"The whole secret of Route 128," Blakeley recalled later, "was the proximity of M.I.T." Like mushrooms after spring rain, they sprouted along the new road that gave such swift and easy access to Boston and surrounding towns. First there was Hytron, then Bomac, then Sylvania, companies whose very names seemed to speak of the future. By 1955, close to forty companies had anchored along the Golden Semicircle, a number of them in the pioneering Cabot, Cabot & Forbes industrial park at Needham, which quickly became an international prototype for such projects. A decade later, the roster of Route 128 companies had grown to nearly six hundred, and included numerous service and distribution outfits as well as the backbone technology companies. Blakeley, meanwhile, had been richly rewarded for his foresight, for anticipating the importance of Route 128 and picking up surrounding land while it was still cheap. In 1956 he bought out the remaining Cabot family shares in Cabot, Cabot & Forbes and became president. By 1960, he'd bought the Forbes interest, too, and taken complete control. The company continued its rapid growth, and by the time industrial development along the Miracle Highway had peaked in the 1970s, Cabot, Cabot & Forbes had done about 85 percent of the building, putting up a total of sixteen industrial parks on Route 128. It had also taken a leading position in development along yet another Boston circumferential highway—Route 495, some fifteen miles out from 128—and was building industrial, commercial, and residential complexes all over the country.

At the same time, the company was doing considerable work in Boston itself, though it had been many years after the resounding early success of new industry on Route 128 before anyone was moved to start sprucing up the Golden Semicircle's

urban core. Meanwhile, it had been business almost as usual—
with a few new twists—in much of Boston, the Boston whose
vocation was the husbandry and employment of capital.

FOUR. "BOSTON MONEY IS THE BEST MONEY"

Boston's fame as a potent father of new enterprise may have
ebbed with the passing of John Murray Forbes and those
touched by his generation's drive and daring, but the city had
steadfastly retained a just renown for attentive money management, for the provident and carefully considered investment and reinvestment—the preservation—of capital. This was
one of the oldest and most honored Boston professions, and
the city's numerous mutual funds, banks and trust companies,
and private trustees were for good reason the caretakers of an
enormous reservoir of funds—a consistent 30 percent or so of
the nation's mutual fund assets have traditionally been in Boston hands. State Street was no Wall Street, to be sure, but that
very difference was part of its allure. In isolated Boston, far
from the frenzied hustle and bustle of the great international
money market and rumor mill of New York, solid, sober, ex-
perienced men could exercise what they were wont to call their
instinctive feel for quality, their nose for the investment with
staying power. As one banker put it, "What we're trying to do
is run a marathon, not a hundred-yard dash." It was frequently
said that even investors itching for speculative action would
turn their "serious money"—money they didn't care to
hazard—over to Boston, where they knew it would be kept
safely in a portfolio darkened with deep-dyed blue chips. So
high was Boston's repute as an investment center—and so large
was the pool of capital in its collective care—that in 1950 leaders
of some of the nation's foremost corporations came to the city
almost in homage to participate in a great civic jubilee celebrat-
ing the half-century mark and hailing Boston's role in the financial life of America.

Solid, that's what Boston was, solid as the granite facing of its
old business buildings, solid as its longtime leading citizen, the
third Charles Francis Adams, who said to his son on the day the

young man set out to his first job: "I believe you've inherited a reputation for honesty—God help you if you lose it." Known as "the Deacon" for his taciturn, simple Boston ways, Adams was a nephew and namesake of the nineteenth-century railroader and real estate speculator—but styled himself "Sr." rather than "III"—and was for years one of Boston's foremost bankers and trustees. At the time of his death in 1954, at the age of eighty-seven, it was noted that he had at one time been a director of a full forty-three corporations, among them American Telephone & Telegraph, John Hancock Mutual Life Insurance, and Pan American World Airways; for thirty years, he was treasurer of Harvard. An avid yachtsman—he skippered the *Resolute* in its 1920 America's Cup victory over Sir Thomas Lipton's *Shamrock IV*—Adams served as secretary of the navy under Herbert Hoover, and went back to Boston in 1933 to be named president of the Union Trust Company. When that institution merged three years later with Allan Forbes's State Street Trust, Adams became chairman of the board, from which post he kept a weather eye on the considerable fortunes and directorships entrusted to his care.

His son might well have followed in his father's footsteps, just as the senior Adams had inherited numerous trusteeships from *his* father, John Quincy Adams, II. Indeed, following World War II service as a seagoing naval commander, Charles Francis Adams, Jr., took up once more his comfortable berth as a partner in the Boston brokerage and investment banking house of Paine, Webber, Jackson & Curtis, and seemed firmly set on a course that would make him a gentleman trustee and director, hard sought for the prestige value of his venerable name. But Adams's navy experience had roused in him a genuine fascination for radar, sonar, and other such electronic gear, and in civilian life he began to take an uncommon interest in his directorship at Raytheon, a company that had been a key wartime supplier of advanced electronic equipment. One of his first moves was to smooth the way for a Raytheon takeover of the Submarine Signal Company, an old-line Boston concern in which Henry Lee Higginson, among others, had taken a strong interest early in the century.

Both Raytheon and Submarine Signal had been suffering

from the postwar slump in defense spending and the pangs of switching from military to civilian markets. Merged, they were still beset with difficulties, and the enlarged Raytheon's directors found themselves eyeball-to-eyeball with impending financial disaster. A special committee of directors set out to find the root of the problem, and determined that the company president—a brilliant engineer, but no great shakes as a businessman—needed a topflight aide to help put Raytheon's rickety corporate house in order. The man of the hour: Charles Francis Adams, Jr., impeccable always in timeless double-breasted suits, marked in his thirties with the high-domed baldness of his illustrious forebears, who had appeared to be so relentlessly headed for a genteel life of Boston-style investment management.

His father—yachtsman, banker, and trustee—warned that it was a mistake to abandon a prestigious partnership for an executive post in a floundering company that had yet to find its way in the world. But Adams stuck to his guns and did what he felt was a duty not only to an ailing company but to an ailing region. "Electronics was new," he explained later. "It was a chance to build a new industry at a time when all the traditional industries of New England—textiles, shoes and the like—were in decline. It was a chance to build a new industry on the ashes of the old, for New England." In May, 1947, Adams took on the job of executive vice-president at Raytheon.

Moving slowly at first—it was his first dip into corporate management waters—Adams felt his way, then began taking action. Shaving operations here, combining functions there, he brought order out of disorganization, gave direction to a company that had been moving out in too many ways at once. Not surprisingly, he frequently locked horns with President Laurence K. Marshall, who, as a founder of the company, was understandably miffed by what he saw as interference. In less than a year Marshall had moved up to the chairmanship, leaving Adams as president, in charge of operations; a year later he was made chief executive officer as well. Under his guidance—and with a timely assist from a rapidly growing national defense budget—Raytheon prospered mightily, and it was not long before the company once known for its radio tubes was known for its Hawk and Sparrow missiles and a host of other electronic marvels.

It had not been an easy task for the broker turned executive. Along the way he had jettisoned a costly entry in the television set market and skillfully sold off, at no loss, an ill-starred data-processing equipment venture. But it had all paid off handsomely, and by 1957, just a decade after he'd given up investment management for corporate command, Adams was presiding over the largest company in New England.

If 1947 had been a prophetic year for Raytheon and Charles Francis Adams, it was a landmark for Edwin Land as well. His Polaroid Corporation had also sunk into the postwar doldrums when its market for glare-proof gunsights and other military optical equipment dried up, but Land had a world-beating ace up his sleeve. In 1944, while shooting snapshots for the family album, Land had been asked by his impatient daughter how soon she could see the finished pictures. As he explained that the film had to be sent out for processing, he was struck with a flash of inspiration of the type that comes to many men, but which is acted upon by only a few. Land was one who acted, and within six months he had worked out the essential principles of what was to become the self-developing Polaroid Land camera. It was, an associate later said, a feat of genius that could probably not be duplicated by a hundred Ph.D.'s working nonstop for a decade.

Land demonstrated his instant photography process to a wondering world in early 1947, and the first of his magic cameras went on sale in Boston in time for the following year's Christmas season, going so fast and furiously that harried clerks found themselves selling display models with missing parts. Land cameras became a nationwide sensation, and so did Polaroid stock, once it was plain that instant photography was more than a fleeting curiosity; from $12 a share in 1956, it vaulted to $100 in three years, making it a speculative favorite of the day.

Polaroid was not, however, the kind of seasoned, tried-and-true blue chip favored by Boston's mainstream money managers, the trustees and mutual fund operators. As a rule, these prudent men—who by the mid-1950s were charged with the care of some $15 billion in investment capital—chose to rely on the long-term, steady returns promised by proven companies rather than take a chance on quick and speculative gain with its attendant risk of equally rapid loss. They were running a marathon, in which victory seldom falls to the merely swift. But they were about to see moving out from their midst a different breed of runner, a devotee of the financial fifty-yard dash, who would introduce mutual funds to a method of stock market wheeling and dealing that would be memorialized in the American lexicon by the decidedly un-Boston term of "go-go."

Gerald Tsai, Jr., was no stranger to Boston when he signed on in early 1952 as a junior stock analyst at one of the city's numerous mutual funds. Born in Shanghai, the thoroughly westernized young man was a 1949 economics graduate of Boston University, and after working for a time in Providence and New York, he came back to Boston and began scouting around for an opening in the city's famed investment management community. He found his niche at the Fidelity Fund, presided over by Edward C. Johnson, II, who took an instant liking to the personable and aggressive young Oriental with a marked knack for getting along with men older than himself. Though every outward inch the proper Boston fiduciary type—even to his well-worn felt hat and hand-knotted bow tie—Johnson was at heart a speculator who had first been inspired to play the stock market after reading as a young man about the career of Wall Street operator Jesse Livermore. Years later, telling stock market chronicler John Brooks about this signal event in his life, Johnson rhapsodized about the few-holds-barred world of the speculator, where it was every man for himself: "And Livermore—what a man, always betting his whole wad! A sure system for losing, of course, but the point was how much he loved it. Operating in the market, he was like Drake sitting on the poop of his vessel in a cannonade. Glorious!"

Glorious, indeed, but if Johnson had been more speculative than most of his fellow Boston mutual fund operators, shun-

ning their inborn habit of buying only for the long haul, he was
still inhibited by class values from giving totally free rein to the
swashbuckling dreams of youth. Tsai, on the other hand, felt
no such qualms, nor did Johnson balk at giving his protégé a
free hand. With gimlet eye for the quick-rising issue, Tsai was
soon buying and selling stocks with a flair that would have been
called almost reckless had it not been so profitable. So stunning
was his performance, in fact, that within five years he asked for,
and was given, a green light to unfurl a fund of his own beneath
the Fidelity umbrella.

Tsai called his new baby the Fidelity Capital Fund and moved
it quickly into the speculative big leagues. Taking what were
judged at the time to be tremendous risks with mutual fund
money, he bought huge lots of stock in such glamorous but still
financially immature companies as Polaroid and Xerox, waited
coolly as his shares moved up a few points, then unloaded them
to move on to something new. Like a star-bound rocket, the
asset value of his fund soared steadily upward, drawing behind
it bales of hopeful money from a public eager for its share of
Tsai's glorious action. Others, inspired by Tsai's example just as
Edward Johnson had been by Jesse Livermore's, jumped on the
bandwagon, and it was not long before Tsai-style growth was
almost the order of the day in much of the mutual fund industry. Money madness—perhaps not quite so manic as that seen by
Charles Ponzi on the faces of his frantic customers, but madness, nonetheless—gripped the land, and go-go moved from
the discotheque to the stock market. Conglomerates; soaring
profits; hot new stock issues that doubled, tripled, quadrupled,
and even more, almost overnight—the Soaring Sixties were
sizzling along with no clear end in sight, and brokers and
mutual fund salesmen from coast to coast were spinning tales of
near-certain riches and assuring neophyte investors that they
really couldn't lose.

For a time, it seemed to many that they couldn't, and Gerald
Tsai, who had done so much to kick off this speculative frenzy,
had every reason to be pleased with his progress. By 1965 he
was a stock market superstar, adored by much of the press and
public, courted by corporate titans in hopes that out of respect

and friendship he would not soften their company stock by unloading huge blocks from his portfolio at a single sweep. It seemed that he could write his own ticket for wherever he wanted to go, but he would soon find that a Boston flexible enough to cradle so great a departure from traditional modes of money management was still Boston, firm and unbending in other of its ways. In the matter of family, for example.

Tsai's ascent as a financial celebrity had neatly coincided with Edward Johnson's arrival at normal retirement age, a circumstance that might reasonably have assured Tsai the role of successor. Except that Johnson had a son, Edward, III, called Ned, who also worked at Fidelity, and who, if he lacked Tsai's dash, was both competent and hardworking. Between the two, Tsai and the younger Johnson, who was destined for the top? To ask the question was almost to answer it, and Johnson minced no words when he at last told his protégé that when the time came, Ned would take his place at the helm of Fidelity.

Tsai, of course, resigned not long after, and with the $2.2 million that he cleared when Fidelity bought back his sizable share in the company, he left Boston for the deeper and more dangerous canyons of Wall Street. His Manhattan Fund, launched with much hoopla in early 1966, was an instant darling of the investing public, but it soon turned fickle. Out of the orbit of Boston, Tsai's magic touch deserted him, and the founder of go-go was outdone by high-rolling imitators. None too soon, still iridescent in the afterglow of his early success, Tsai sold off his operation at a fabulous profit and retired from mutual fund management; he bailed out just in time to miss the late-1960s crash that left Wall Street littered with the thread-bare reputations of go-go "gunslingers" done in by a plague of falling prices. Dodging disaster, his fortune assured, the onetime sprinter had slowed almost to marathon speed.

At about the same time that Gerald Tsai's star was mounting high in the speculative sky, the venerable First National Bank of Boston was quietly looking into the affairs of Serge Semenenko. Despite a heavy accent and the exotic timbre of his name, Semenenko was not a dissident Russian author or composer, nor the claimant to some obscure grand ducal title. He was, in fact, the bank's vice-chairman, known far and wide for his deft hand at reorganizing ailing companies and engineering complicated mergers. He was known, too, as something of a worldly jet-setter, and as the "mystery man of the financial world." These were odd distinctions for a Boston banker, but then, Semenenko was not really "from" Boston, nor was he, despite his high post in the city's largest bank, of it. Born in the Black Sea port of Odessa in 1903—his father was a wealthy banker, landowner, and philanthropist—he fled with his family to Constantinople when the Bolsheviks took over and was educated in that Byzantine city's Classical College. At a professor's urging, he then left for the United States and the Harvard Graduate School of Business Administration. He liked Boston—it was, in its way, the most American of cities, and stood close enough to the real center of things in New York—and in 1926 joined the First National Bank as a $100-a-month credit clerk. It was a lowly post, but the young immigrant's quick mind and smooth charm eased the way upward. In two years he was an assistant vice-president, and he made vice-president five years later. By 1947 he was a senior vice-president and member of the board, of which he was named vice-chairman in 1959.

Along the way the bank had given him a rare autonomy, allowed him to operate so independently that he and his small staff became almost a bank within a bank. If he was slightly unorthodox by Boston standards—he maintained a plush office suite in New York's Pierre Hotel and was frequently seen in chichi Acapulco and on the French Riviera—Semenenko was good for business and had a brilliant knack for putting deals together in ways that enabled the First to compete successfully with banking giants of New York and Chicago. His very difference from the starched and stuffy Boston stereotype seemed to work to his advantage, and by the mid-1960s it was widely reported that he had arranged more than $5 billion in loans without ever suffering a loss. It was a record for which a Boston bank would gladly overlook a few eccentricities, and even the quiet resentment of Semenenko's peers.

Along the way, too, Semenenko had gathered a sizable fortune of his own, largely through private investments in companies to which, as a banker, he had lent money. There seemed to be something slightly irregular about this practice, though Semenenko would always maintain that his dealings were neither illegal nor unethical. Then in 1963, Democratic Congressman Wright Patman of Texas disclosed that mystery man Semenenko was tapping a group of New York charitable foundations, which just happened to be controlled by a close business associate, to finance his personal ventures in companies that he was servicing as a bank officer. But after a round of discreet inquiries from his fellow bank executives, Semenenko went about his business as usual.

Semenenko had frequently moved the First National Bank into situations that seemed a bit too glamorous, not to mention dangerous, for a Boston bank. He had arranged numerous loans to communications and entertainment companies—among them the Hearst Corporation, Columbia Pictures, Metro-Goldwyn-Mayer, and Warner Brothers—and was widely credited with saving the movie industry after World War II. The Hollywood ventures had made Boston a major source of movie capital and Semenenko a kind of shadow movie mogul; at one time, with money purportedly borrowed from the charitable foundations spotlighted by Wright Patman, Semenenko bought enough stock in Warner Brothers to make himself the company's second largest shareholder. Then in late 1963, he made a much-ballyhooed move to save the floundering Curtis Publishing Company and its flagship property, the *Saturday Evening Post*. So famed was he then that he knew his name carried more weight in some circles than did the name of his bank; when a frantic Matthew "Joe" Culligan, president of Curtis, rushed to the imperturbable Boston banker's hotel suite with a stern letter from New York's First National City Bank, demanding prompt payment of an outstanding loan, Semenenko could smile and observe that Curtis creditors would take a different view of things when they learned that Serge Semenenko had arrived on the scene.

Indeed he had. With First National of Boston supplying $10.5 million, Semenenko put together a lightning-fast six-bank loan of $35 million, enough to keep the sinking publishing company above water for a while. Among other benefits, Semenenko also arranged for the transfer of $38 million in Curtis pension funds to the Old Colony Trust Company, an arm of his bank. In the bargain, he bought a considerable number of Curtis shares for his own account, managing later to sell them at a handsome profit. But what was good for Semenenko and his bank was not necessarily good for Curtis and the doomed *Saturday Evening Post*, which drifted to disaster despite the infusion of cash and a flurry of last-ditch retrenchments.

But by then, Serge Semenenko was out of the Curtis picture, and out of the First National Bank as well, the apparent victim of one too many private deals. In the summer of 1967, the First's mystery man left the bank quite suddenly, a year short of normal retirement age. He was retiring, Semenenko explained, to devote more time to other affairs, and was becoming a business consultant; in best Boston banker form, the First's board chairman hailed Semenenko for the "outstanding services he rendered during his long and distinguished career with the bank." It was the kind of terse statement that corporations frequently make when high-ranking officers leave under a cloud, and many bank officials were surprised and a little bit embarrassed years later when their former vice-chairman appeared for old times' sake at an annual shareholders meeting.

Serge Semenenko and Gerald Tsai may have brought a certain dash, an exotic flavor, to the Boston financial community, but such seasonings were hardly standard fare in State Street. Mavericks of the Semenenko-Tsai stripe were generally regarded as "New York guys" who chose for reasons of their own to live and work in Boston, and who were accepted because their matchlessly brilliant performance left no other choice. It came as little surprise in Boston when Tsai hied himself to Manhattan, nor did waves of wonderment sweep through the financial district at the news of Semenenko's abrupt departure from the First National Bank. To many, it merely seemed that some ineffable providence was at work, pruning away elements uncongenial to the accepted Boston way of doing things.

Not that financial Boston was totally inhospitable to strangers. The executive suites and board rooms of its banks and other financial institutions were heavily leavened with "outsiders"—men from as far afield as Indiana, Iowa, and Nebraska—who had been drawn at an early age by Boston's high repute as a solid investment center, then worked their way up the corporate ladder. But these newcomers had in the main become thoroughly Bostonized, tastefully knotting passable facsimiles of the old school tie and embracing Boston's ways in both outward thought and visible deed. Boston remained Boston, its prevailing spirit formed and jelled—not to say solidified—over many generations. The upper reaches of the city's financial establishment had opened of necessity to talented and ambitious men from other parts of the country, but the old traditions had been little disturbed. Prudence and integrity, qualities frequently honored elsewhere in their breach, were still scrupulously maintained in Boston, and if the city's investment community was sometimes chided for an excess of caution, it was never charged with stinting on rectitude—or with losing sight of its past. At in-town clubs such as the Somerset and Union, at The Country Club—*The* Country Club, the first such club in America, whose emblem is the frisky but provident squirrel—proven fealty to Boston values was a prerequisite for membership, and these congregations of influential men with shared beliefs tended both to ratify and to reinforce traditional ways. And on a more superficial level, but perhaps nonetheless telling, conservative business attire, highlighted by a vest and ponderous watch chain and topped by an indifferently blocked hat, seemed to remain a downtown Boston fashion long after it had loosened its grip in other quarters.

And even if, taken as a class, the old trade- and textile-based aristocracy was no longer totally dominant, the continuing presence and influence of first-family members seemed living proof of the old virtues. Amid all change and alteration, *Fortune* magazine, in its 1957 catalogue of Americans with personal fortunes of more than $50 million, listed only one Bostonian, the ninety-six-year-old Godfrey Lowell Cabot—whose wealth was reckoned at between $75 million and $100 million. (Joseph P. Kennedy was listed, too, but with his city of origin carefully hyphenated as Boston–New York.) Coolidges and Gardners had put Bostonians at the helm of United Fruit once more; the large-scale management of money was a distinctly Brahmin enterprise whose undisputed paradigm was the banker Ralph Lowell, fifth-generation descendant of the Old Judge, successor of Harvard President Abbott Lawrence Lowell as sole trustee of the Lowell Institute, and heir to the Charles Francis Adams, Sr., mantle as corporate director par excellence—in his prime, Lowell was director, trustee, or treasurer of more than sixty corporations and institutions.

He was well prepared for such a role. A 1912 graduate of Harvard, where he specialized in Egyptology and earned a Phi Beta Kappa key, Lowell had taken a grand tour retracing some of the travels of Lowell Institute founder John Lowell, Jr., stopping at the Philippines for a visit with Governor Cameron Forbes, son of William Hathaway Forbes. Back in Boston, he took a lowly job with a State Street brokerage house, and after learning a few ropes moved on to the First National Bank as secretary to its president, Daniel G. Wing. Following stateside teaching duty in World War I—he'd been one of the first to rally to the Plattsburgh officer training program in 1915— Lowell stalked out of the bank on his first day back after the acerbic Wing remarked pointedly that he'd fallen behind his contemporaries who had stayed out of uniform. The reception was a bit warmer at Lee, Higginson & Company, which Lowell joined in 1919. Moving steadily upward, he was named a partner in the late 1920s and began assuming the inevitable directorships, trusteeships, and treasurerships that come to prudent men with good family and financial connections. He was as surprised as everyone else when Ivar Kreuger's pistol shot brought down the match king's shaky empire and Lee, Higginson along with it, and when the venerable firm went under Lowell surfaced as Boston manager for the firm of Clark, Dodge & Company, and was soon a partner. And as trustee Abbott Lawrence Lowell advanced in age, Ralph Lowell also became active in the affairs of the Lowell Institute, in whose interest he would soon show that old-school Bostonians could change with the times.

Since its beginnings in 1836 as a sponsor of public lectures, the Lowell Institute had branched into a variety of university extension courses and other such educational ventures, and by the eve of World War II, wise and prudent management had swelled the original bequest to some $2 million. But the formal lectures themselves had fallen on bad times, brought on both by a decline in the public's interest in the lecture as an art form, and by A. Lawrence Lowell's seeming preference for opaque speakers and subjects. The younger Ralph Lowell, even before taking complete control of the institute on his elder kinsman's death in 1943, had managed to bring some fresh air to the lectures; among the speakers appearing at his invitation was Arthur M. Schlesinger, Jr., whose series on "Jacksonian Democracy" became the backbone of his Pulitzer Prize-winning *The Age of Jackson*. But Lowell was quick to see that the institute's main mission could best be performed, not in lecture halls, but on the airwaves. Shortly after World War II, in company with Harvard, M.I.T., and four other Boston-area universities, he set up the Lowell Institute Cooperative Broadcasting Council to carry out a two-year trial at developing educational programs for broadcast over commercial radio stations. So successful was the experiment that it was continued beyond the trial period, and it was soon apparent to Lowell and his associates that their next logical step, to assure continuity and good time-slots, was to acquire a radio station of their own. By the fall of 1951, WGBH-FM went on the air with its maiden broadcast, a live performance of the Boston Symphony Orchestra. The Lowell Institute had put up most of the needed funds.

In laying down guidelines for future trustees, John Lowell, Jr., had given them freedom to choose lecture topics in keeping with "the wants and taste of the age." Now Ralph Lowell, having moved the institute into radio, prepared to take the founder's injunction a step further by expanding into television, a move surely in tune with public wants and taste of the early 1950s. So it was that the nonprofit WGBH Educational Foundation, formed to operate the radio venture, applied to the Federal Communications Commission for a Boston television channel. The request granted, WGBH-TV went on the air in May, 1955, its initial backing supplied by the Lowell Institute, a public fund-raising drive, and generous foundation grants pulled in largely by Ralph Lowell, whose unstinting efforts on the station's behalf would continue even beyond his retirement in 1966. Not for nothing did WGBH dedicate its new studio complex, opened in 1965, to Ralph Lowell; not for nothing, either, was Lowell once called "the Pope of educational television."

He was also—though he lived in surburban Westwood— called Mr. Boston, in combined recognition of his family heritage, his civic activities, and his post as chairman of the solid and prestigious Boston Safe Deposit & Trust Company, an office he had assumed in 1943. No mere figurehead, Lowell was a skillful money manager in his own right; after taking over the Lowell Institute investments in the mid-1940s, he moved them out of their heavy position in bonds and real estate and switched to well-chosen common stocks that increased the fund's value from about $2 million to some $5 million within a decade, laying a strong base for the 1970s' value of more than $7 million. And like others before him—like the merchant prince Thomas Handasyd Perkins; like assorted Lowells and Lawrences of the nineteenth century; like Henry Lee Higginson, James Jackson Storrow, Jr., and Charles Francis Adams, Sr.—Lowell seemed the very personification of Boston and its long traditions. Beyond any aristocratic or cultural claims, his Boston was a city of wealth, an investment center known worldwide for skillful management of large sums of money. If Boston's financial community took its lumps from time to time from those who accused it of being stuffy or timid, the city had at the same time harbored its Serge Semenenkos and Gerald Tsais, and the Boston money manager was deservedly draped with a respectful mystique. Even Semenenko, hardly cut from Boston cloth, could capitalize on this aura, and he observed at the height of his celebrity as a corporate savior that he frequently tried to "convince people that Boston money is the best money, for we stay with it through thick and thin."

But it was Howard Hughes, one of the richest and most

enigmatic of Americans, who may well have given Boston-style money management its greatest accolade when he paid a mysterious visit to the city in 1966. Taking over the entire fifth floor of the Ritz Carlton Hotel, glimpsed only by those he summoned to his side, Hughes remained closeted for four months before stealing out of the city as furtively as he had arrived. Indeed, even after the death of the phantom capitalist, it was not known who saw him in Boston, or why he had come—nor would Cabot, Cabot & Forbes, owner of the Ritz, even acknowledge the identity of its shadowy guest. It was widely believed at the time that Hughes had journeyed to Boston to consult with some of the city's renowned medical specialists about his worsening deafness, but that was not the only explanation. Not long before arriving in Boston Hughes had sold his majority interest in Trans World Airlines for a staggering $566 million, probably the largest sum ever to fall into the hands of one man at a single stroke. The orderly investment of so large a treasure would have taxed even the imagination of a Howard Hughes, and there were those who said that the reclusive billionaire had come to Boston for advice on what to do with all his sudden extra millions.

FIVE. "A NEW BOSTON"

Holed up in his closely curtained hotel suite, whether seeking medical treatment or financial counsel, Howard Hughes could see little of the Boston whose golden-domed Bulfinch State House Oliver Wendell Holmes had once dubbed "the hub of the solar system"—adding with satiric impartiality that "The axis of the earth sticks out visibly through the center of each and every town and city." It was a fetching image, made more cosmic by succeeding Boston boosters who extended their city's fanciful radius to make it the hub of the whole universe. Seldom if ever used in spoken conversation, the term became beloved by headline writers ("Hub Sailor Stabs Four") and writers seeking to avoid constant repetition of the city's name. During Boston's long decades of decline, terming the city "the Hub" was almost to call ironic attention to Boston's fall from grandeur, if not from a certain shabbily genteel grace.

Holmes had written of a Boston that was a focal point of culture and manners; by the mid-1950s the city was not only a financial and cultural center but the literal hub of a great and still-growing research and development complex. Near miracles were being worked in those trimly tailored buildings perched along Route 128's wooded and landscaped periphery, and Boston was the ultimate source of it all, had made it all possible by generations of building and achievement that began when the first captains set out to trade with the Indies. But Boston itself, good gray Boston so filled with memories and renewed promise, had not changed with the times, had seen no miracles on its own streets. Seedy, ancient buildings—ancient, at least, by American standards—seemed to stamp the city still, to press it firmly into a mold unsuited to the needs of new and venturesome twentieth-century enterprise. Unlike most American cities, Boston looked much the same as it had for generations, with few tangible signs of impending change; a stroller down nearly any block of midtown Manhattan—Gotham to Boston's Hub—would pass more new construction projects than in the whole city of Boston. Boston's money managers, with all the billions in their care, bore the dubious distinction of being beyond challenge the most poorly housed financial community in the nation, if not the whole world. There were those who likened metropolitan Boston to a gleaming apple with a rotten core, or called the ailing city "the patient," as if it suffered from some progressive disease more subject to remission than to cure.

Such talk was not new—there was little that was really new in Boston, it seemed. Calls for renewal had been heard in the dismal decade of national economic depression and during the war, too, when it appeared that nothing short of massive rebuilding could prevent Boston from becoming a quaint, tumble-down relic of better days that had fled beyond all returning. Speaking at a Faneuil Hall meeting in the closing month of 1944, architect William Roger Greeley had gone unchallenged when he lamented that Boston had not shared with

London the "advantage" of widespread destruction by aerial bombardment, leaving behind the rubble of an old city as a foundation for the new. In the absence of such wholesale but healthy razing, Greeley went on with graphically clinical metaphor, Bostonians needed to "destroy our own diseased tissues and by heroic will-power rebuild our community as a worthy competitor of the newer type of city."

It was a brave call to action, but one that would remain unheeded for some time to come. Still in the clutches of James Michael Curley's corrupt cronyism, Boston seemed hardly the place to invest in major building projects. The twenty-six story office tower opened up by the John Hancock Mutual Life Insurance Company in 1949 had seemed at first a harbinger of a better future, of a new Boston rising alongside the old. Indeed, the building's first tenants were the Massachusetts Investors Trust and the American Research & Development Corporation, twin symbols of the capital and brainpower that were combining to fire a renewed spirit of Boston enterprise. In a fine display of harmony between tradition and fast-paced change, an early visitor to ARD President Georges Doriot's office had been his Beacon Hill neighbor Allan Forbes, banker and devotee of his city's past, who brought with him the gift of a framed print of bygone Boston. But instead of providing inspiration, the building stood for years as a monolithic caution to those tempted to put their faith and their money behind a rebuilt Boston; when they got their first tax bill, startled Hancock officials discovered that they had been hit with considerably more than the amount that had been agreed upon with the city when the building was on the drawing boards. Stung by this duplicity, Boston's insurance companies—almost essential sources of funds for large-scale building—shied away from financing major construction in their home city for more than a decade and a half.

Not that anyone was much interested in building, in reversing the city's physical collapse. A writer for *Fortune*, noting matter-of-factly in 1957 that "the center of Boston is rotting away," was told by Raytheon's Charles Francis Adams that "Bostonians would rather watch the city crumble than rise," that the old-guard beneficiaries of past enterprise were "protecting the status quo rather than reaching out as in the days of the clippers." Nor would salvation come from the new entrepreneurs, the high priests of the new technology that was transforming greater Boston. Among them, said Adams, who was himself deeply immersed in the affairs of Raytheon, there was "no one with enough flair, time, or money to give leadership."

Then came a jolt of recognition. Its tax base eroded by declining property values, its population filtering across the city line to the suburbs, decrepit old Boston found itself doddering at the margin of bankruptcy. When the city went to the investing public in late 1959 with a bond issue, the highly respected Moody's Investors Service examined Boston's creaky condition and ranked its bonds at the lowest level of any United States city with a population of more than 500,000. The hub of the solar system, the Athens of America, found itself with a credit rating lower than Baltimore's or Cincinnati's. Fearing the worst, a group of business and financial leaders—pressed by blueblood attorney Charles A. Coolidge and Mr. Boston himself, Ralph Lowell—formed a coordinating committee to scoop up the pieces and act as receivers in the event of the financial collapse that seemed a distinct possibility. Significantly, few of the committee members—numbering generally a dozen and more—were Bostonians by birth or early breeding, though all had reached commanding positions in the city's business and financial community.

The feared disaster did not come. John F. Collins, the upset victor in a 1959 mayoral race held amid murmurings of impending fiscal ruin, determined not to take the bankruptcy route, but to plump instead for a rebuilding program that would restore Boston to good health. Burying the traditional animosity between Irish politicians and the State Street establishment, Collins persuaded the crisis-born coordinating committee—popularly known as The Vault after its meeting place in a basement board room of Ralph Lowell's Boston Safe Deposit & Trust Company—to work with him for needed change. If Boston were to survive, there was little other choice.

Actually, engines of renewal were already in motion, though

they were not running particularly smoothly. Work had finally begun on the Prudential Center, a long-planned and much-delayed office-, hotel-, and apartment-complex on the blighted site of a onetime Back Bay railway freight yard, and there was much brave talk that this would lead to a movement of the business district from downtown to the newer Back Bay. And the bulldozers and wrecking balls were finishing up their ruthless work in the old West End, an ethnic neighborhood destroyed to make room for high-rise, high-rent apartments, an enterprise that would become a textbook example of how not to go about urban renewal.

The new mayor, surprising critics and supporters alike, had bigger and better plans. Encouraged by the uncustomary backing from the business community, his eye on the great store of urban renewal funds available from the federal treasury, he hired Edward J. Logue, first as a consultant, then as head of the Boston Redevelopment Authority, at a salary half again as large as the mayor's. Logue had already made a name for himself with his renewal work in New Haven, and would make an even bigger name in Boston before going on to New York. Soon he and Collins moved ahead with plans for Government Center, a complex of state and federal office buildings and a new City Hall, to be built on the site of a once-fashionable Scollay Square that had become a congeries of sleazy bars, burlesque houses, shooting galleries, and tattoo parlors. Located hard by the degenerating central business district, the project was seen as a goad to development throughout the surrounding area, a seed for what was called the New Boston.

The architect I. M. Pei was hired to do a master plan for the Government Center, which he scaled to avoid undue intrusion on neighboring older buildings such as Faneuil Hall. The design of the new City Hall was thrown open to national architectural competition—the first such contest held for a public building in the United States in half a century—and though there were some who called the winning entry a ponderous disaster, others praised it as one of the century's most significant buildings. When final plans for the sixty-acre site were unwrapped in early 1963, the project was said to be one of the most far-reaching and ambitious urban facelifts yet undertaken in an American city. Included in the design: a thirty-five-story commercial office tower to be built by Cabot, Cabot & Forbes.

The city's demonstrated commitment to renew itself, to become a suitable home for a great financial center and a fit companion of the dynamic age of new technology spawning along Route 128, had indeed become a spur to increased downtown development. Confidence generated confidence, and the same breed of chain reaction that had been touched off by the early research-based enterprises began crackling through the streets of Boston. Not long after the long-awaited Prudential tower was dedicated in 1965—and more than two years before City Hall was ready for its first occupants—the thirty-four-story State Street Bank Building was completed at Franklin and Pearl streets, the same corner where once had stood the home of Thomas Handasyd Perkins. Others followed on its heels, and the downtown Boston skyline, for decades dominated by the pre–World War I Custom House tower, was punctuated by the mid-1970s with ranks of tall new buildings that spoke of the proud old Hub's resiliency and of its place among cities.

It was indeed a new Boston, risen on the remnants of the old, and much that had made the city what it was and what it had become was changed or gone forever. The port was of relatively small commercial consequence now; the mills of Lowell and Lawrence and other textile towns that had enriched Boston for generations were largely quiet and stripped of their machinery. The city's renown as an investment center continued unabated, but United Fruit and United Shoe, once twin pillars of Boston business might, had joined the roster of homegrown concerns taken over by outside financial interests. Even the Route 128 companies that had done so much to bring about the rebirth of Boston found themselves falling on hard times, squeezed since the early 1970s by the fall-off in space and defense spending. But as they had in the past when the China trade had paled and textiles faded, and when the end of World War II found Boston nearly crippled from decades of lassitude, Bostonians were casting about for alternative ways to mobilize their city's resources in new and productive fields. There was talk of yet another revolution of technology, of large-scale industrial growth in such dynamic areas as holography, solar energy, oceanography, biomedical instrumentation, pollution control, and many more. And Boston, a new Boston now, would be the source and center of it all.

Yet, for all the newness, for all the glimmering buildings rising over the old city, much of the past remains. Faneuil Hall, refurbished along with the neighboring Quincy Market and its adjoining brick and granite warehouses, is still maintained as Peter Faneuil had intended—shops on the ground floor, public meeting hall above. Not far away, visible as always from the window of banker Allan Forbes's carefully assembled counting-room-office—untouched since the banker's death more than two decades ago—the Old State House stands as it has for more than two centuries, dwarfed but somehow not overpowered by three adjacent skyscrapers developed by Cabot, Cabot & Forbes. And down at the water end of State Street, called King Street in the days of British dominion and colonial enterprise, lies the old harbor, where forests of masts once swayed to the lapping tides, where young boys clerking for merchant princes dreamed of distant ports and fortunes of their own. More recently, empty winds had skittered bits of wayward trash between vacant buildings and along weed-grown wharves doing tired duty as parking lots, but now a new and different life has come. Old wharf buildings, the ones that survived decades of neglect and decrepitude, have been reclaimed and converted into stores and restaurants, apartments and office space. Where India Wharf—its last proud vestige beaten down in the 1960s—once probed a busy harbor to receive the rich cargoes of China and the Indies, a tall apartment complex now stands, flanked on the bones of Central Wharf by an aquarium for display of exotic creatures of the sea. So long a melancholy reminder of braver days long past, the waterfront with its storied wharves is thronged once more, if not with maritime commerce, then with tourists and with the people of Boston, who owe so much to what began there so many years ago.

Notes on Sources and Further Reading

Any student of Boston history will find a wealth of original letters, records, and other materials at the Massachusetts Historical Society and the Bostonian Society, both of whose *Proceedings* are invaluable sources of information. The Boston Athenaeum, certainly the most comfortable and congenial library in America, is also a trove of material on Boston past and present—as is, of course, the Boston Public Library. The Manuscript Division of the Harvard Business School's Baker Library is a rich mine of data on industrial and commercial history. For the overall feel and flavor of Boston and Bostonians, the following are particularly useful:

Cleveland Amory, *The Proper Bostonians* (New York, 1947).

Lucius Beebe, *Boston and the Boston Legend* (New York, 1935).

Mary Caroline Crawford, *Famous Families of Massachusetts* (Boston, 1930).

Gene Farmer, *Massachusetts: The Anatomy of Quality* (Boston, 1967).

Martin Green, *The Problem of Boston* (New York, 1966).

Ferris Greenslet, *The Lowells and their Seven Worlds* (Boston, 1946).

Oscar Handlin, *Boston's Immigrants, 1790–1880* (Cambridge, 1959).

Howard Mumford Jones and Bessie Zaban Jones, *The Many Voices of Boston* (Boston, 1975).

John P. Marquand, *The Late George Apley* (Boston, 1936).

Samuel Eliot Morison, *The Maritime History of Massachusetts* (Boston, 1921; 1961).

————, *One Boy's Boston* (Boston, 1962).

Nathaniel B. Shurtleff, *A Topographical and Historical Description of Boston* (Boston, 1871).

Walter Muir Whitehill, *Boston: A Topographical History* (Cambridge, 1959; 1968).

Justin Winsor, *Memorial History of Boston* (Boston, 1881–1883).

Chapter 1. The Colonial Enterprise &
Chapter 2. Comes the Revolution

Herbert S. Allan, *John Hancock, Patriot in Purple* (New York, 1948).

Charles M. Andrews, *The Boston Merchants and the Non-Importation Movement* (New York, 1968).

Bernard Bailyn, *The New England Merchants in the 17th Century* (Cambridge, 1955).

W. T. Baxter, *The House of Hancock: Business in Boston, 1724–1775* (Cambridge, 1945).

Carl Bridenbaugh, *Cities in Revolt* (New York, 1955).

————, *Cities in the Wilderness* (New York, 1938).

A. E. Brown, *Faneuil Hall and Faneuil Hall Market* (Boston, 1900).

Wallace Brown, *The King's Friends* (Providence, 1966).

Robert McC. Calhoon, *The Loyalists in Revolutionary America, 1760–1781* (New York, 1973).

Peter J. Duignan and Clarence C. Clendenen, *The United States and the African Slave Trade, 1619–1862* (Palo Alto, 1963).

Robert A. East, *Business Enterprise in the American Revolutionary Era* (New York, 1938).

James A. Henretta, "Economic Development and Social Structure in Colonial Boston," *William & Mary Quarterly*, January, 1965.

Daniel P. Mannix and Malcolm Cowley, *Black Cargoes* (New York, 1962).

Samuel Eliot Morison, *Builders of the Bay Colony* (Boston, 1930).

James Pope-Hennesy, *Sins of the Fathers* (London, 1967).

Lucius Manlius Sargent, *Dealings with the Dead* (Boston, 1855).

Arthur M. Schlesinger, Sr., *The Colonial Merchants and the American Revolution* (New York, 1918).

William Babcock Weeden, *Economic and Social History of New England, 1620–1789* (New York, 1890).

Chapter 3. Voyages of Adventure:
The Old China Trade Days &
Chapter 5. China Traders, Old and New

Samuel Breck, *Recollections of Samuel Breck* (Philadelphia, 1877).

Thomas G. Cary, *Memoir of Thomas Handasyd Perkins* (Boston, 1856).

Richard J. Cleveland, *A Narrative of Voyages and Commercial Enterprises* (Cambridge, 1842).

Tyler Dennett, *Americans in Eastern Asia* (New York, 1922).

Jacques M. Downs, "American Merchants and the China Opium Trade, 1800–1843," *Business History Review*, Winter, 1968.

Foster Rhea Dulles, *The Old China Trade* (Boston, 1930).

Robert Bennet Forbes, *Personal Reminiscences* (Boston, 1878).

Sydney Greenbie and Mrs. Marjorie Greenbie, *Gold of Ophir; or, the Lure that Made America* (Garden City, 1925).

Frederic W. Howay, *Voyages of the "Columbia" to the Northwest Coast; 1787–1790 and 1790–1793* (Boston, 1941).

William C. Hunter, *Bits of Old China* (London, 1885).

———, *The "Fan-Kwae" at Canton* (London, 1882).

Henrietta M. Larson, "A China Trader Turns Investor," *Harvard Business Review*, April, 1934.

Richard O'Connor, *Pacific Destiny* (Boston, 1969).

Josiah Quincy, *The Journals of Major Samuel Shaw* (Boston, 1847).

Carl Seaburg and Stanley Patterson, *Merchant Prince of Boston: Colonel T. H. Perkins, 1764–1854* (Cambridge, 1971).

Charles C. Stelle, "American Trade in Opium to China, 1821–1839," *Pacific Historical Review*, March, 1941.

J. R. Sturgis, *From Books and Papers of Russell Sturgis* (Oxford, 1893).

Chapter 4. Mills on the Merrimack:
The Textile Kings

Nathan Appleton, *Introduction of the Power Loom, and Origin of Lowell* (Lowell, 1858).

William Appleton, *Selections from Diaries, 1786–1862* (Boston, 1922).

William R. Bagnall, *The Textile Industries of the United States* (Cambridge, 1893).

Thomas G. Cary, *Result of Manufactures at Lowell* (Boston, 1845).

Frederick W. Coburn, *History of Lowell and its People* (New York, 1921).

John Coolidge, *Mill and Mansion* (New York, 1942).

Melvin T. Copeland, *The Cotton Manufacturing Industry in the United States* (Cambridge, 1912).

Charles Cowley, *A Handbook of Business in Lowell* (Lowell, 1856).

Abner Forbes and J. W. Greene, *The Rich Men of Massachusetts* (Boston, 1851).

Hamilton Andrews Hill, *Memoir of Abbott Lawrence* (Boston, 1884).

Hannah Josephson, *The Golden Threads: New England's Mill Girls and Magnates* (New York, 1949).

Edward C. Kirkland, *Men, Cities and Transportation* (Cambridge, 1928).

Lucy Larcom, "Among Lowell Mill Girls: a Reminiscence," *Atlantic Monthly*, November, 1881.

William Lawrence, *Life of Amos A. Lawrence* (Boston, 1888).

———, *Memories of a Happy Life* (Boston, 1926).

William R. Lawrence, *Extracts from the Diary and Correspondence of the Late Amos Lawrence* (Boston, 1855).

Paul F. McGouldrick, *New England Textiles in the 19th Century* (Cambridge, 1968).

C. Robbins, *Memoir of William Appleton* (Boston, 1863).

Harriet H. Robinson, *Loom and Spindle, or Life Among the Early Mill Girls* (New York, 1898).

William Scoresby, *American Factories and Their Female Operatives* (Boston, 1845).

Harriet Knight Smith, *The History of the Lowell Institute* (Boston, 1898).

Louise Hall Tharp, *The Appletons of Beacon Hill* (Boston, 1973).

Caroline Farrar Ware, *The Early New England Cotton Manufacture* (Boston, 1931).

Thomas L. V. Wilson, *The Aristocracy of Boston: Who They Are and What They Were* (Boston, 1848).

R. C. Winthrop, *Memoir of Nathan Appleton* (Boston, 1861).

Chapter 6. The Years of Building & Chapter 7. The Financiers

Charles Francis Adams, "Boston," *North American Review*, January, April, 1868.

———, *Charles Francis Adams, 1835–1915* (Boston, 1916).

——— "The Railroad System," *North American Review*, April, 1867.

Frederick Upham Adams, *Conquest of the Tropics* (New York, 1914).

Alexander Agassiz, *Letters and Recollections of Alexander Agassiz* (Boston, 1913).

Oakes Ames, A Memoir (Cambridge, 1883).

John Brooks, *Telephone, The First Hundred Years* (New York, 1976).

Thomas C. Cochran, *Railroad Leaders* (Cambridge, 1953).

T. Jefferson Coolidge, *The Autobiography of T. Jefferson Coolidge, 1831–1920* (Boston, 1923).

Horace Coon, *American Tel & Tel* (New York, 1939).

N. R. Danielian, *A.T. & T.: The Story of Industrial Conquest* (New York, 1939).

John Murray Forbes, *Letters and Recollections of J. M. Forbes* (Boston, 1899).

William B. Gates, *Michigan Copper and Boston Dollars* (Cambridge, 1951).

Paul Goodman, "Ethics and Enterprise: the Values of the Boston Elite, 1800–1860," *American Quarterly*, Fall, 1966.

John Winthrop Hammond, *Men and Volts: The Story of General Electric* (Philadelphia, 1941).

Frederick C. Jaher, "Businessman and Gentleman: Nathan and Thomas Gold Appleton—An Exploration in Intergenerational History," *Explorations in Entrepreneurial History*, Fall, 1966.

Arthur Menzies Johnson and Barry E. Supple, *Boston Capitalists and Western Railroads* (Cambridge, 1967).

Edward C. Kirkland, *Charles Francis Adams, Jr., 1835–1915: The Patrician at Bay* (Cambridge, 1965).

Isaac F. Marcosson, "The Millionaire Yield of Boston," *Munsey's Magazine*, August, 1912.

Joseph Gregory Martin, *A Century of Finance* (Boston, 1898).

Henry G. Pearson, *An American Railroad Builder: John Murray Forbes* (Boston, 1911).

Bliss Perry, *Life and Letters of Henry Lee Higginson* (Boston, 1921).

Arthur Stanwood Pier, *Forbes: Telephone Pioneer* (New York, 1953).

Jonas W. Stehman, *The Financial History of the American Telephone & Telegraph Company* (Boston, 1925).

Edward Weeks, *Men, Money and Responsibility; A History of Lee, Higginson Corp., 1848–1962* (Boston, 1962).

Barrett Wendell, *A History of Lee, Higginson & Co.* (Boston, 1921).

Gerald Taylor White, *A History of the Massachusetts Hospital Life Insurance Company* (Cambridge, 1955).

Charles M. Wilson, *Empire in Green and Gold* (New York, 1947).

Chapter 8. Decline and Disintegration

Trevor Allen, *Ivar Kreuger, Match King, Croesus and Crook* (London, 1932).

"Boston," *Fortune*, February, 1933.

Allen Churchill, *The Incredible Ivar Kreuger* (New York, 1957).

Elmer Davis, "Boston, Notes on a Barbarian Invasion," *Harper's*, January, 1928.

Donald H. Dunn, *Ponzi! The Boston Swindler* (New York, 1975).

Manfred Georg, *The Case of Ivar Kreuger* (London, 1933).

N. S. B. Gras, *The Massachusetts First National Bank of Boston, 1785–1934* (Cambridge, 1937).

Leon A. Harris, *Only to God; The Extraordinary Life of Godfrey Lowell Cabot* (New York, 1967).

Donald Holbrook, *The Boston Trustee* (Boston, 1937).

Mark DeWolfe Howe, *The Boston Symphony Orchestra* (Boston, 1931).

———, "Boston—Why Is It and What?" *Harper's Weekly*, November 21, 1908.

Frederic C. Jaher, "The Boston Brahmins in the Age of Industrial Capitalism," in: *The Age of Industrialism in America: Essays in Social Structure and Cultural Analysis* (New York, 1968).

David E. Koskoff, *Joseph P. Kennedy: A Life and Times* (Englewood Cliffs, N. J., 1974).

Henry G. Pearson, *Son of New England: James Jackson Storrow, 1864–1926* (Boston, 1932).

Charles Ponzi, *The Rise of Mr. Ponzi* (New York and Rome, 1937).

Samuel C. Prescott, *When M.I.T. Was "Boston Tech," 1861–1916* (Cambridge, 1954).

Robert Shaplen, *Kreuger, Genius and Swindler* (New York, 1960).

Frederic Jesup Stimson, *My United States* (New York, 1931).

Richard J. Whalen, *The Founding Father* (New York, 1964).

Chapter 9. Awakening

John Brooks, *The Go-Go Years* (New York, 1973).

J. E. Burchard, *M.I.T. in World War II* (New York, 1948).

Martin Meyerson and Edward C. Banfield, *Boston: the Job Ahead* (Cambridge, 1966).

Christopher Rand, *Cambridge, U.S.A.; Hub of a New World* (New York, 1964).

Otto J. Scott, *The Creative Ordeal: The Story of Raytheon* (New York, 1974).

H. Lee Silberman, *50 Years of Trust; Massachusetts Investors Trust, 1925–1974* (Boston, 1974).

Walter Muir Whitehill, *Boston in the Age of John Fitzgerald Kennedy* (Norman, Oklahoma, 1966).

Bernard Taper, *The Arts in Boston: An Outsider's View of the Cultural Estate* (Cambridge, 1970).

Edward Weeks, *The Lowells and Their Institute* (Boston, 1966).

INDEX

Adams, Brooks, 232
Adams, Charles Francis (ambassador), 189, 191
Adams, Charles Francis (railroad developer):
career of, 166, 188–194, 196–197, 220, 228
Civil War experiences of, 147, 186
educational views of, 240
"money-getting" evaluated by, 194, 235
"society" life evaluated by, 198–199, 232
Adams, Charles Francis, Sr. ("the Deacon"; banker and trustee), 290–292
Adams, Charles Francis, Jr. (Raytheon developer), 275, 291–293, 306–307
Adams, Henry, 232
Adams, John, 26, 29
Adams, John Quincy, 51, 131
Adams, John Quincy, II, 196–197, 291
Adams family, 188–189, 290–291
Agassiz, Alexander, 85, 162–167, 184, 212, 214–215
Agassiz, Ida, 186
Agassiz, Louis, 85, 162, 197
Agassiz family, 165
Age of Jackson, The (Schlesinger), 302
Aldrich, Richard, 237
Alford, William, 4
Allen, Frederic W., 259, 265
American Appliance Company, 275
American Electric Company, 211
American Research and Development Corporation (ARD), 279–283, 285, 306

American Revolution, Boston's part in, 21, 25–37
American Telephone & Telegraph Company (A.T.&T.), 207, 267, 291
Ames, F. Lothrop, 211
Ames, Oakes, 173–177
Ames, Oliver, 173–177
Ammidon, Philip, 105
Amory, Cleveland, 98
Amory, Francis, 227
Amory, Jonathan, 33, 227
Amory, Thomas, 18, 24, 56
Amoskeag Mills, 191
Anaconda Company, 214
Anderson, Harlan E., 285
Anthology Society, 93
Appleton, Eben, 70–71
Appleton, Nathan ("the Great Manufacturer"), 61–73, 99–100, 120, 222–225, 230, 242
Appleton, Samuel, 70, 152
Appleton, Sarah Elizabeth, 151
Appleton, Thomas Gold, 218, 221
Appleton, Warren, 151
Appleton, William, 82–83, 91, 92, 108, 156, 225, 231
Appleton, Wisconsin, naming of, 152
Appleton Company, 75, 104
Apthorp, Thomas, 31
Association of American Geologists and Naturalists, 242
Astor, John Jacob, 109
Atchison, Topeka & Santa Fe, 190
Atlantic textile mill, 88

317

DATE DUE

OCT 01 1998	